Teach Yourself

VISUALLY™

PowerPoint® 2002

W9-DDO-528

Visual

From
maranGraphics®

&

Wiley Publishing, Inc.

Teach Yourself VISUALLY™ PowerPoint® 2002

Published by
Wiley Publishing, Inc.
909 Third Avenue
New York, NY 10022

Published simultaneously in Canada

Copyright © 2002 by maranGraphics Inc.
5755 Coopers Avenue
Mississauga, Ontario, Canada
L4Z 1R9

Library of Congress Control Number: 2002100393

ISBN: 0-7645-3660-5

Manufactured in the United States of America

10 9 8 7 6 5 4 3 2

1K/SU/QX/QT/MG

Trademark Acknowledgments

Important Numbers

For U.S. corporate orders, please call maranGraphics at 800-469-6616
or fax 905-890-9434.

For general information on our other products and services or
to obtain technical support, please contact our Customer Care
Department within the U.S. at 800-762-2974, outside the U.S.
at 317-572-3993 or fax 317-572-4002.

Permissions

U.S. Corporate Sales	**U.S. Trade Sales**
Contact maranGraphics at (800) 469-6616 or fax (905) 890-9434.	Contact Wiley at (800) 762-2974 or fax (317) 572-4002.

Some comments from our readers...

"I have to praise you and your company on the fine products you turn out. I have twelve of the *Teach Yourself VISUALLY* and *Simplified* books in my house. They were instrumental in helping me pass a difficult computer course. Thank you for creating books that are easy to follow."

–Gordon Justin (Brielle, NJ)

"I commend your efforts and your success. I teach in an outreach program for the Dr. Eugene Clark Library in Lockhart, TX. Your *Teach Yourself VISUALLY* books are incredible and I use them in my computer classes. All my students love them!"

–Michele Schalin (Lockhart, TX)

"Thank you so much for helping people like me learn about computers. The Maran family is just what the doctor ordered. Thank you, thank you, thank you."

–Carol Moten (New Kensington, PA)

"I would like to take this time to compliment maranGraphics on creating such great books. Thank you for making it clear. Keep up the good work."

–Kirk Santoro (Burbank, CA)

"I write to extend my thanks and appreciation for your books. They are clear, easy to follow, and straight to the point. Keep up the good work!"

–Seward Kollie (Dakar, Senegal)

"What fantastic teaching books you have produced! Congratulations to you and your staff. You deserve the Nobel prize in Education in the Software category. Thanks for helping me to understand computers."

–Bruno Tonon (Melbourne, Australia)

"Over time, I have bought a number of your 'Read Less-Learn More' books. For me, they are THE way to learn anything easily."

–José A. Mazón (Cuba, NY)

"I was introduced to maranGraphics about four years ago and YOU ARE THE GREATEST THING THAT EVER HAPPENED TO INTRODUCTORY COMPUTER BOOKS!"

–Glenn Nettleton (Huntsville, AL)

"Compliments To The Chef!! Your books are extraordinary! Or, simply put, Extra-Ordinary, meaning way above the rest! THANK YOU THANK YOU THANK YOU! for creating these."

–Christine J. Manfrin (Castle Rock, CO)

"I'm a grandma who was pushed by an 11-year-old grandson to join the computer age. I found myself hopelessly confused and frustrated until I discovered the Visual series. I'm no expert by any means now, but I'm a lot further along than I would have been otherwise. Thank you!"

–Carol Louthain (Logansport, IN)

"Thank you, thank you, thank you...for making it so easy for me to break into this high-tech world. I now own four of your books. I recommend them to anyone who is a beginner like myself. Now... if you could just do one for programming VCR's, it would make my day!"

–Gay O'Donnell (Calgary, Alberta, Canada)

"You're marvelous! I am greatly in your debt."

–Patrick Baird (Lacey, WA)

maranGraphics is a family-run business
located near Toronto, Canada.

At **maranGraphics**, we believe in producing great computer books—one book at a time.

Each maranGraphics book uses the award-winning communication process that we have been developing over the last 25 years. Using this process, we organize screen shots, text and illustrations in a way that makes it easy for you to learn new concepts and tasks.

We spend hours deciding the best way to perform each task, so you don't have to! Our clear, easy-to-follow screen shots and instructions walk you through each task from beginning to end.

Our detailed illustrations go hand-in-hand with the text to help reinforce the information. Each illustration is a labor of love—some take up to a week to draw!

We want to thank you for purchasing what we feel are the best computer books money can buy. We hope you enjoy using this book as much as we enjoyed creating it!

Sincerely,

The Maran Family

Please visit us on the Web at:
www.maran.com

CREDITS

Authors:
Kelleigh Johnson
Ruth Maran

Copy Developer & Indexer:
Roxanne Van Damme

Project Manager:
Judy Maran

Editing & Screen Captures:
Roderick Anatalio
Norm Schumacher
Megan Kirby

Layout Design & Overview Illustrations:
Treena Lees

Illustrators
Russ Marini
Steven Schaerer

Screen Artist & Illustrator:
Darryl Grossi

Wiley Vice President & Executive Group Publisher:
Richard Swadley

Wiley Vice President & Publisher:
Barry Pruett

Wiley Editorial Support:
Jennifer Dorsey
Sandy Rodrigues
Lindsay Sandman

Post Production:
Robert Maran

ACKNOWLEDGMENTS

Thanks to the dedicated staff of maranGraphics, including
Roderick Anatalio, Darryl Grossi, Kelleigh Johnson,
Megan Kirby, Wanda Lawrie, Treena Lees, Cathy Lo,
Jill Maran, Judy Maran, Robert Maran, Ruth Maran,
Russ Marini, Steven Schaerer, Norm Schumacher,
Raquel Scott, Roxanne Van Damme and Paul Whitehead.

Finally, to Richard Maran who originated the easy-to-use graphic
format of this guide. Thank you for your inspiration and guidance.

TABLE OF CONTENTS

Chapter 1

Chapter 2

Chapter 3

EDIT TEXT

Chapter 4

FORMAT TEXT

TABLE OF CONTENTS

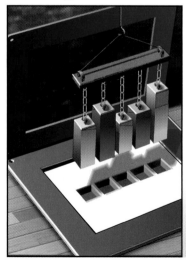

Chapter 8

Chapter 9

Chapter 10

TABLE OF CONTENTS

Chapter 11

ADD SPECIAL EFFECTS

Chapter 12

FINE-TUNE A PRESENTATION

Chapter 13

DELIVER A PRESENTATION

Chapter 14

POWERPOINT AND THE INTERNET

CHAPTER 1

Getting Started

Are you ready to begin using Microsoft PowerPoint 2002? This chapter will show you the way.

INTRODUCTION TO POWERPOINT

PowerPoint helps you plan, organize, design and deliver professional presentations.

You can use PowerPoint to create presentations that you will deliver using a computer screen, overheads, 35mm slides or on the Web. PowerPoint includes a wizard and pre-designed templates to help you quickly create presentations.

Edit Text

PowerPoint offers many features to help you work with the text in your presentation. You can add, delete, move and copy text on your slides. You can also insert symbols, find and replace text and check for spelling mistakes.

Format Slides

There are many ways you can change the appearance of text in your presentation. For example, you can change the font, color and alignment of the text. You can also change the slide design, color scheme and background of slides to enhance the overall appearance of your presentation. PowerPoint includes Slide Masters and Title Masters that allow you to make formatting changes to all the slides in your presentation at once.

Add Objects to Slides

You can add objects to slides to illustrate important concepts and make your slides more interesting. You can add objects such as AutoShapes, pictures, charts, diagrams and tables. PowerPoint also allows you to create a photo album to neatly display several pictures in a presentation.

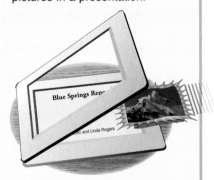

Add Multimedia to Slides

Adding multimedia to slides can make your presentation more entertaining. You can add sounds, movies and voice narration to slides. You can also play a music CD during your presentation to add background music to the slides.

Add Special Effects to Slides

PowerPoint includes special effects you can use to enhance your presentation and help direct the audience's attention to important information. You can apply one of PowerPoint's preset animation schemes to a slide or add custom animations to specific objects you want to highlight on a slide. You can also add transitions to help introduce slides in your presentation.

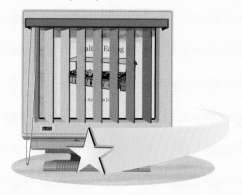

Fine-Tune Presentations

PowerPoint includes many features that allow you to put finishing touches on your presentation. You can add slides from another presentation or work with your presentation in Microsoft Word. PowerPoint also allows you to save a presentation for other people to review and then decide which changes you want to incorporate into the presentation.

Deliver Presentations

You can rehearse and view a presentation on your computer screen. During your presentation, you can take notes, called meeting minutes, that you can review once your presentation is complete. PowerPoint also helps you present a slide show using two monitors and package your presentation so you can easily deliver it on another computer.

CREATING GREAT PRESENTATIONS

Consider the Audience

You should consider your audience when developing the content and tone of your presentation. For example, a presentation for the engineering department of a company should be different than a presentation for the sales department.

Organize the Text

➢ Use uppercase and lowercase text, not ALL UPPERCASE.

➢ Ensure the punctuation is consistent on all slides.

➢ Discuss only one concept per slide.

➢ Include only main ideas on each slide.

➢ Do not include more than six points on a slide.

➢ Each point or slide title should be no more than two lines long.

➢ Spell check your presentation.

Choose Colors and Fonts

➢ Choose colors and fonts that match the mood of your presentation. For example, use bright colors to convey good news.

➢ Choose colors and fonts that make your text easy to read.

➢ Avoid using more than five colors per slide.

➢ Avoid using more than three fonts per slide.

Add Visuals

Add visuals, such as pictures, charts, diagrams, tables or movies, to your slides. Visuals can help enhance your presentation, but you should try to avoid cluttering your slides with visuals that have no purpose.

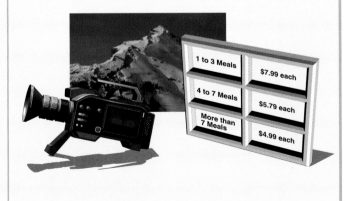

TIPS FOR DELIVERING A GREAT PRESENTATION

Rehearse the Presentation

Make sure you rehearse your presentation before you deliver it in front of an audience. This will help your presentation flow smoothly and can help ensure that you will complete the presentation in the time provided. If possible, practice your presentation in front of a friend or colleague.

Check the Hardware

Before you deliver your presentation, check all the hardware you plan to use. Make sure you know how to operate the hardware and you have all the parts you need, such as spare bulbs or an extension cord. In case of a hardware failure, you should always have a paper copy of your presentation with you.

Check the Presentation Room

You should check the room you will be presenting in before the presentation. Make sure the audience will be able to read the slides from all areas of the room. If necessary, determine the location of electrical outlets and light switches.

Check Your Body Language

When delivering a presentation, your posture should convey a relaxed and confident manner. Make eye contact with your audience while presenting and avoid hiding or clasping your hands.

CREATING GREAT PRESENTATIONS

View on a Computer Screen

You can deliver your presentation on a computer screen. This method is ideal for delivering a presentation to a small audience and allows you to add multimedia such as sounds, movies or animations, to your slides.

View on Two Monitors

You can present a slide show to an audience using one monitor while you view the presentation on another monitor. This allows you to see your notes and a miniature version of each slide in your presentation while the audience views only the slides.

Use a Slide Projector

You can use a slide projector to deliver a presentation on 35mm slides. 35mm slides offer better color and crisper images than a presentation shown on a computer screen. A service bureau can output your presentation to 35mm slides.

Use a Computer Projector

You can connect a computer to a computer projector to display your presentation on a screen or wall. The presentation will appear as it would appear on the computer screen.

Use an Overhead Projector

You can use an overhead projector to display your presentation on a screen or wall. Many office supply stores sell overhead transparencies that you can print your presentation on. A service bureau can also print your presentation on overhead transparencies.

Use an LCD Panel

You can connect an LCD (Liquid Crystal Display) panel to your computer and then place the LCD panel on an overhead projector to display your presentation. The presentation will appear on a screen or wall as it would appear on a computer screen.

View at a Kiosk

You can create a self-running presentation that people can view at a kiosk. Kiosks are often found at trade shows and shopping malls.

View on the Internet

You can save your presentation as a Web page. You can then publish the presentation on the Internet to make the presentation available to people around the world.

USING THE MOUSE

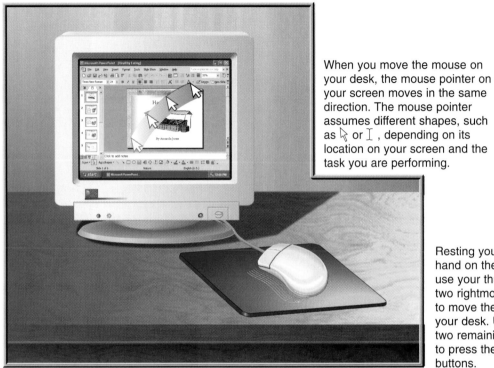

A mouse is a handheld device that allows you to select and move items on your screen.

When you move the mouse on your desk, the mouse pointer on your screen moves in the same direction. The mouse pointer assumes different shapes, such as ⬚ or I , depending on its location on your screen and the task you are performing.

Resting your right hand on the mouse, use your thumb and two rightmost fingers to move the mouse on your desk. Use your two remaining fingers to press the mouse buttons.

MOUSE ACTIONS

Click

Press and release the left mouse button. A click is usually used to select an item on the screen.

Double-click

Quickly press and release the left mouse button twice. A double-click is usually used to open an item.

Right-click

Press and release the right mouse button. A right-click is usually used to display a list of frequently used commands for an item.

Drag

Position the mouse pointer over an item on your screen and then press and hold down the left mouse button as you move the mouse to where you want to place the item. Then release the mouse button.

THE POWERPOINT WINDOW

The PowerPoint window displays several items to help you perform tasks efficiently.

Title Bar

Shows the name of the displayed presentation.

Menu Bar

Provides access to lists of commands available in PowerPoint and displays an area where you can type a question to get help information.

Standard Toolbar

Contains buttons you can use to select common commands, such as Save and Open.

Formatting Toolbar

Contains buttons you can use to select common formatting commands, such as Bold and Underline.

Outline and Slides Tabs

Provide two ways of viewing the slides in your presentation.

Slide Pane

Displays the current slide.

View Buttons

Allow you to quickly change the way your presentation is displayed on the screen.

Notes Pane

Displays the notes for the current slide.

Drawing Toolbar

Contains buttons to help you work with objects in your presentation.

Status Bar

Provides information about the slide displayed on the screen and the current presentation.

Task Pane

Contains links you can select to perform common tasks, such as opening or creating a presentation.

START POWERPOINT

You can start PowerPoint to create a new presentation or work with a presentation you previously created.

When you start PowerPoint, a blank slide appears on your screen. You can type text into this slide.

START POWERPOINT

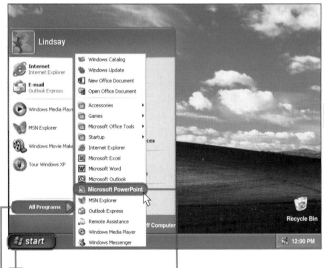

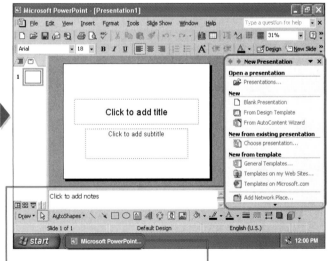

1 Click **start**.

2 Click **All Programs** to view a list of the programs on your computer.

*Note: If you are using an earlier version of Windows, click **Programs** in step 2.*

3 Click **Microsoft PowerPoint**.

■ The Microsoft PowerPoint window appears, displaying a blank slide.

■ This area displays a task pane, which allows you to quickly perform common tasks. For information on using the task pane, see page 16.

■ A button for the Microsoft PowerPoint window appears on the taskbar.

When you finish using PowerPoint, you can exit the program.

You should always exit all open programs before turning off your computer.

EXIT POWERPOINT

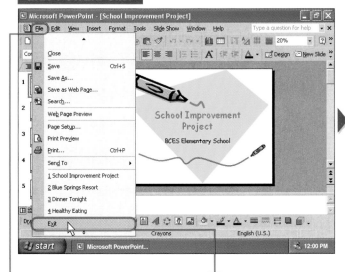

■ Before exiting PowerPoint, you should save all your open presentations. To save a presentation, see page 26.

1 Click **File**.

2 Click **Exit**.

Note: If Exit does not appear on the menu, position the mouse ▷ over the bottom of the menu to display the menu option.

■ The Microsoft PowerPoint window disappears from your screen.

■ The button for the Microsoft PowerPoint window disappears from the taskbar.

13

SELECT COMMANDS

You can select commands from menus or toolbars to perform tasks in PowerPoint.

When you first start PowerPoint, the most commonly used commands and buttons appear on each menu and toolbar. As you work, PowerPoint customizes the menus and toolbars to display the commands and buttons you use most often.

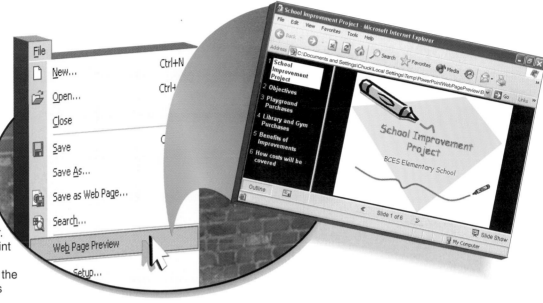

SELECT COMMANDS

USING MENUS

1 Click the name of the menu you want to display.

■ A short version of the menu appears, displaying the most commonly used commands.

2 To expand the menu and display all the commands, position the mouse ⌖ over ⌄.

Note: If you do not perform step 2, the expanded menu will automatically appear after a few seconds.

■ The expanded menu appears, displaying all the commands.

3 Click the command you want to use.

Note: A dimmed command is currently not available.

■ To close a menu without selecting a command, click outside the menu.

14

How can I make a command appear on the short version of a menu?

When you select a command from an expanded menu, PowerPoint automatically adds the command to the short version of the menu. The next time you display the short version of the menu, the command you selected will appear.

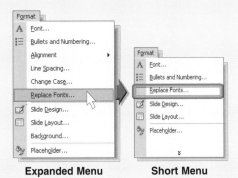

Expanded Menu   **Short Menu**

How can I quickly select a command?

You can use a shortcut menu to quickly select a command.

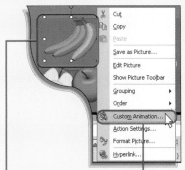

1 Right-click an item to display a shortcut menu. The shortcut menu displays the most frequently used commands for the item.

2 Click the command you want to use.

■ To close a shortcut menu without selecting a command, click outside the menu.

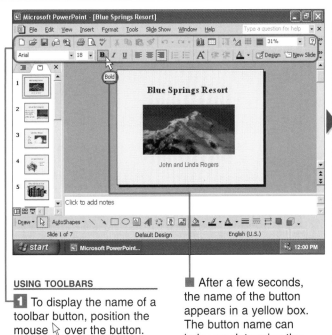

USING TOOLBARS

1 To display the name of a toolbar button, position the mouse ⬚ over the button.

■ After a few seconds, the name of the button appears in a yellow box. The button name can help you determine the task the button performs.

2 A toolbar may not be able to display all of its buttons. Click ⬚ to display additional buttons for the toolbar.

■ Additional buttons for the toolbar appear.

3 To use a toolbar button to select a command, click the button.

USING THE TASK PANE

You can use the task pane to perform common tasks in PowerPoint. The task pane appears each time you start PowerPoint.

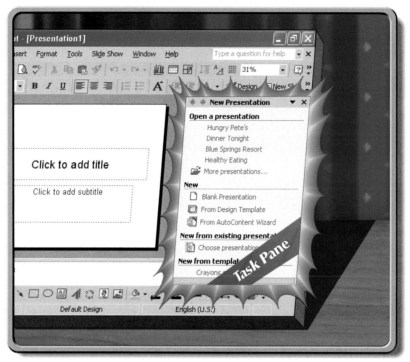

You can display or hide a task pane at any time. When you perform some tasks, such as searching for a presentation, the task pane will automatically appear.

USING THE TASK PANE

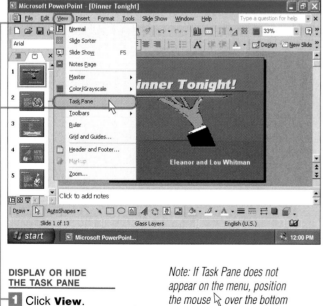

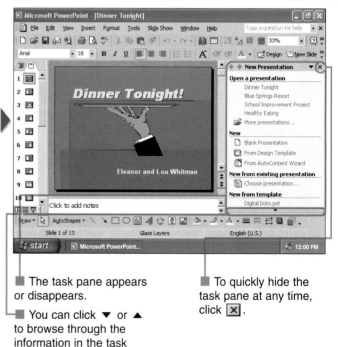

DISPLAY OR HIDE THE TASK PANE

■1 Click **View**.

■2 Click **Task Pane**.

Note: If Task Pane does not appear on the menu, position the mouse ⫦ over the bottom of the menu to display the menu option.

■ The task pane appears or disappears.

■ You can click ▼ or ▲ to browse through the information in the task pane.

■ To quickly hide the task pane at any time, click ⊠.

What are some of the task panes available in PowerPoint?

New Presentation

Allows you to open presentations and create new presentations. For information on opening a presentation, see page 28.

Search

Allows you to search for presentations on your computer. For information on searching for presentations, see page 32.

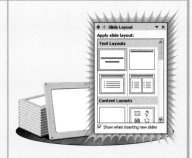

Slide Layout

Allows you to select the slide layout you want to use for the current slide. For information on changing the slide layout, see page 46.

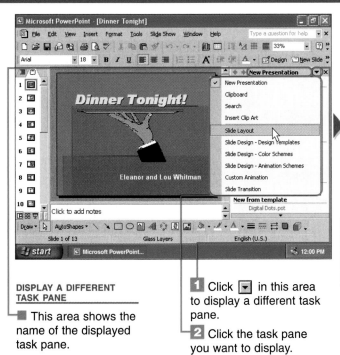

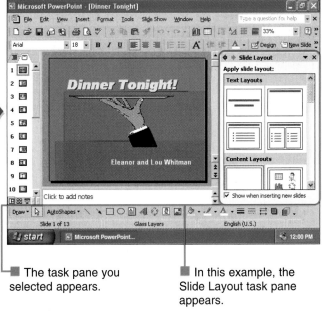

DISPLAY A DIFFERENT TASK PANE

■ This area shows the name of the displayed task pane.

1 Click ▾ in this area to display a different task pane.

2 Click the task pane you want to display.

■ The task pane you selected appears.

■ In this example, the Slide Layout task pane appears.

CREATE A PRESENTATION USING THE AUTOCONTENT WIZARD

You can use the AutoContent Wizard to create a presentation. The wizard asks you a series of questions and then sets up a presentation based on your answers.

USING THE AUTOCONTENT WIZARD

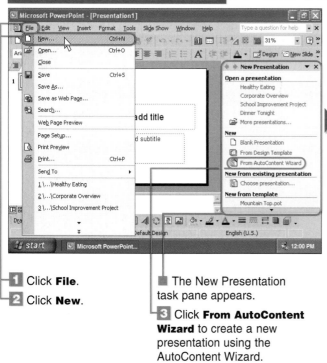

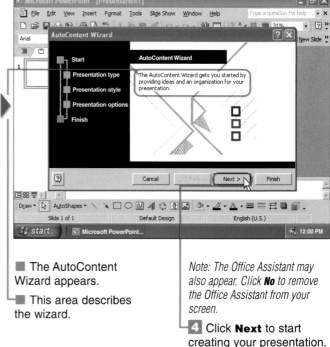

■⬛ Click **File**.

■⬛ Click **New**.

■ The New Presentation task pane appears.

⬛ Click **From AutoContent Wizard** to create a new presentation using the AutoContent Wizard.

■ The AutoContent Wizard appears.

■ This area describes the wizard.

*Note: The Office Assistant may also appear. Click **No** to remove the Office Assistant from your screen.*

⬛ Click **Next** to start creating your presentation.

Why did a dialog box appear after I selected a presentation in the AutoContent Wizard?

A dialog box appears if the presentation you selected is not installed on your computer. Insert the CD-ROM disc you used to install PowerPoint into your computer's CD-ROM drive. Then click **Yes** to install the presentation.

Note: A window may appear on your screen. Click ⊠ in the top right corner of the window to close the window.

Is there another way to create a presentation?

If you want to design your own presentation without using the content PowerPoint suggests, you can create a blank presentation. Creating a blank presentation allows you to create and design each slide individually. To create a blank presentation, see page 24.

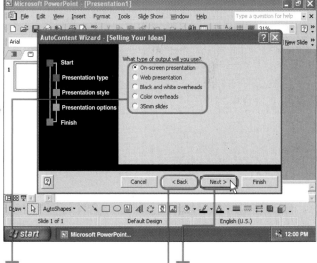

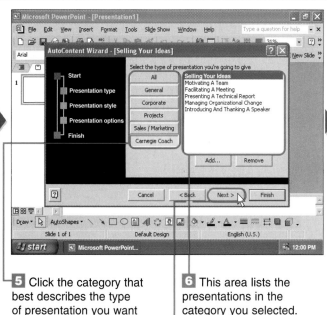

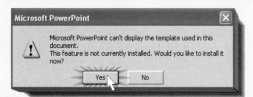

5 Click the category that best describes the type of presentation you want to create.

*Note: If you are not sure which category to select, click **All** to display all the available presentations.*

6 This area lists the presentations in the category you selected. Click the presentation that best suits your needs.

7 Click **Next** to continue.

8 Click the type of output you want to use for your presentation (○ changes to ⦿).

9 Click **Next** to continue.

■ You can click **Back** at any time to return to a previous step and change your answers.

CONTINUED

CREATE A PRESENTATION USING THE AUTOCONTENT WIZARD

The AutoContent Wizard allows you to specify a title for the first slide in your presentation. You can also specify information you want to appear on each slide.

Presentation title
Footer
Date last updated
Slide number

USING THE AUTOCONTENT WIZARD (CONTINUED)

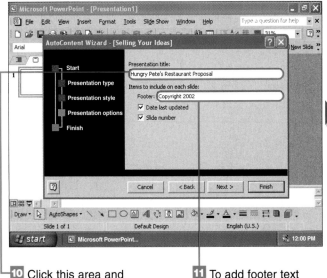

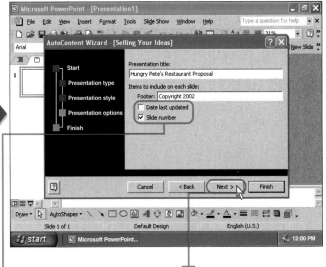

10 Click this area and type the title you want to appear on the first slide in your presentation.

11 To add footer text to each slide in your presentation, click this area and then type the text.

■ PowerPoint will add the current date and slide number to each slide in your presentation.

12 If you do not want to add the current date or slide number, click the option you do not want to add (☑ changes to ☐).

13 Click **Next** to continue.

How do I replace the sample text PowerPoint provides?

To replace the sample text, drag the mouse ⊥ over the text until you highlight the text and then type the new text you want to use.

Can I change the design of the presentation I created using the AutoContent Wizard?

The design PowerPoint uses for the presentation depends on the presentation type you selected in the AutoContent Wizard. You can change the design of the presentation to give the presentation a new appearance. To change the design, see page 102.

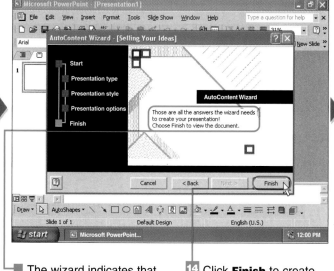

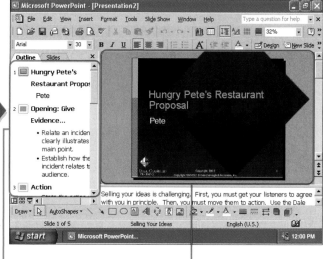

■ The wizard indicates that you have provided all the answers needed to create your presentation.

14 Click **Finish** to create your presentation.

■ This area displays the sample text PowerPoint provides for each slide in your presentation. You can replace the sample text with your own text. For more information, see the top of this page.

■ This area displays the current slide.

CREATE A PRESENTATION USING A DESIGN TEMPLATE

You can use a design template to create a professional-looking presentation. Each design template uses fonts, backgrounds and colors to create a particular look.

CREATE A PRESENTATION USING A DESIGN TEMPLATE

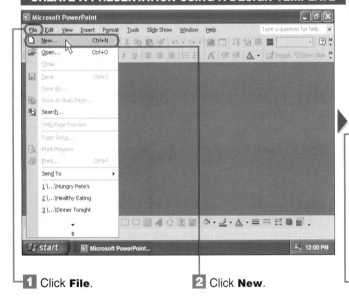

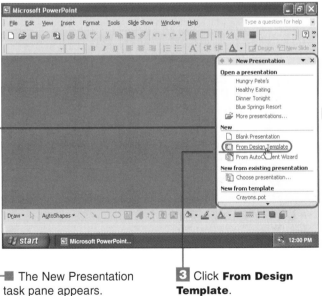

1 Click **File**.

2 Click **New**.

■ The New Presentation task pane appears.

3 Click **From Design Template**.

■ PowerPoint creates a new presentation.

Only one slide appeared in the presentation I created. What is wrong?

When you create a presentation using a design template, PowerPoint creates only the first slide. You can add additional slides to your presentation as you need them. To add a slide to your presentation, see page 48.

 Can I later change the design template for my presentation?

You can change the design template for your entire presentation or for a single slide at any time. To change the design template, see page 102.

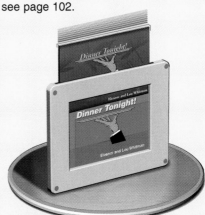

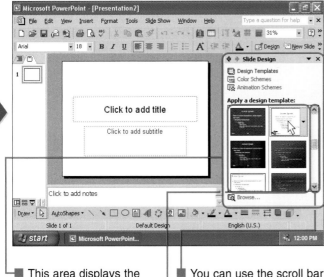

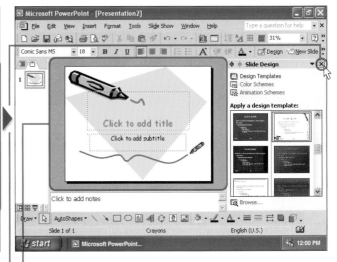

■ This area displays the Slide Design task pane, which you can use to select a design template for the presentation.

■ You can use the scroll bar to browse through the design templates.

4 Click the design template you want to use.

■ The slide displays the design template you selected.

Note: To select a different design template, repeat step 4.

5 When the slide displays the design template you want to use, you can click **X** to hide the Slide Design task pane.

■ You can now change the layout of the slide or add text to the slide. To change the layout, see page 46. To add text, see page 60.

CREATE A BLANK PRESENTATION

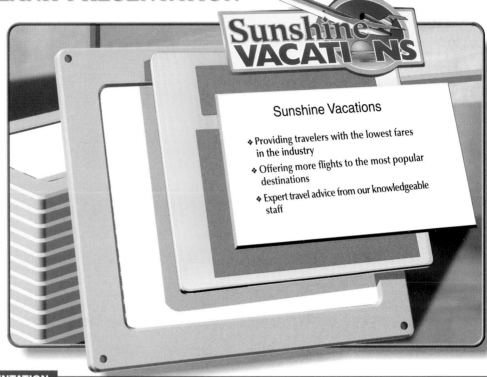

You can use PowerPoint to create a blank presentation. Blank presentations are useful when you want to create your own design and content for your slides.

CREATE A BLANK PRESENTATION

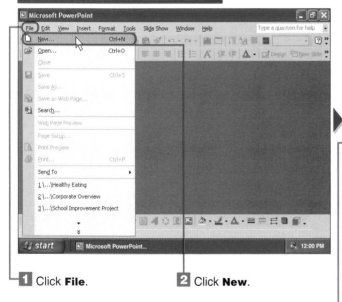

1 Click **File**.

2 Click **New**.

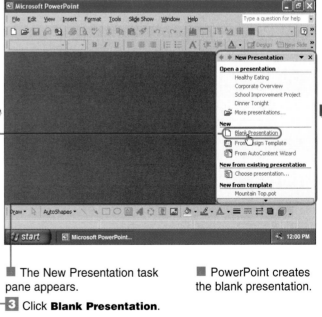

■ The New Presentation task pane appears.

3 Click **Blank Presentation**.

■ PowerPoint creates the blank presentation.

Why did PowerPoint create only one slide in my presentation?

When you create a blank presentation, PowerPoint creates only the first slide. You can add additional slides to your presentation as you need them. To add a slide to your presentation, see page 48.

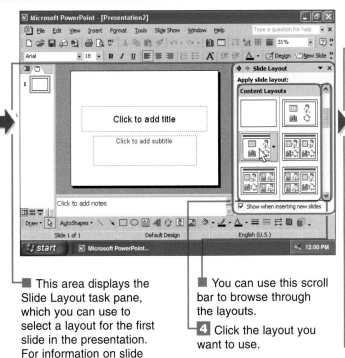

SLIDE 1

How can I quickly create a blank presentation?

While working in PowerPoint, you can click to create a blank presentation at any time.

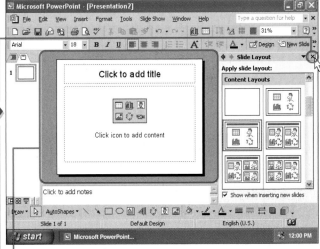

■ This area displays the Slide Layout task pane, which you can use to select a layout for the first slide in the presentation. For information on slide layouts, see page 46.

■ You can use this scroll bar to browse through the layouts.

4 Click the layout you want to use.

■ The slide displays the layout you selected.

Note: To select a different layout, repeat step 4.

5 When the slide displays the layout you want to use, you can click ☒ to hide the Slide Layout task pane.

■ You can now add text and objects to the slide. To add text, see page 60. To add objects, see pages 120 to 129.

SAVE A PRESENTATION

You can save your presentation to store the presentation for future use. This allows you to later review and edit the presentation.

SAVE A PRESENTATION

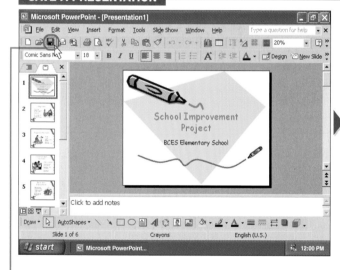

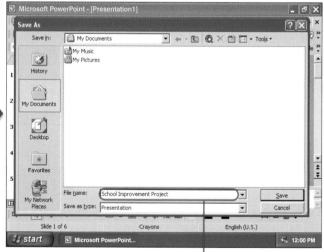

1 Click 🖫 to save your presentation.

Note: If 🖫 is not displayed, click ⟫ on the Standard toolbar to display the button.

■ The Save As dialog box appears.

Note: If you previously saved your presentation, the Save As dialog box will not appear since you have already named the presentation.

2 Type a name for the presentation.

Note: A presentation name cannot contain the * : ? > < | or " characters.

What are the commonly used locations that I can access?

History	**My Documents**	**Desktop**	**Favorites**	**My Network Places**
Provides access to folders and presentations you recently worked with.	Provides a convenient place to store a presentation.	Allows you to store a presentation on the Windows desktop.	Provides a place to store a presentation you will frequently use.	Allows you to store a presentation on your network.

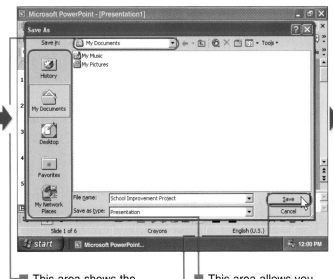

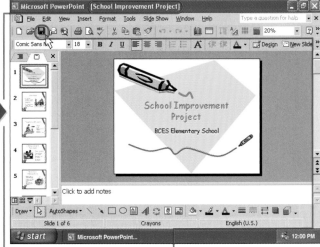

■ This area shows the location where PowerPoint will store your presentation. You can click this area to change the location.

■ This area allows you to access commonly used locations. You can click a location to save your presentation in the location.

3 Click **Save** to save your presentation.

■ PowerPoint saves your presentation.

■ This area displays the name of the presentation.

SAVE CHANGES

You should regularly save changes you make to a presentation to avoid losing your work.

1 Click 🖫 to save your changes.

OPEN A PRESENTATION

You can open a saved presentation to view the presentation on your screen. This allows you to review and make changes to the presentation.

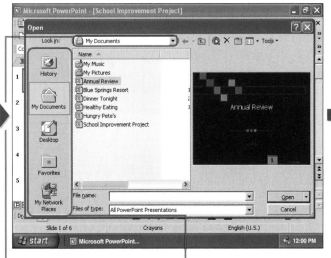

1 Click 📂 to open a presentation.

Note: If 📂 is not displayed, click 📧 on the Standard toolbar to display the button.

■ The Open dialog box appears.

■ This area shows the location of the displayed presentations. You can click this area to change the location.

■ This area allows you to access presentations in commonly used locations. You can click a location to display the presentations stored in the location.

Note: For information on the commonly used locations, see the top of page 27.

28

How can I quickly open a presentation I recently worked with?

PowerPoint remembers the names of the last four presentations you worked with. You can use one of the following methods to quickly open any of these presentations.

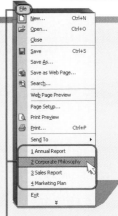

Use the Task Pane

The New Presentation task pane appears each time you start PowerPoint. To display the New Presentation task pane, see page 16.

1 Click the name of the presentation you want to open.

Use the File Menu

1 Click **File**.

2 Click the name of the presentation you want to open.

Note: If the names of the last four presentations you worked with are not all displayed, position the mouse ⌖ over the bottom of the menu to display all the names.

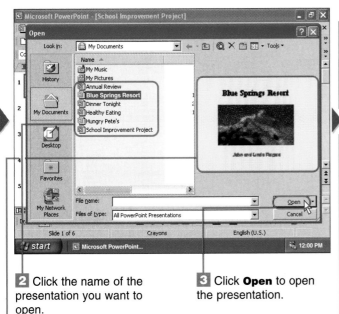

2 Click the name of the presentation you want to open.

■ This area displays the first slide in the presentation you selected.

3 Click **Open** to open the presentation.

■ The presentation opens and appears on your screen. You can now review and make changes to the presentation.

■ This area displays the name of the presentation.

■ If you already had a presentation open, the new presentation appears in a new Microsoft PowerPoint window. For information on switching between presentations, see page 30.

SWITCH BETWEEN PRESENTATIONS

You can have several presentations open at once. PowerPoint allows you to easily switch from one open presentation to another.

SWITCH BETWEEN PRESENTATIONS

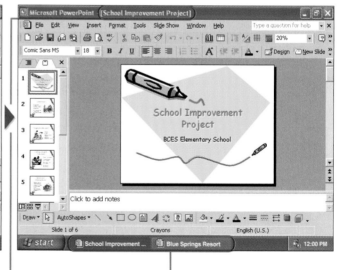

1 Click **Window** to display a list of all the presentations you have open.

2 Click the name of the presentation you want to switch to.

■ The presentation appears.

■ This area shows the name of the displayed presentation.

■ The taskbar displays a button for each open presentation. You can also click the button for a presentation you want to work with to display the presentation.

Note: If a menu appears displaying the name of each open presentation, click the name of the presentation you want to display.

CLOSE A PRESENTATION

When you finish working with a presentation, you can close the presentation to remove it from your screen.

When you close a presentation, you do not exit the PowerPoint program. You can continue to work with other presentations.

CLOSE A PRESENTATION

■ Before closing a presentation, you should save any changes you made to the presentation. To save a presentation, see page 26.

1 Click **File**.

2 Click **Close** to close the presentation.

■ The presentation disappears from your screen.

■ If you had more than one presentation open, the second last presentation you worked with appears on your screen.

SEARCH FOR A PRESENTATION

If you cannot remember the name or location of a presentation you want to work with, you can search for the presentation.

SEARCH FOR A PRESENTATION

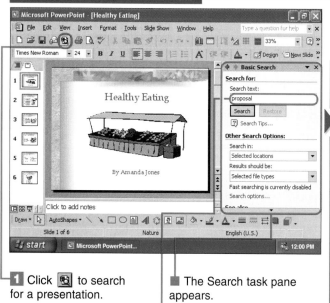

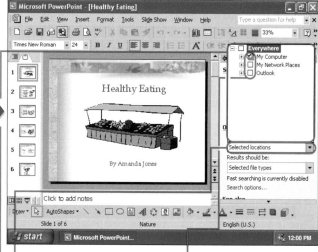

1 Click 🔍 to search for a presentation.

Note: If 🔍 is not displayed, click ⁈ on the Standard toolbar to display the button.

■ The Search task pane appears.

2 Click this area and type one or more words you want to search for.

Note: If this area already contains text, drag the mouse I over the existing text and then press the Delete key. Then perform step 2.

3 Click ▼ in this area to select the locations you want to search.

■ A check mark (✔) appears beside each location PowerPoint will search.

Note: By default, PowerPoint will search all the drives and folders on your computer.

4 You can click the box beside a location to add (✔) or remove (☐) a check mark.

5 To close the list of locations, click outside the list.

How will PowerPoint use the words I specify to search for presentations?

PowerPoint will search the contents and names of presentations for the words you specify. When searching the contents of presentations, PowerPoint will search for various forms of the words. For example, searching for "run" will find "run," "running" and "ran."

When selecting the locations and types of files I want to search for, how can I display more items?

Each item that displays a plus sign (⊞) contains hidden items. To display the hidden items, click the plus sign (⊞) beside the item (⊞ changes to ⊟). To once again hide the items, click the minus sign (⊟) beside the item.

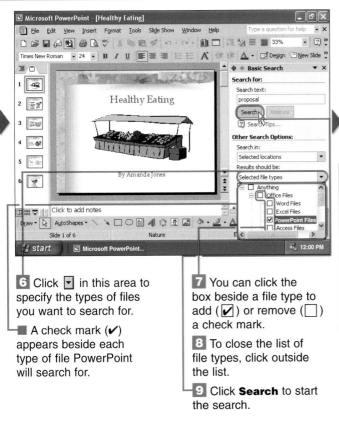

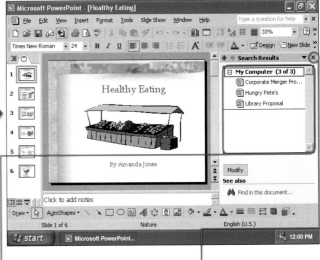

■ **6** Click ▾ in this area to specify the types of files you want to search for.

■ A check mark (✔) appears beside each type of file PowerPoint will search for.

7 You can click the box beside a file type to add (☑) or remove (☐) a check mark.

8 To close the list of file types, click outside the list.

9 Click **Search** to start the search.

■ This area lists the presentations that contain the words you specified.

■ To open a presentation in the list, click the presentation.

■ To hide the Search task pane at any time, click ☒ .

33

PROTECT A PRESENTATION

You can prevent other people from opening or making changes to a presentation by protecting it with a password.

PROTECT A PRESENTATION

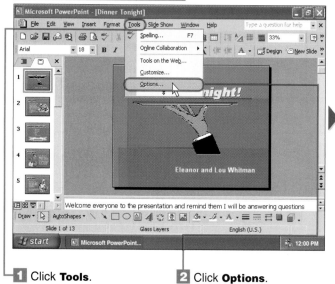

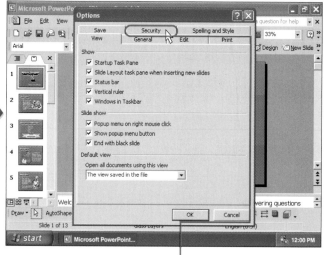

1 Click **Tools**.

2 Click **Options**.

■ The Options dialog box appears.

3 Click the **Security** tab.

What password should I use to protect my presentation?

When choosing a password, you should not use words that people can easily associate with you, such as your name or favorite sport. The most effective passwords connect two words or numbers with a special character (example: **car#123**). A password can contain up to 15 characters and can be any combination of letters, numbers and symbols.

Should I take any special precautions with my password?

You should write down your password and keep it in a safe place. If you forget the password, you may not be able to open or modify the presentation.

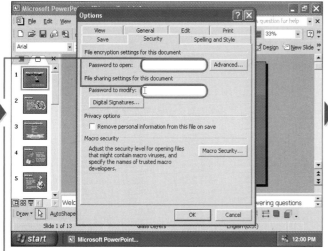

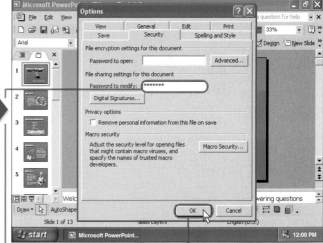

4 Click the box for the type of password you want to enter.

Password to open
Prevents people from opening the presentation without entering the correct password.

Password to modify
Prevents people from making changes to the presentation without entering the correct password.

5 Type the password you want to use.

6 Click **OK** to continue.

CONTINUED

PROTECT A PRESENTATION

After you protect a presentation with a password, PowerPoint will ask you to enter the password each time you open the presentation.

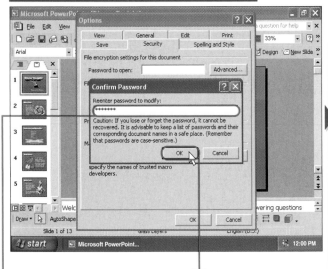

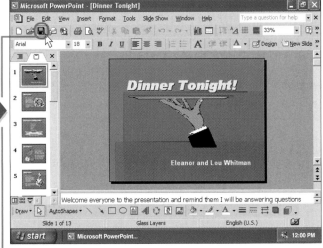

■ The Confirm Password dialog box appears, asking you to confirm the password you entered.

7 Type the password again to confirm the password.

8 Click **OK** to protect the presentation.

9 Click 🔲 to save the changes you made to the presentation.

Note: If you have not previously saved the presentation, the Save As dialog box will appear. To save a presentation, see page 26.

I typed the correct password, but PowerPoint will not open my presentation. What is wrong?

Passwords in PowerPoint are case sensitive. If you do not enter the correct uppercase and lowercase letters, PowerPoint will not accept the password. For example, if your password is **car#123**, you cannot enter **Car#123** or **CAR#123** to open the presentation.

How do I unprotect a presentation?

To unprotect a presentation, perform steps **1** to **3** on page 34. Drag the mouse I over the existing password in the Options dialog box until you highlight the password and then press the Delete key. Then perform step **9** below.

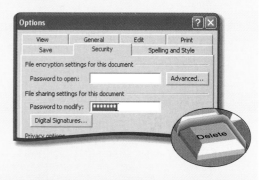

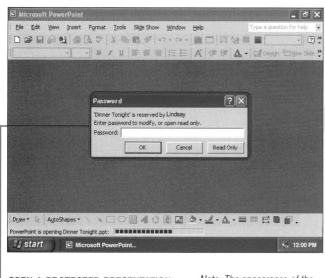

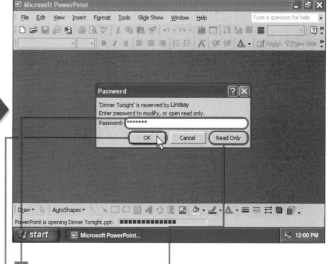

OPEN A PROTECTED PRESENTATION

■ A Password dialog box appears each time you open a protected presentation. To open a presentation, see page 28.

Note: The appearance of the dialog box depends on the type of password assigned to the presentation.

1 Type the correct password.

2 Click **OK**.

■ If the **Read Only** button is available, you can click the button to open the presentation without entering a password. You will not be able to make changes to the presentation.

GETTING HELP

If you do not know how to perform a task in PowerPoint, you can ask a question to find help information for the task. Asking a question allows you to quickly find help information of interest.

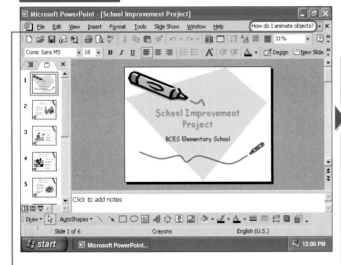

1 Click this area and type your question. Then press the Enter key.

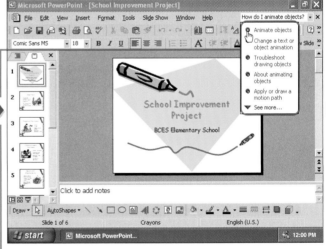

■ A list of help topics related to your question appears.

2 Click a help topic of interest.

*Note: If more help topics exist, you can click **See more** to view the additional topics.*

What other ways can I obtain help?

In the Microsoft PowerPoint Help window, you can use the following tabs to obtain help information.

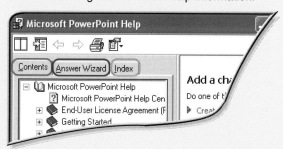

Index

You can type a word of interest and then press the `Enter` key or double-click a word in the alphabetical list of keywords to display help topics related to the word.

Contents

You can double-click a book icon (📖) or click a page icon (📄) to browse through the contents of Microsoft PowerPoint Help.

Answer Wizard

You can type a question and then press the `Enter` key to display help topics related to the question.

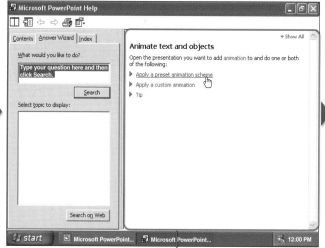

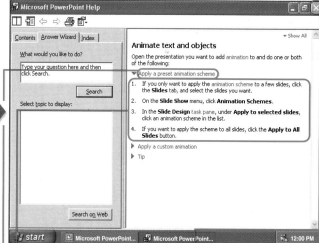

■ The Microsoft PowerPoint Help window appears.

Note: To maximize the Microsoft PowerPoint Help window to fill your screen, click ▣ in the top right corner of the window.

■ This area displays information about the help topic you selected.

3 To display additional information for a word or phrase that appears in color, click the word or phrase.

■ The additional information appears.

Note: The additional information may be a definition, a series of steps or a tip.

■ To once again hide the additional information, click the colored word or phrase.

4 When you finish reviewing the help information, click ⊠ to close the Microsoft PowerPoint Help window.

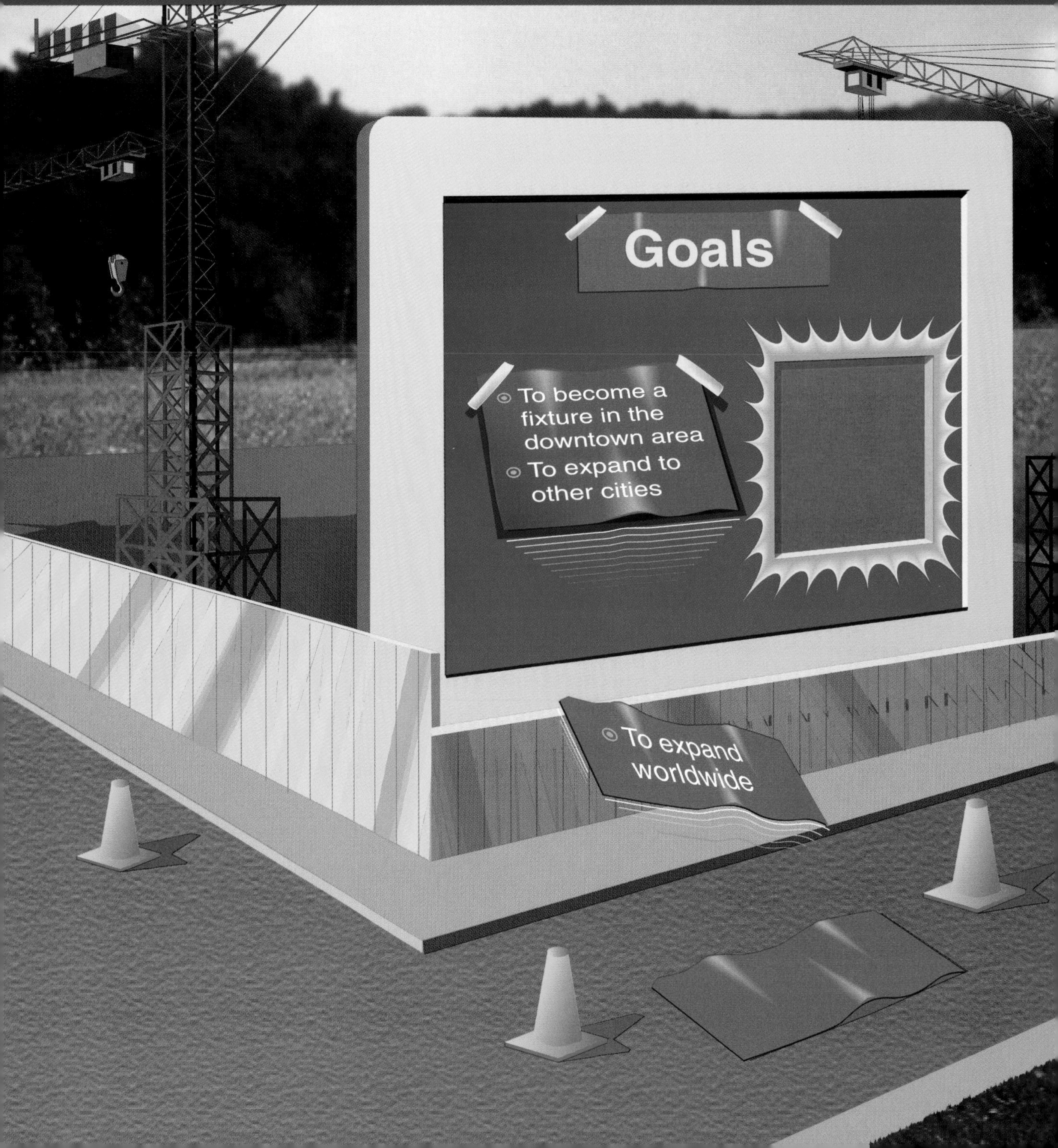
Goals
To become a fixture in the downtown area
To expand to other cities
To expand worldwide

CHAPTER 2

PowerPoint Basics

Are you wondering how to start working with your presentation? In this chapter, you will learn how to change the view of a presentation, change the slide layout and more.

CHANGE THE VIEW OF A PRESENTATION

PowerPoint offers several ways that you can view a presentation on your screen.

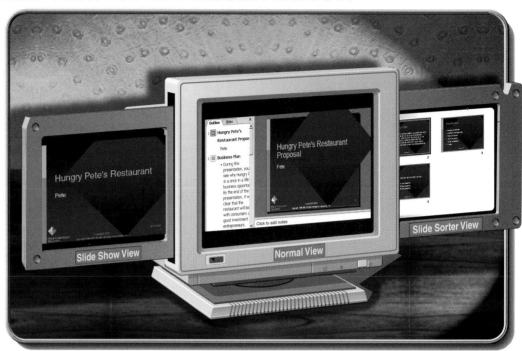

Slide Show View   Normal View   Slide Sorter View

Each view displays the same presentation. If you make changes to your presentation in one view, the other views will also display the changes.

CHANGE THE VIEW OF A PRESENTATION

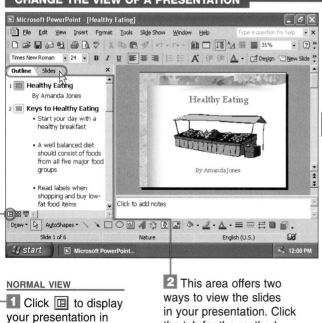

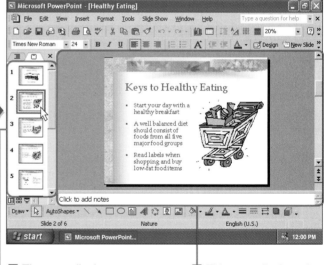

NORMAL VIEW

1 Click 🔲 to display your presentation in the Normal view.

2 This area offers two ways to view the slides in your presentation. Click the tab for the method you want to use.

▤ **Outline**–Display the text on each slide

▥ **Slides**–Display a miniature version of each slide

■ The area displays text or a miniature version of each slide, depending on the tab you selected.

3 Click a slide of interest.

■ This area displays the slide you selected and the notes for the slide. For information on notes, see page 238.

42

When would I use each view?

Normal View

Useful for creating and editing your presentation. This view allows you to see different parts of your presentation, such as the current slide and your notes, on a single screen.

Slide Sorter View

Useful for reorganizing and deleting slides. This view allows you to see the overall organization of your presentation.

Slide Show View

Useful for previewing your presentation. This view allows you to see how your audience will view your presentation.

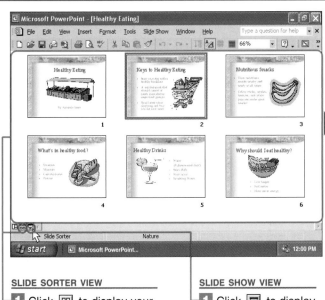

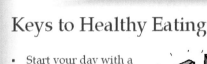

SLIDE SORTER VIEW

1 Click ⊞ to display your presentation in the Slide Sorter view.

■ This area displays miniature versions of all the slides in your presentation.

SLIDE SHOW VIEW

1 Click 🖵 to display your presentation in the Slide Show view.

■ A full-screen version of the current slide appears on your screen.

■ You can click anywhere on the current slide to move through the slides in your presentation and view your entire slide show. For more information on viewing a slide show, see page 266.

BROWSE THROUGH A PRESENTATION

Your computer screen cannot display your entire presentation at once. You can browse through your presentation to view other areas of the presentation.

BROWSE THROUGH A PRESENTATION

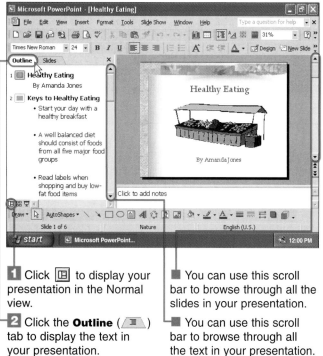

1 Click 🖿 to display your presentation in the Normal view.

2 Click the **Outline** (☰) tab to display the text in your presentation.

■ You can use this scroll bar to browse through all the slides in your presentation.

■ You can use this scroll bar to browse through all the text in your presentation.

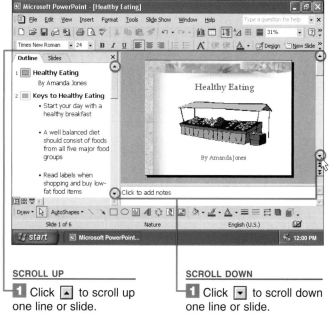

SCROLL UP

1 Click ▲ to scroll up one line or slide.

SCROLL DOWN

1 Click ▼ to scroll down one line or slide.

How can I browse through the notes in my presentation?

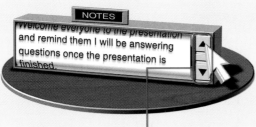

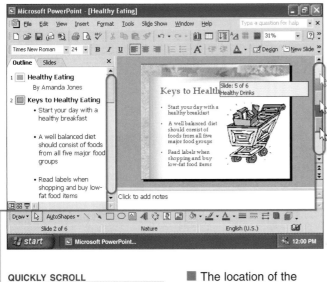

■ Any notes you have created for the current slide appear in the Notes pane.

1 To browse through the notes, click ▲ or ▼.

Note: For information on creating notes, see page 238.

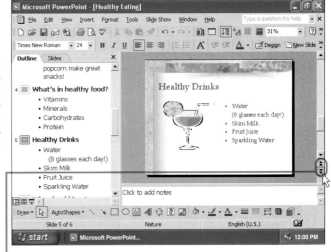

How do I use a wheeled mouse to browse through my presentation?

A wheeled mouse has a wheel between the left and right mouse buttons. Moving this wheel lets you quickly browse through your presentation. The Microsoft IntelliMouse is a popular example of a wheeled mouse.

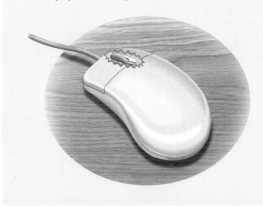

QUICKLY SCROLL

1 To quickly scroll through your presentation, drag the scroll box along the scroll bar.

■ The location of the scroll box indicates which part of your presentation you are viewing. To view the middle of your presentation, drag the scroll box halfway down the scroll bar.

DISPLAY PREVIOUS OR NEXT SLIDE

1 Click one of the following buttons.

▲ Display previous slide

▼ Display next slide

CHANGE THE SLIDE LAYOUT

You can change the layout of a slide in your presentation to accommodate text and objects you want to add.

Each slide layout displays a different arrangement of placeholders. Placeholders allow you to easily add objects you want to appear on a slide, such as a clip art image or a chart.

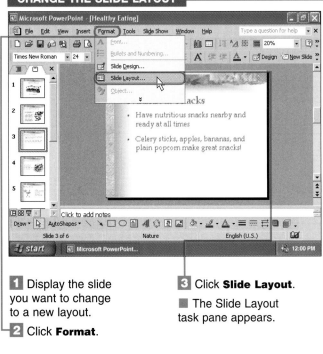

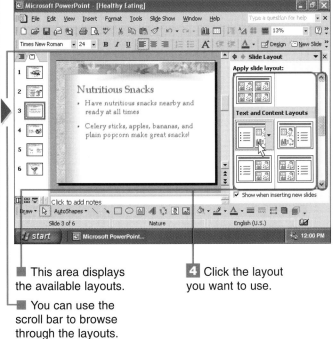

1 Display the slide you want to change to a new layout.

2 Click **Format**.

3 Click **Slide Layout**.

■ The Slide Layout task pane appears.

■ This area displays the available layouts.

■ You can use the scroll bar to browse through the layouts.

4 Click the layout you want to use.

How can I determine the types of placeholders a slide layout contains?

The icons displayed on each slide layout indicate the types of placeholders in the layout.

—	Title
☰	List of points
🖼	Object such as a table, chart, clip art image or diagram
👤	Clip art image
📊	Chart
🎞	Media clip
▦	Table
🗂	Diagram or organization chart

If a slide already contains text or an object, do I have to change the slide layout before adding a new object?

No. You can add a new object to the slide without first adding a placeholder for the object. PowerPoint will automatically adjust the slide layout for you and display the Automatic Layout Options button (📋). If you do not want to use the new slide layout, click the Automatic Layout Options button to display a list of options and then select **Undo Automatic Layout**. The Automatic Layout Options button is available only until you perform another task.

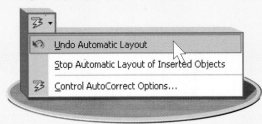

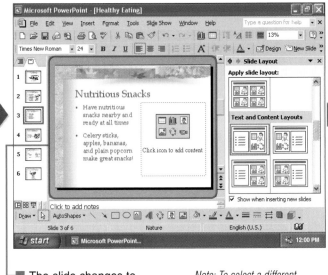

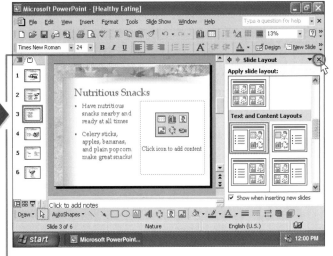

■ The slide changes to the layout you selected.

Note: To select a different layout, repeat step 4.

5 When you finish selecting a slide layout, you can click ✕ to hide the Slide Layout task pane.

ADD A NEW SLIDE

You can insert a new slide into your presentation to add a new topic you want to discuss.

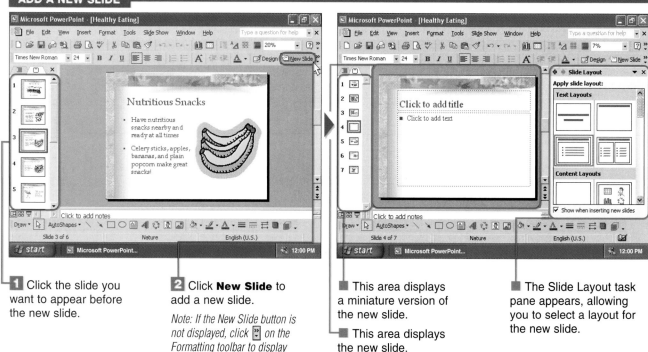

1 Click the slide you want to appear before the new slide.

2 Click **New Slide** to add a new slide.

Note: If the New Slide button is not displayed, click ⁉ on the Formatting toolbar to display the button.

■ This area displays a miniature version of the new slide.

■ This area displays the new slide.

■ The Slide Layout task pane appears, allowing you to select a layout for the new slide.

How much text should I display on a slide?

You should be careful not to include too much text on a slide in your presentation. If you add too much text to a slide, the slide may be difficult to read and you will minimize the impact of important ideas. If a slide contains too much text, you should add a new slide to accommodate some of the text.

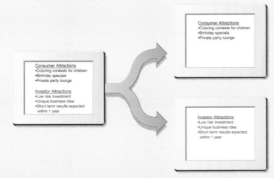

What types of layouts can I use for a new slide?

Each slide layout displays a different arrangement of placeholders, which determine the position of text and objects on a slide. The icons in the placeholders indicate the type of information you can add to the placeholder.

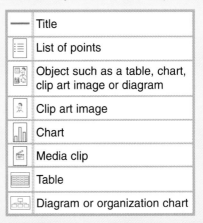

—	Title
☰	List of points
🖼	Object such as a table, chart, clip art image or diagram
👤	Clip art image
📊	Chart
🎬	Media clip
▦	Table
🗂	Diagram or organization chart

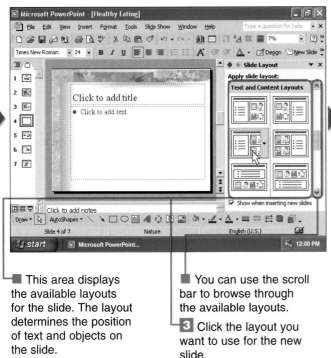

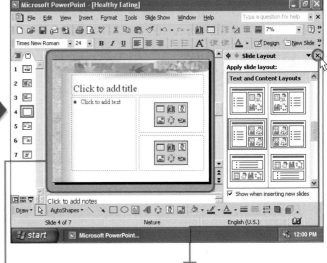

■ This area displays the available layouts for the slide. The layout determines the position of text and objects on the slide.

■ You can use the scroll bar to browse through the available layouts.

3 Click the layout you want to use for the new slide.

■ The slide changes to the layout you selected.

Note: To select a different layout, repeat step 3.

4 When the slide displays the layout you want to use, you can click ✖ to hide the Slide Layout task pane.

ZOOM IN OR OUT

PowerPoint allows you to enlarge or reduce the display of information on your screen.

You can increase the zoom setting to view an area of your presentation in more detail or decrease the zoom setting to see more information at once.

ZOOM IN OR OUT

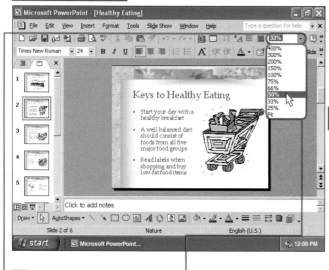

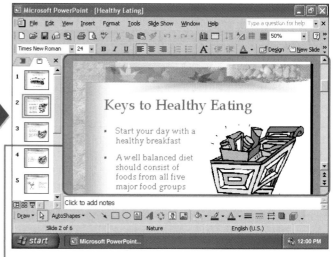

1 Click the area you want to enlarge or reduce. You can enlarge or reduce the area displaying the outline, current slide or notes.

2 Click ▾ in this area to display a list of zoom settings.

Note: If the Zoom area is not displayed, click ▸▸ on the Standard toolbar to display the area.

3 Click the zoom setting you want to use.

■ The area appears in the new zoom setting. You can edit the information in the area as usual.

■ Changing the zoom setting will not affect the way information appears on a printed page.

*Note: To return the current slide to the normal zoom setting, repeat steps 1 to 3, selecting **Fit** in step 3.*

DISPLAY OR HIDE A TOOLBAR

PowerPoint offers several toolbars that you can display or hide to suit your needs. Toolbars contain buttons that you can select to quickly perform common tasks.

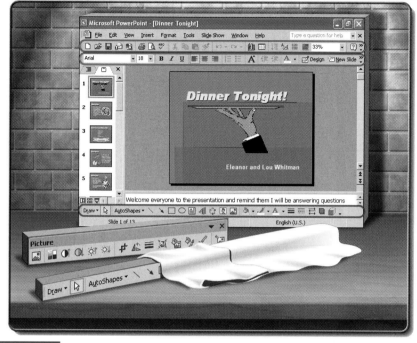

When you first start PowerPoint, the **Standard**, **Formatting** and **Drawing** toolbars appear on your screen.

DISPLAY OR HIDE A TOOLBAR

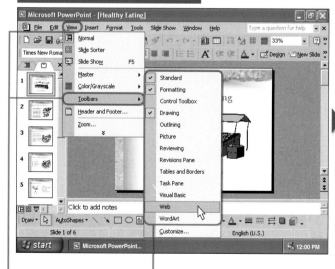

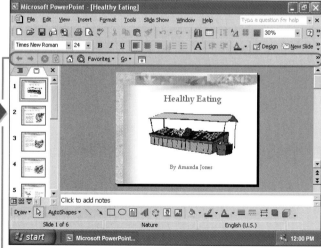

1 Click **View**.

2 Click **Toolbars**.

■ A list of toolbars appears. A check mark (✔) appears beside the name of each toolbar that is currently displayed.

3 Click the name of the toolbar you want to display or hide.

■ PowerPoint displays or hides the toolbar you selected.

Note: A screen displaying fewer toolbars provides a larger and less cluttered working area.

51

MOVE A TOOLBAR

You can move a toolbar to the top, bottom, right or left edge of your screen.

You can move a toolbar to the same row as another toolbar or to its own row.

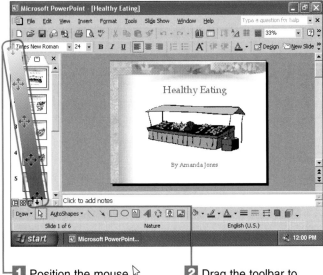

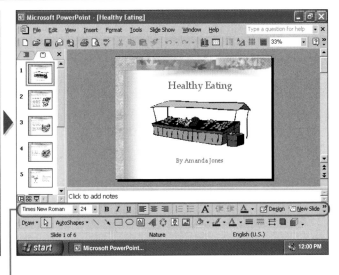

1 Position the mouse ⏳ over the move handle (⫾) of the toolbar you want to move (⏳ changes to ✛).

2 Drag the toolbar to a new location.

■ The toolbar appears in the new location.

52

SIZE A TOOLBAR

You can increase the size of a toolbar to display more buttons on the toolbar. This is useful when a toolbar appears on the same row as another toolbar and cannot display all its buttons.

You cannot size a toolbar that appears on its own row.

SIZE A TOOLBAR

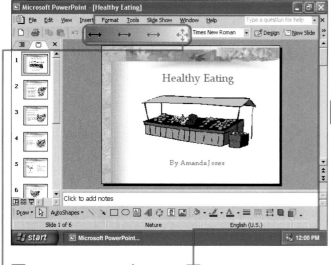

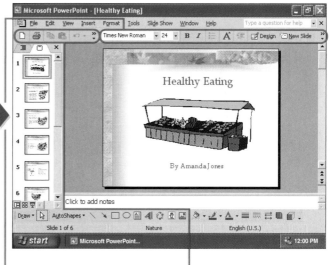

1 Position the mouse ⟍ over the move handle (⫾) of the toolbar you want to size (⟍ changes to ✛).

2 Drag the mouse ↔ until the toolbar is the size you want.

■ The toolbar displays the new size.

■ The new toolbar size affects the location and size of other toolbars on the same row.

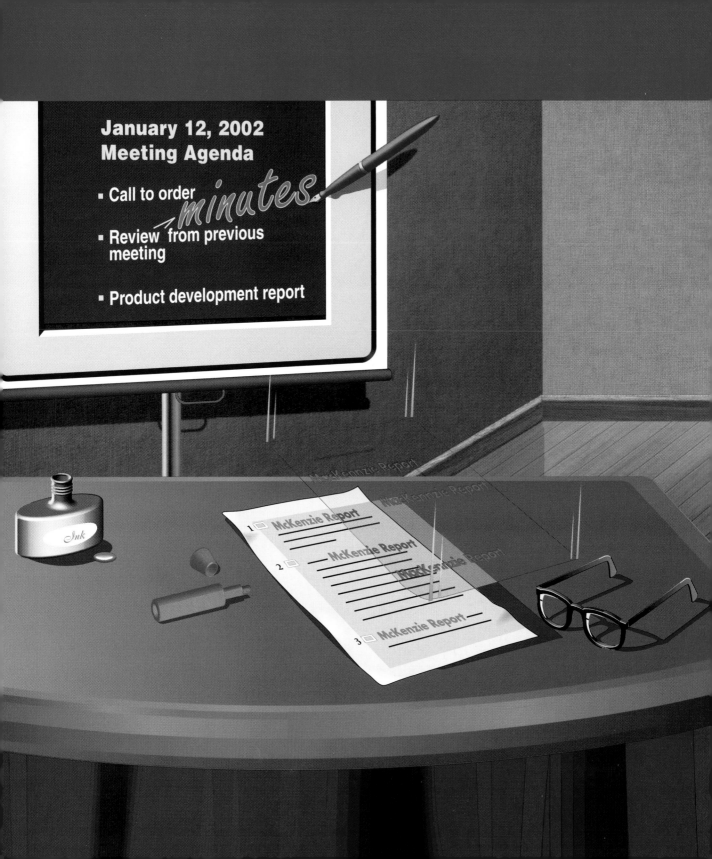

CHAPTER 3

Edit Text

Do you want to edit the text in your presentation or check the text for spelling errors? This chapter teaches you how.

Overview

We provide meals for th
handicapped, and peo   ly too busy
to prepare a deliciou   n that is
nutritious, satisfying   d low in fat!

ans available to suit
heeds. We can
evening meals a week.

SELECT TEXT

Before making changes to text in your presentation, you will often need to select the text you want to work with. Selected text appears highlighted on your screen.

SELECT TEXT

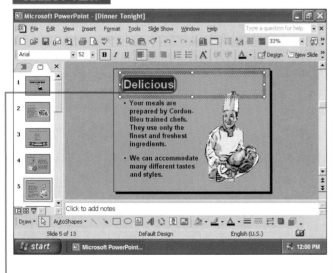

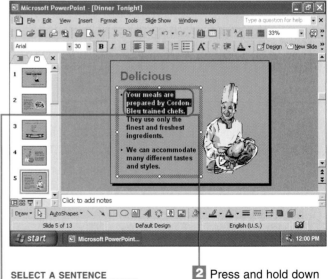

SELECT A WORD

1 Double-click the word you want to select.

■ To deselect text, click outside the selected area.

SELECT A SENTENCE

1 Click in the sentence you want to select.

2 Press and hold down the **Ctrl** key as you click the sentence again.

56

Is there another way to select text in my presentation?

You can also perform the steps below to select text on the Outline tab in the Normal view. The Outline tab displays the text for all the slides in your presentation. For information on the Outline tab, see page 42.

■ To display the Outline tab in the Normal view, click the **Outline** (▥) tab.

How can I quickly select all the text on a slide?

You can quickly select all the text on a slide displayed on the Outline tab. For information on the Outline tab, see page 42.

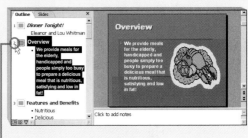

1 To select all the text for a slide, click the number of the slide that contains the text you want to select.

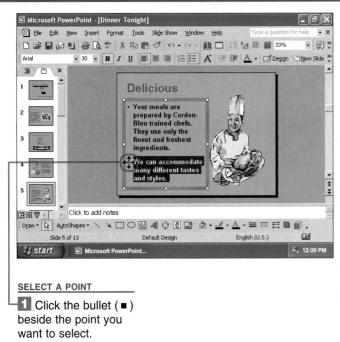

SELECT A POINT

1 Click the bullet (■) beside the point you want to select.

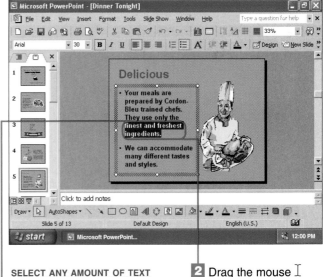

SELECT ANY AMOUNT OF TEXT

1 Position the mouse I over the first word you want to select.

2 Drag the mouse I until you highlight the text you want to select.

REPLACE SELECTED TEXT

You can replace text you have selected in your presentation with new text. Replacing selected text allows you to change all the text for a slide title or an entire point at once.

When you use the AutoContent Wizard to create a presentation, you need to replace the sample text provided by the wizard with your own text. For information on the AutoContent Wizard, see page 18.

REPLACE SELECTED TEXT

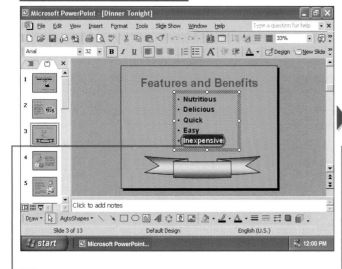

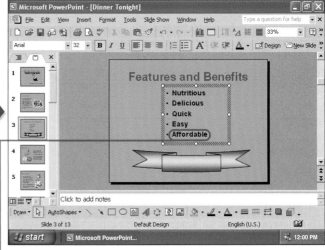

1 Select the text you want to replace with new text. To select text, see page 56.

2 Type the new text.

■ The text you type replaces the text you selected.

Note: You can also perform these steps to replace text on the Outline tab in the Normal view. The Outline tab displays the text for all the slides in your presentation.

UNDO CHANGES

PowerPoint remembers the last changes you made to your presentation. If you regret these changes, you can cancel them by using the Undo feature.

The Undo feature can cancel your last editing and formatting changes.

UNDO CHANGES

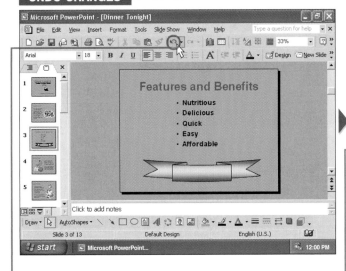

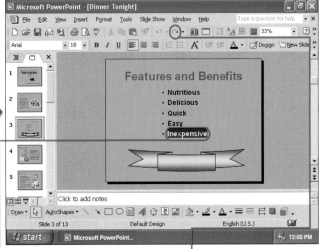

1 Click 🖎 to undo the last change you made to your presentation.

Note: If 🖎 is not displayed, click ⏵ on the Standard toolbar to display the button.

■ PowerPoint cancels the last change you made to your presentation.

■ You can repeat step **1** to cancel previous changes you made.

■ To reverse the results of using the Undo feature, click 🖎.

Note: If 🖎 is not displayed, click ⏵ on the Standard toolbar to display the button.

INSERT TEXT

PowerPoint allows you to type text onto a slide in your presentation quickly and easily.

INSERT CHARACTERS

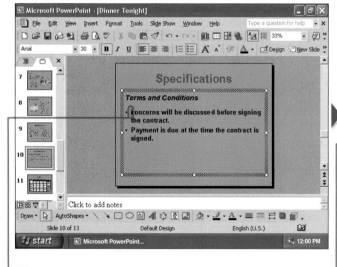

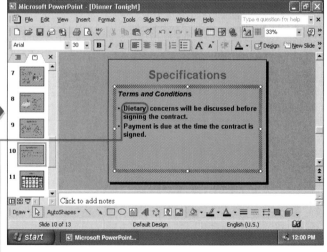

1 Click where you want to insert the new text.

■ The text you type will appear where the insertion point flashes on your screen.

Note: You can press the ←, ↓, ↑ or → key to move the insertion point.

2 Type the text you want to insert.

■ To insert a blank space, press the **Spacebar**.

Is there another way to insert text?

You can also insert text on the Outline tab in the Normal view. The Outline tab displays all the text for your presentation. Text you insert on the Outline tab will automatically appear on the slide in the Slide pane. For more information on the Outline tab, see page 42.

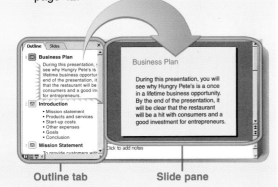

Outline tab   **Slide pane**

Why does the AutoFit Options button ( ) appear when I insert text in a placeholder on a slide?

If you insert more text than a placeholder can hold, PowerPoint will automatically change the line spacing and resize the text to fit in the placeholder. The AutoFit Options button ( ) also appears, allowing you to change how text fits in the placeholder. For example, you may be able to specify whether you want PowerPoint to keep the new spacing and text size or continue the text on a new slide.

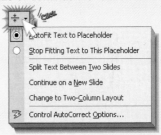

INSERT A NEW POINT

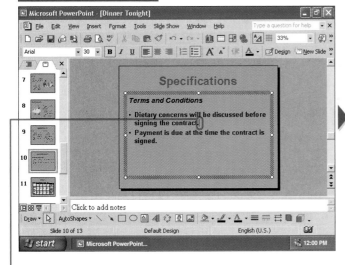

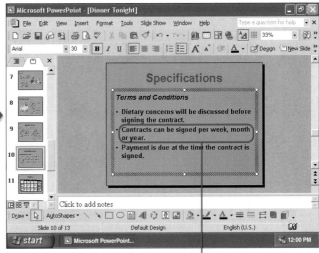

1 Click at the end of the point directly above where you want to insert a new point.

2 Press the **Enter** key to insert a blank line for the new point.

3 Type the text for the new point.

DELETE TEXT

You can delete text from a slide to remove information that you no longer need in your presentation.

DELETE TEXT

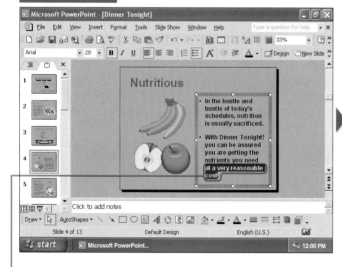

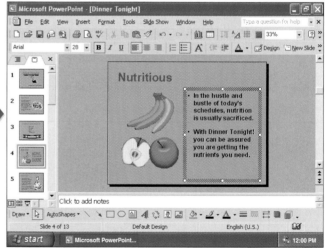

1 Select the text you want to delete. To select text, see page 56.

2 Press the Delete key to remove the text from your presentation.

■ The text disappears.

■ To delete a single character, click to the right of the character you want to delete and then press the +Backspace key. PowerPoint will delete the character to the left of the flashing insertion point.

Note: You can also perform these steps to delete text on the Outline tab in the Normal view. The Outline tab displays the text for all the slides in your presentation.

You can display
only the titles
for each slide
in your outline
and hide the
remaining text.

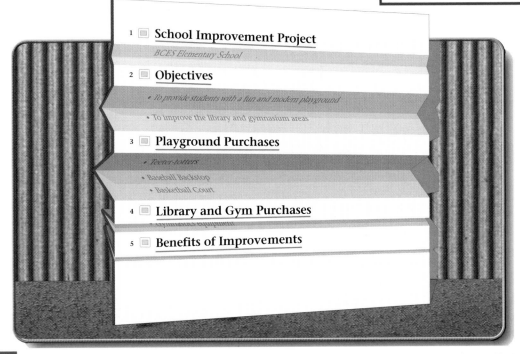

Hiding the text
on the slides lets
you focus on the
main ideas of your
presentation.

HIDE SLIDE TEXT

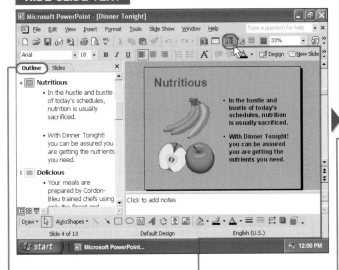

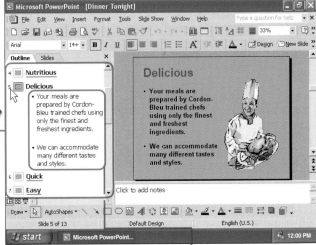

1 Click the **Outline** (▤)
tab to display the text on each
slide in your presentation.

2 Click 🔢 to hide the
text on all the slides in
your outline.

*Note: If 🔢 is not displayed,
click ▾ on the Standard toolbar
to display the button.*

■ A gray line appears
below each slide title to
indicate the text on the
slide is hidden.

3 To display the text
on a slide, double-click
the number of the slide.

■ The text on the slide
appears. You can repeat
step **3** to once again hide
the text.

■ To once again display
the text on all the slides,
repeat step **2**.

MOVE OR COPY TEXT

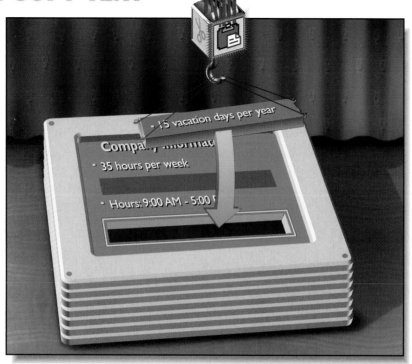

You can move or copy text to a new location in your presentation. You can move or copy text directly on your slides or in the outline of your presentation.

Moving text is useful when you want to reorganize the ideas on a slide. When you move text, the text disappears from its original location.

Copying text allows you to repeat information in your presentation without having to retype the text. When you copy text, the text appears in both the original and new locations.

MOVE OR COPY TEXT

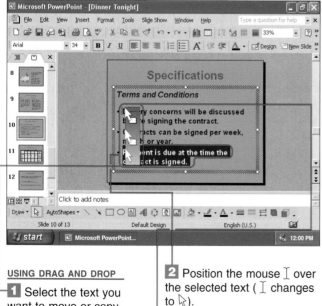

USING DRAG AND DROP

1 Select the text you want to move or copy. To select text, see page 56.

2 Position the mouse I over the selected text (I changes to ⬓).

3 To move the text, drag the mouse ⬓ to where you want to place the text.

Note: The text will appear where you position the dotted insertion point on your screen.

■ The text moves to the new location.

■ To copy text, perform steps **1** to **3**, except press and hold down the **Ctrl** key as you perform step **3**.

64

How can I use the Clipboard task pane to move or copy text?

The Clipboard task pane displays up to the last 24 items you have selected to move or copy. To place a clipboard item in your presentation, click the location where you

want the item to appear and then click the item in the task pane. For more information on the task pane, see page 16.

Why does the Paste Options button ( ) appear when I move or copy text?

You can use the Paste Options button ( ) to change the format of the text you have moved or copied. For example, you can choose to keep the original formatting of the text. Click the Paste Options button to display a list of options and then select the option you want to use. The Paste Options button is available only until you perform another task.

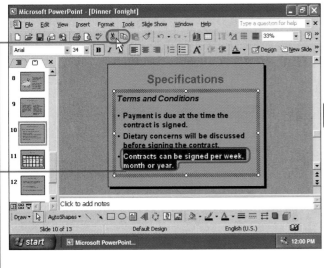

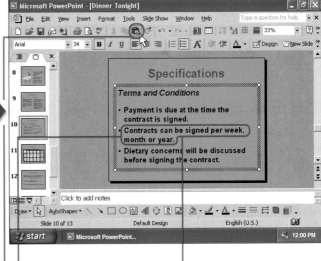

USING THE TOOLBAR BUTTONS

1 Select the text you want to move or copy. To select text, see page 56.

2 Click one of the following buttons.

✂ Move text

📋 Copy text

Note: If the button you want is not displayed, click ⯯ on the Standard toolbar to display the button.

■ The Clipboard task pane may appear. To use the Clipboard task pane, see the top of this page.

3 Click the location where you want to place the text.

4 Click 📋 to place the text in the new location.

Note: If 📋 is not displayed, click ⯯ on the Standard toolbar to display the button.

■ The text appears in the new location.

INSERT SYMBOLS

You can add symbols that do not appear on your keyboard to your slides.

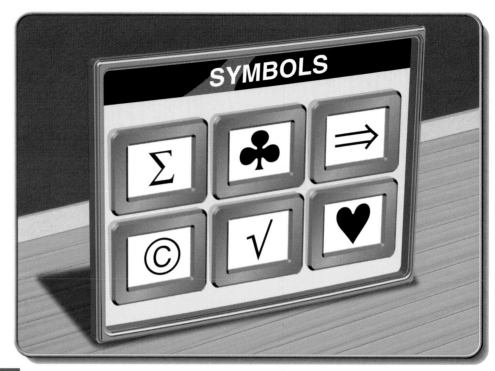

INSERT SYMBOLS

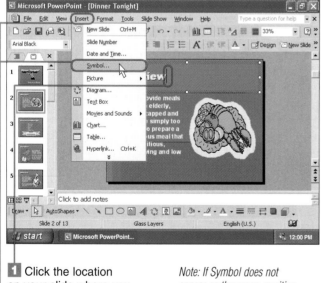

1 Click the location on your slide where you want a symbol to appear.

2 Click **Insert**.

3 Click **Symbol**.

Note: If Symbol does not appear on the menu, position the mouse ⍩ over the bottom of the menu to display the menu option.

■ The Symbol dialog box appears, displaying the symbols for the current font.

4 To display the symbols for another font, click ▼ in this area.

5 Click the font that provides the symbols you want to display.

66

Which font should I select in the Symbol dialog box?

The Symbol and Wingdings fonts are popular fonts available in the Symbol dialog box. The Symbol font contains a selection of symbols for mathematical equations. The Wingdings fonts contain a variety of bullet and arrow symbols.

Is there another way to add symbols to my slides?

When you type one of the following sets of characters, PowerPoint automatically replaces the characters with a symbol.

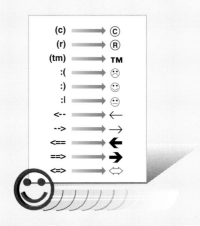

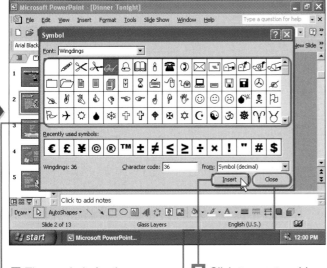

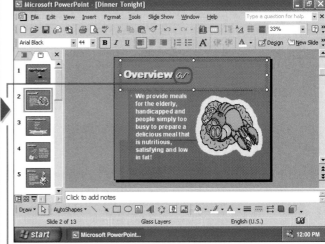

■ The symbols for the font you selected appear in this area.

6 Click the symbol you want to place on your slide.

7 Click **Insert** to add the symbol to your slide.

8 Click **Close** to close the Symbol dialog box.

■ The symbol appears on your slide.

■ To remove a symbol from a slide, drag the mouse I over the symbol until you highlight the symbol and then press the Delete key.

FIND TEXT

You can use the Find feature to quickly locate every occurrence of a word or phrase in your presentation.

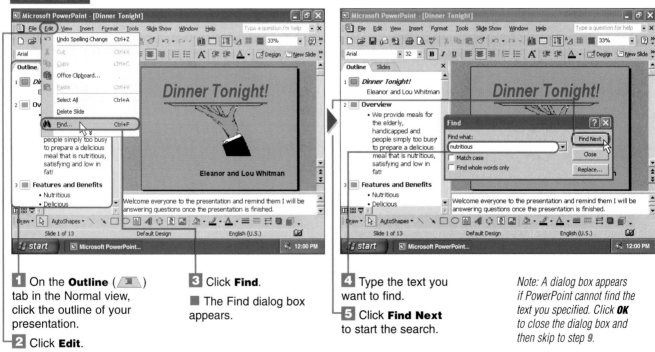

1 On the **Outline** ( ) tab in the Normal view, click the outline of your presentation.

2 Click **Edit**.

3 Click **Find**.

■ The Find dialog box appears.

4 Type the text you want to find.

5 Click **Find Next** to start the search.

*Note: A dialog box appears if PowerPoint cannot find the text you specified. Click **OK** to close the dialog box and then skip to step 9.*

Can I search for part of a word?

When you search for text in your presentation, PowerPoint will find the text even when the text is part of a larger word. For example, if you search for **place**, PowerPoint will also find **place**s, **place**ment and common**place**.

Why does this dialog box appear when I search for text in my presentation?

This dialog box appears if your presentation contains text that does not appear on the Outline (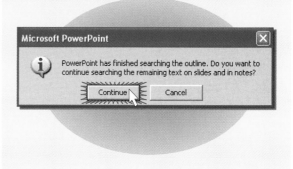) tab, such as notes. Click **Continue** to search the additional text in your presentation.

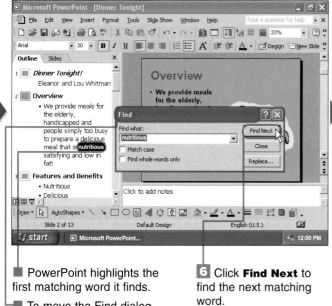

■ PowerPoint highlights the first matching word it finds.

■ To move the Find dialog box so you can clearly view the highlighted text, position the mouse ⇗ over the title bar and then drag the dialog box to a new location.

6 Click **Find Next** to find the next matching word.

*Note: To end the search at any time, click **Close**.*

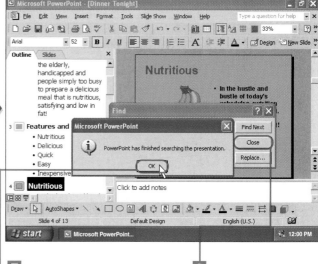

7 Repeat step **6** until a dialog box appears, telling you the search is complete.

8 Click **OK** to close the dialog box.

9 Click **Close** to close the Find dialog box.

REPLACE TEXT

You can find and replace every occurrence of a word or phrase in your presentation. This is useful if you have frequently misspelled a name.

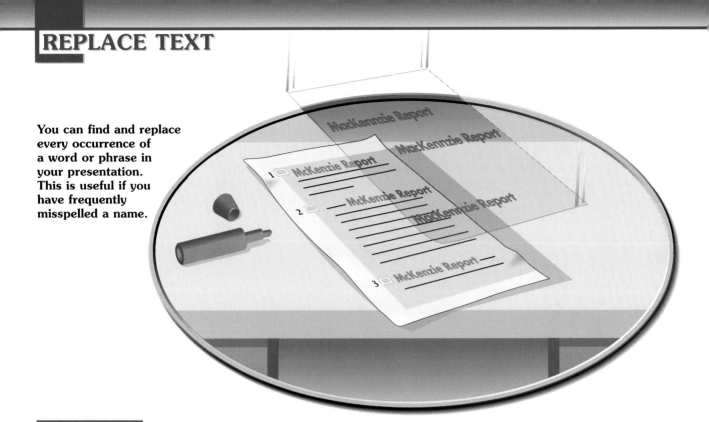

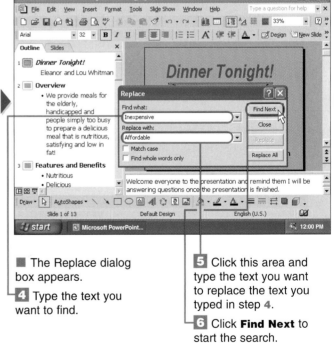

1 On the **Outline** ( ) tab in the Normal view, click the outline of your presentation.

2 Click **Edit**.

3 Click **Replace**.

Note: If Replace does not appear on the menu, position the mouse ⓚ over the bottom of the menu to display the menu option.

■ The Replace dialog box appears.

4 Type the text you want to find.

5 Click this area and type the text you want to replace the text you typed in step **4**.

6 Click **Find Next** to start the search.

Why does this dialog box appear when I am using the Replace feature?

This dialog box appears if your presentation contains additional text that is not included on the Outline ( ) tab, such as an AutoShape. Click **Continue** to search the additional text in your presentation.

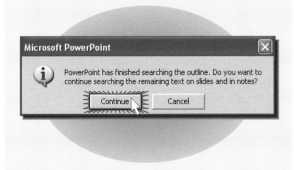

Can the Replace feature help me quickly enter text?

Yes. When you need to type a long word or phrase, such as **University of Massachusetts**, many times in a presentation, you can use the Replace feature to simplify the task. You can type a short form of the word or phrase, such as **UM**, throughout your presentation and then have PowerPoint replace the short form with the full word or phrase.

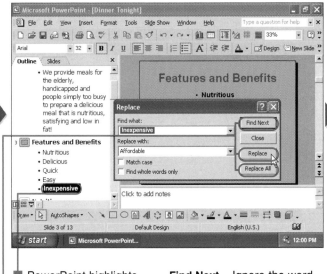

■ PowerPoint highlights the first matching word it finds.

7 Click one of the following options.

Find Next – Ignore the word

Replace – Replace the word

Replace All – Replace all occurrences of the word in the presentation

Note: To cancel the search at any time, press the Esc key.

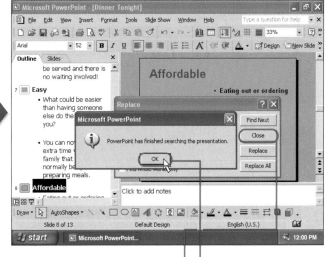

■ In this example, PowerPoint replaces the word and searches for the next matching word.

8 Replace or ignore matching words until a dialog box appears, telling you the search is complete.

9 Click **OK** to close the dialog box.

10 Click **Close** to close the Replace dialog box.

CHECK SPELLING

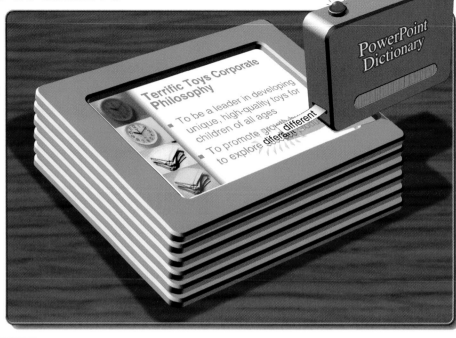

You can find and correct all the spelling errors in your presentation.

PowerPoint automatically underlines misspelled words in red. The underlines will not appear when you print your presentation or view the slide show.

CHECK SPELLING

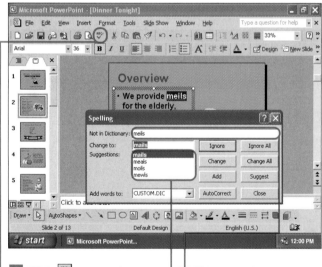

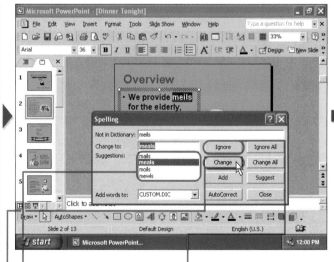

1 Click 🖍 to start the spell check.

Note: If 🖍 is not displayed, click ⯆ on the Standard toolbar to display the button.

■ The Spelling dialog box appears if PowerPoint finds a misspelled word in your presentation.

■ This area displays the first misspelled word.

■ This area displays suggestions for correcting the word.

2 Click the word you want to use to correct the misspelled word.

3 Click **Change** to replace the misspelled word with the word you selected.

■ To skip the word and continue checking your presentation, click **Ignore**.

*Note: To skip the word and all other occurrences of the word in your presentation, click **Ignore All**.*

Can PowerPoint automatically correct my typing mistakes?

PowerPoint automatically corrects common spelling errors as you type. For more information on the AutoCorrect feature, see page 74.

acheive	→ achieve
claer	→ clear
developement	→ development
foriegn	→ foreign
hte	→ the
occassion	→ occasion
recomend	→ recommend
statment	→ statement
wtih	→ with

How does PowerPoint find spelling errors in my presentation?

PowerPoint compares every word in your presentation to words in its dictionary. If a word in your presentation does not exist in the dictionary, the word is considered misspelled.

PowerPoint will not find a correctly spelled word used in the wrong context, such as "We have been in business for **sit** years." You should carefully review your presentation to find this type of error.

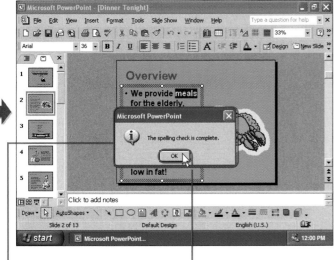

4 Correct or ignore misspelled words until this dialog box appears, telling you the spell check is complete.

5 Click **OK** to close the dialog box.

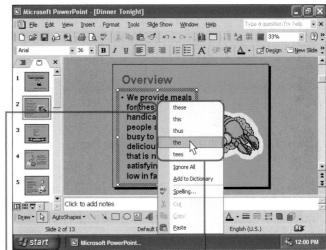

CORRECT ONE MISSPELLED WORD

1 Right-click the misspelled word you want to correct.

■ A menu appears with suggestions to correct the word.

2 To replace the misspelled word with one of the suggestions, click the suggestion.

Note: If you do not want to use any of the suggestions to correct the word, click outside the menu to close the menu.

USING AUTOCORRECT

PowerPoint automatically corrects hundreds of typing and spelling errors as you type. You can create an AutoCorrect entry to add your own words and phrases to the list of errors that PowerPoint corrects.

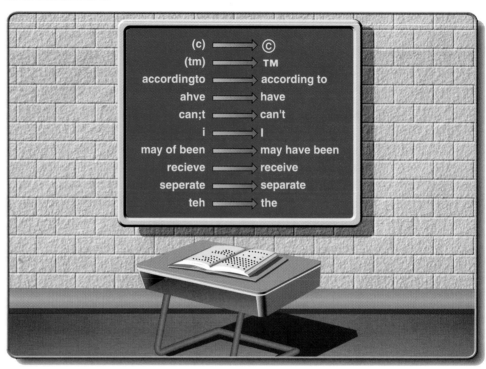

USING AUTOCORRECT

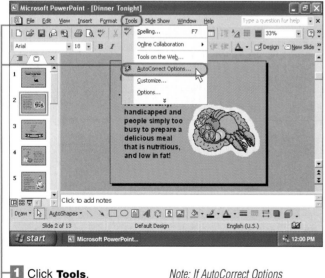

1 Click **Tools**.

2 Click **AutoCorrect Options**.

Note: If AutoCorrect Options does not appear on the menu, position the mouse ⇧ over the bottom of the menu to display the menu option.

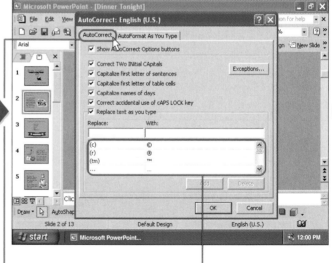

■ The AutoCorrect dialog box appears.

3 Click the **AutoCorrect** tab.

■ This area displays the list of AutoCorrect entries included with PowerPoint.

What other types of errors does PowerPoint automatically correct?

When you type two consecutive uppercase letters, PowerPoint automatically converts the second letter to lowercase. When you type a lowercase letter for the first letter of a sentence or the name of a day, PowerPoint automatically converts the letter to uppercase.

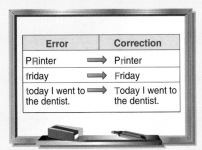

Error		Correction
PRinter	➡	Printer
friday	➡	Friday
today I went to the dentist.	➡	Today I went to the dentist.

Why does a blue rectangle (▭) appear when I position the mouse ⌖ over a word in my presentation?

A blue rectangle appears below a word that has been automatically corrected.

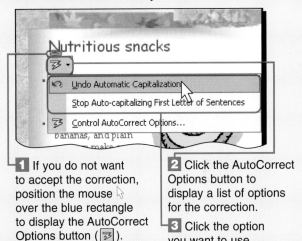

1 If you do not want to accept the correction, position the mouse ⌖ over the blue rectangle to display the AutoCorrect Options button (⚡).

2 Click the AutoCorrect Options button to display a list of options for the correction.

3 Click the option you want to use.

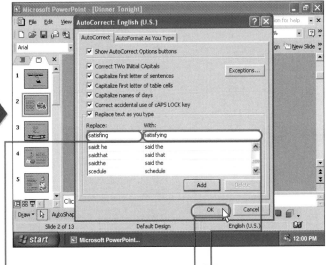

4 To add a new entry to the list, type the text you want PowerPoint to replace automatically. The text should not contain spaces and should not be a real word.

5 Click this area and type the text you want PowerPoint to automatically insert into your presentations.

6 Click **OK** to confirm your change.

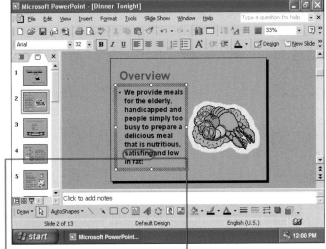

INSERT AN AUTOCORRECT ENTRY

■ After you create an AutoCorrect entry, PowerPoint will automatically insert the entry each time you type the corresponding text.

1 Click the location where you want the AutoCorrect entry to appear.

2 Type the text PowerPoint will automatically replace and then press the **Spacebar**.

■ PowerPoint automatically replaces the text with the AutoCorrect entry.

CHAPTER 4

Format Text

Would you like to improve the appearance of the text on your slides? This chapter shows you how to change the style and color of text, work with bullets and numbers and much more.

CHANGE FONT OF TEXT

You can change the font of text to enhance the appearance of a slide.

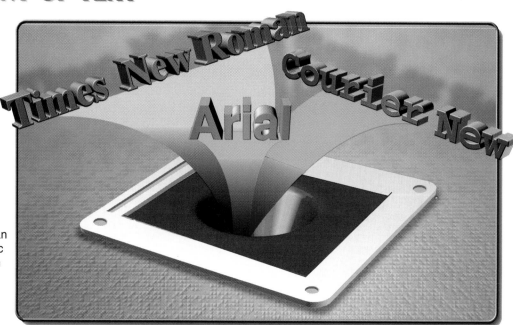

You should consider your audience when choosing a font. For example, choose an informal font, such as Comic Sans MS, for a presentation to your co-workers and a conservative font, such as Times New Roman, for a presentation to your clients.

CHANGE FONT OF TEXT

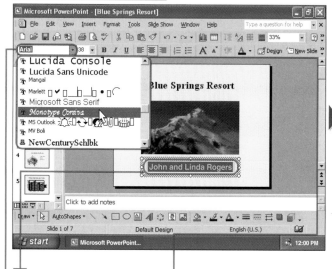

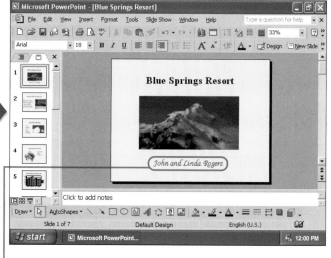

1 Select the text you want to change to a different font. To select text, see page 56.

2 Click ▼ in this area to display a list of the available fonts.

Note: If the Font area is not displayed, click ⟩⟩ *on the Formatting toolbar to display the area.*

3 Click the font you want to use.

Note: PowerPoint displays the fonts you have recently used at the top of the list.

■ The text you selected changes to a new font.

■ To deselect text, click outside the selected area.

CHANGE SIZE OF TEXT

You can increase
or decrease the
size of text on a
slide.

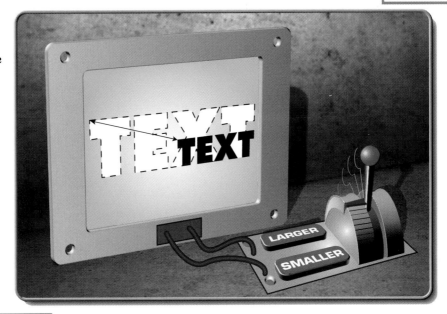

Larger text is
easier to read,
but smaller text
allows you to fit
more information
on a slide.

PowerPoint
measures the
size of text in
points. There
are 72 points
in an inch.

CHANGE SIZE OF TEXT

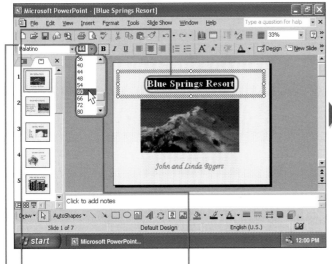

1 Select the text you
want to change to a
new size. To select text,
see page 56.

2 Click ▼ in this area
to display a list of the
available sizes.

*Note: If the Font Size area is
not displayed, click* ⟩⟩ *on the
Formatting toolbar to display
the area.*

3 Click the size you
want to use.

■ The text you selected
changes to the new size.

■ To deselect text, click
outside the selected area.

QUICKLY CHANGE SIZE OF TEXT

1 Select the text you want
to change to a new size.

2 Click **A** or **A** to
increase or decrease the
size of the text.

*Note: If the button you want is
not displayed, click* ⟩⟩ *on the
Formatting toolbar to display
the button.*

CHANGE STYLE OF TEXT

You can bold, italicize, underline or add a shadow to text to emphasize information on a slide.

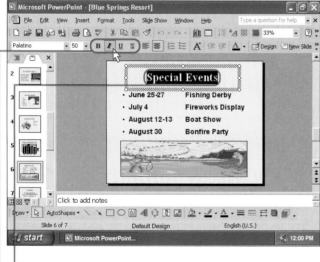

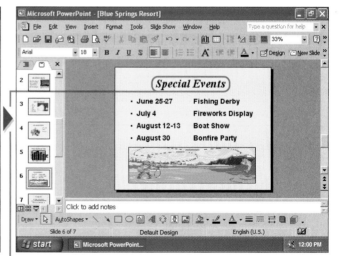

1 Select the text you want to bold, italicize, underline or add a shadow to. To select text, see page 56.

2 Click one of the following buttons.

B	Bold
I	Italic
U	Underline
S	Shadow

Note: If the button you want is not displayed, click ⟫ on the Formatting toolbar to display the button.

■ The text you selected appears in the new style.

■ To deselect text, click outside the selected area.

■ To remove a bold, italic, underline or shadow style, repeat steps **1** and **2**.

CHANGE TEXT COLOR

You can change the color of text on a slide to enhance the appearance of the slide and draw attention to important information.

CHANGE TEXT COLOR

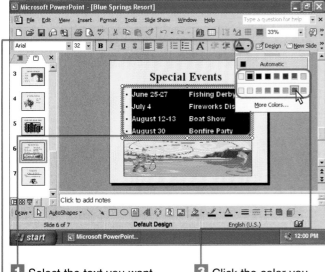

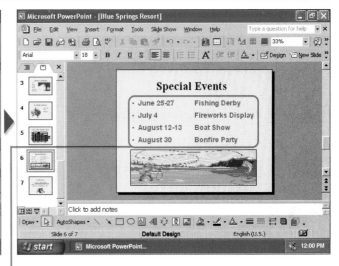

1 Select the text you want to change to a different color. To select text, see page 56.

2 Click ⏷ in this area to display the available colors.

Note: If 🅰⏷ is not displayed, click ⏷ on the Formatting toolbar to display the button.

3 Click the color you want to use.

Note: The available colors depend on the color scheme of the slide. For information on color schemes, see page 104.

■ The text appears in the color you selected.

■ To deselect text, click outside the selected area.

■ To return the text to the default color, repeat steps **1** to **3**, selecting **Automatic** in step **3**.

CHANGE APPEARANCE OF TEXT

You can make text in your presentation look more attractive by using various fonts, styles, sizes, effects and colors.

CHANGE APPEARANCE OF TEXT

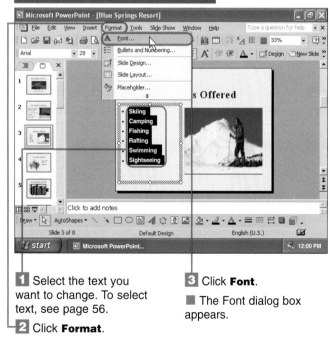

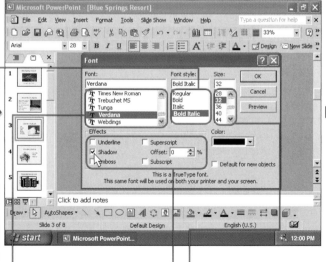

1 Select the text you want to change. To select text, see page 56.

2 Click **Format**.

3 Click **Font**.

■ The Font dialog box appears.

4 To select a font for the text, click the font you want to use.

5 To select a style for the text, click the style you want to use.

6 To select a size for the text, click the size you want to use.

7 To select effects for the text, click each effect you want to use (☐ changes to ☑).

What determines which fonts are available on my computer?

The fonts available on your computer depend on the programs installed on your computer, the setup of your computer and your printer. You can obtain additional fonts at computer stores and on the Internet.

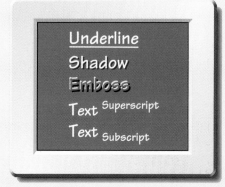

What effects can I add to text in my presentation?

PowerPoint offers many effects that you can use to change the appearance of text in your presentation.

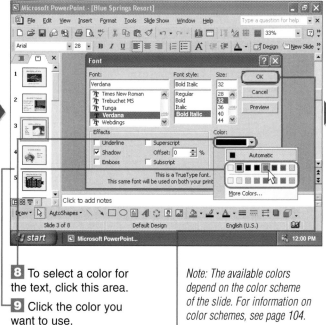

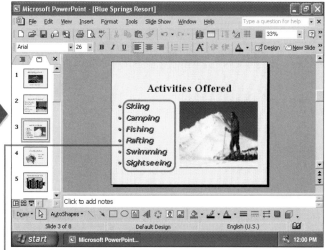

8 To select a color for the text, click this area.

9 Click the color you want to use.

Note: The available colors depend on the color scheme of the slide. For information on color schemes, see page 104.

10 Click **OK** to apply your changes.

■ The text you selected displays the changes.

■ To deselect text, click outside the selected area.

CHANGE CASE OF TEXT

You can change the case of text in your presentation without retyping the text. PowerPoint offers five case styles for you to choose from.

CHANGE CASE OF TEXT

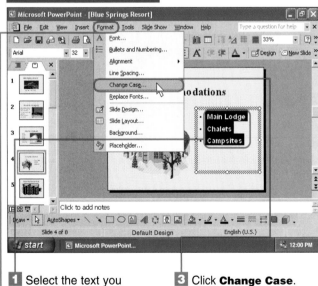

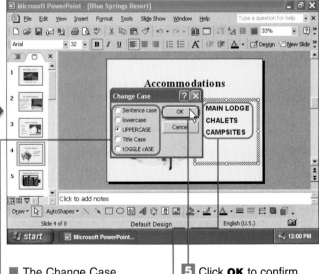

1 Select the text you want to change to a new case style. To select text, see page 56.

2 Click **Format**.

3 Click **Change Case**.

Note: If Change Case does not appear on the menu, position the mouse ⓚ over the bottom of the menu to display the menu option.

■ The Change Case dialog box appears.

4 Click the case style you want to use (○ changes to ⊙).

5 Click **OK** to confirm your selection.

■ The text you selected changes to the new case style.

■ To deselect text, click outside the selected area.

You can change
the alignment of
text on a slide
to enhance the
appearance of
the slide.

CHANGE ALIGNMENT OF TEXT

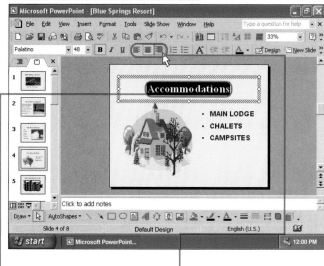

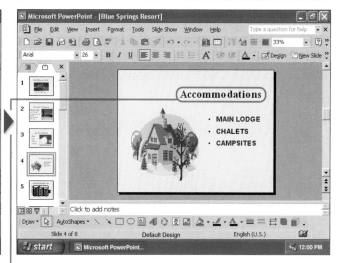

1 Select the text you
want to align differently.
To select text, see
page 56.

2 Click one of the
following buttons.

- Left align
- Center
- Right align

*Note: If the button you want
is not displayed, click* ⯈
*on the Formatting toolbar
to display the button.*

■ The text displays the
new alignment.

■ To deselect text, click
outside the selected area.

You can change the appearance of bullets or numbers on a slide.

You can also remove bullets or numbers from points on a slide. This is useful when a slide contains text you do not want to appear in a bulleted list, such as a quotation or a single point.

CHANGE BULLET OR NUMBER STYLE

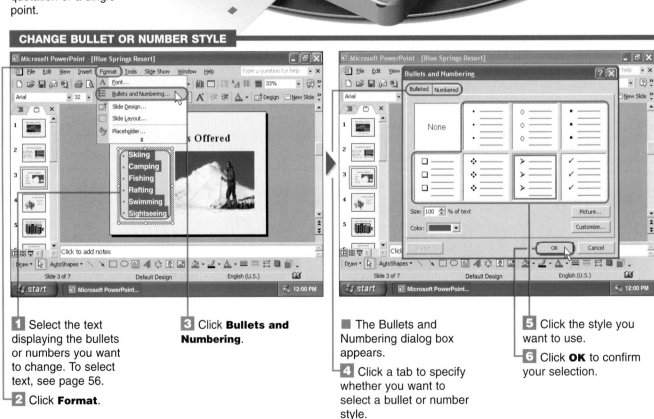

1 Select the text displaying the bullets or numbers you want to change. To select text, see page 56.

2 Click **Format**.

3 Click **Bullets and Numbering**.

■ The Bullets and Numbering dialog box appears.

4 Click a tab to specify whether you want to select a bullet or number style.

5 Click the style you want to use.

6 Click **OK** to confirm your selection.

Can I customize the bullets or numbers on my slides?

Yes. You can change the size or color of the bullets or numbers displayed on your slides.

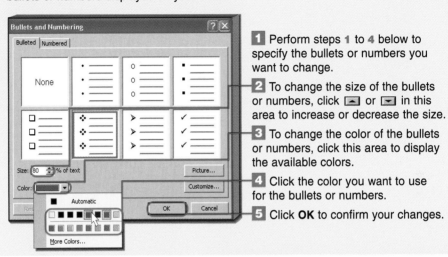

1 Perform steps **1** to **4** below to specify the bullets or numbers you want to change.

2 To change the size of the bullets or numbers, click ▲ or ▼ in this area to increase or decrease the size.

3 To change the color of the bullets or numbers, click this area to display the available colors.

4 Click the color you want to use for the bullets or numbers.

5 Click **OK** to confirm your changes.

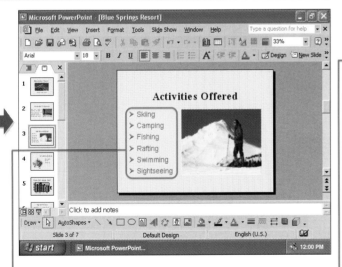

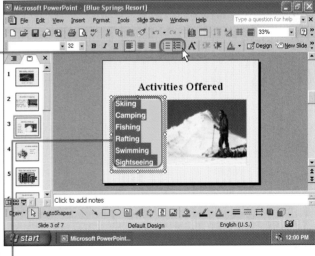

QUICKLY ADD OR REMOVE BULLETS OR NUMBERS

■ The text you selected displays the new bullets or numbers.

■ To deselect text, click outside the selected area.

■ To remove bullets or numbers, repeat steps **1** to **6**, selecting **None** in step **5**.

1 Select the text where you want to add or remove bullets or numbers. To select text, see page 56.

2 Click one of the following buttons.

▤ Numbers

▤ Bullets

Note: If the button you want is not displayed, click ▧ on the Formatting toolbar to display the button.

WORK WITH BULLETS AND NUMBERS

You can enhance a bulleted list on a slide by beginning each point with a picture bullet.

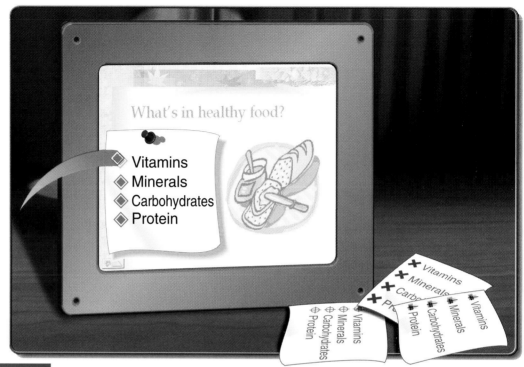

ADD PICTURE BULLETS

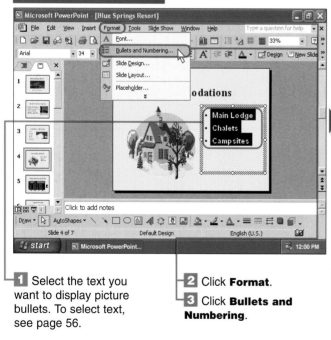

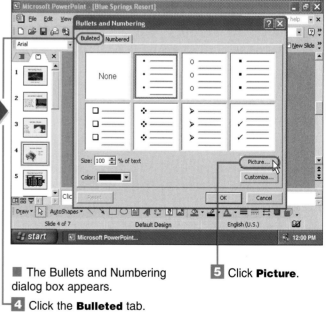

1 Select the text you want to display picture bullets. To select text, see page 56.

2 Click **Format**.

3 Click **Bullets and Numbering**.

■ The Bullets and Numbering dialog box appears.

4 Click the **Bulleted** tab.

5 Click **Picture**.

Can I make changes to the bullets on all my slides at once?

You can make changes to the bullets on the Slide Master to change the bullets on all the slides in your presentation. PowerPoint will not change bullets you have already changed on your slides. For information on the Slide Master, see page 114.

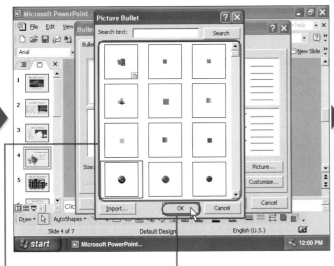

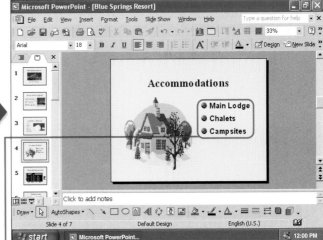

■ The Picture Bullet dialog box appears.

6 Click the picture bullet you want to use.

Note: You can use the scroll bar to browse through the available picture bullets.

7 Click **OK** to confirm your selection.

■ The text you selected displays the picture bullets.

■ To deselect text, click outside the selected area.

■ To remove the picture bullets, repeat steps **1** to **6** on page 86, selecting **None** in step **5**.

CHANGE LINE SPACING

You can change the amount of space between the lines of text on a slide.

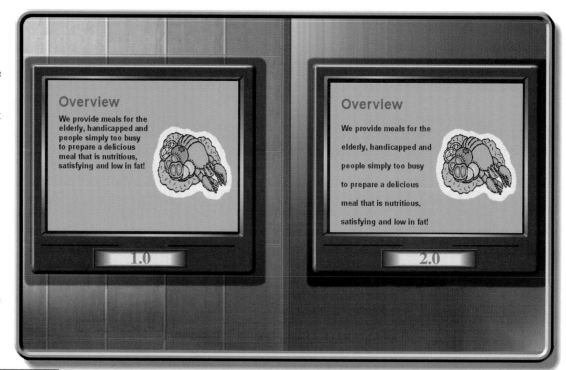

Changing the line spacing can help make the text on a slide easier to read.

CHANGE LINE SPACING

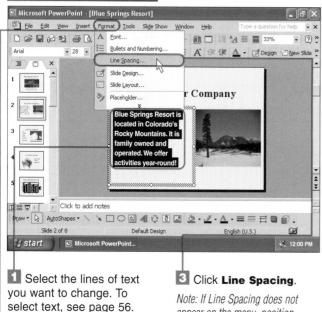

■1 Select the lines of text you want to change. To select text, see page 56.

■2 Click **Format**.

■3 Click **Line Spacing**.

Note: If Line Spacing does not appear on the menu, position the mouse ⬉ over the bottom of the menu to display the menu option.

■ The Line Spacing dialog box appears.

■4 Click ▲ or ▼ in this area to increase or decrease the amount of space between the lines of text you selected.

■5 Click **OK** to confirm your change.

■ PowerPoint will display the text you selected with the new line spacing.

DISPLAY TEXT FORMATTING

You can display
the formatting
of all the text in
your presentation.
Displaying the
formatting of text
allows you to see
how the text in
your outline or
notes will appear
when printed.

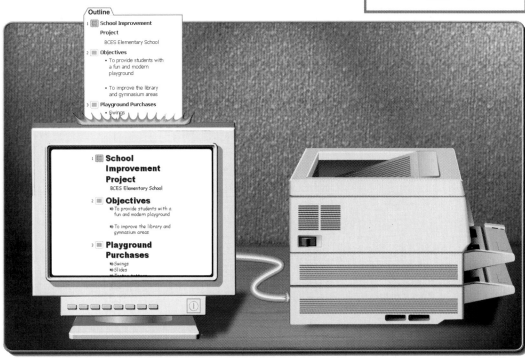

DISPLAY TEXT FORMATTING

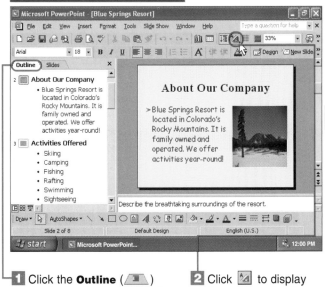

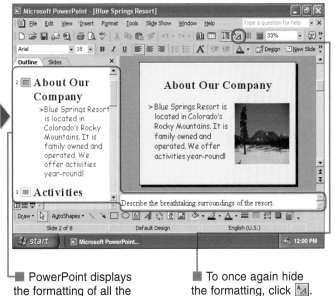

1 Click the **Outline** (▱) tab to display the text on each slide in your presentation.

2 Click ⁴⁄ₐ to display the formatting of all the text in your presentation.

Note: If ⁴⁄ₐ is not displayed, click ⁇ on the Standard toolbar to display the button.

■ PowerPoint displays the formatting of all the text in your presentation.

■ To once again hide the formatting, click ⁴⁄ₐ.

COPY FORMATTING

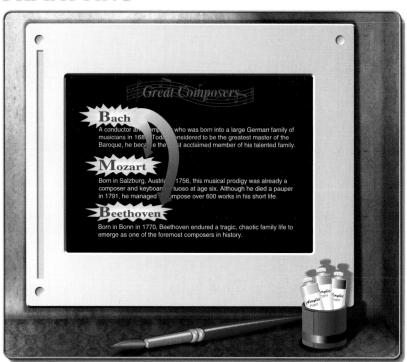

You can copy the formatting of text to make one area of text in your presentation look exactly like another.

You may want to copy the formatting of text to make all the headings or important words in your presentation look the same. This will give the text in your presentation a consistent appearance.

COPY FORMATTING

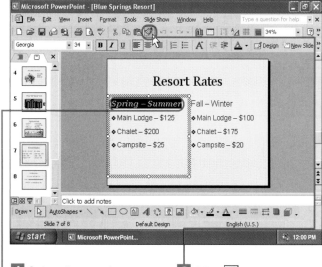

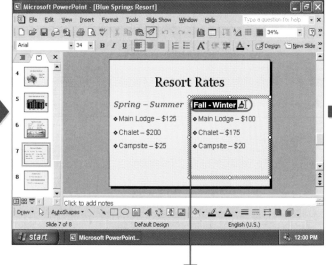

1 Select the text that displays the formatting you want to copy. To select text, see page 56.

2 Click 🖌 to copy the formatting of the text.

Note: If 🖌 is not displayed, click ┊ on the Standard toolbar to display the button.

■ The mouse ⌖ changes to 🖌 when over the slide.

3 Select the text you want to display the formatting.

How do I copy formatting between slides in my presentation?

To copy formatting between slides, perform steps 1 and 2 on page 92. Display the slide containing the text you want to display the same formatting and then select the text.

What types of formatting can I copy?

You can copy text formatting, such as the font, font size, style and color of text. PowerPoint may not be able to copy some text formatting features, such as the alignment or case of text.

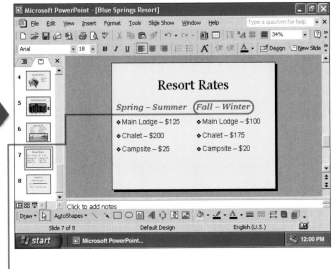

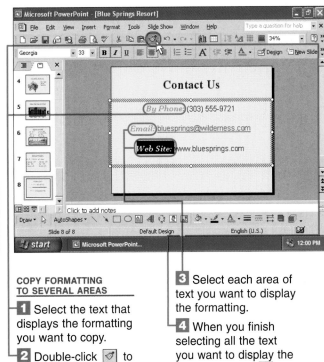

■ The text you selected displays the formatting.

■ To deselect text, click outside the selected area.

COPY FORMATTING TO SEVERAL AREAS

1 Select the text that displays the formatting you want to copy.

2 Double-click to copy the formatting of the text.

3 Select each area of text you want to display the formatting.

4 When you finish selecting all the text you want to display the formatting, click or press the Esc key.

93

REPLACE A FONT

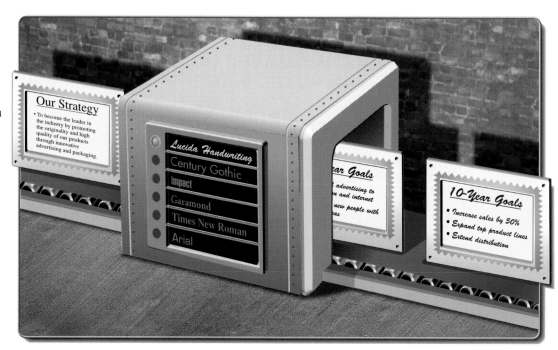

If you do not like a font used throughout your presentation, you can replace all occurrences of the font with a font you prefer.

REPLACE A FONT

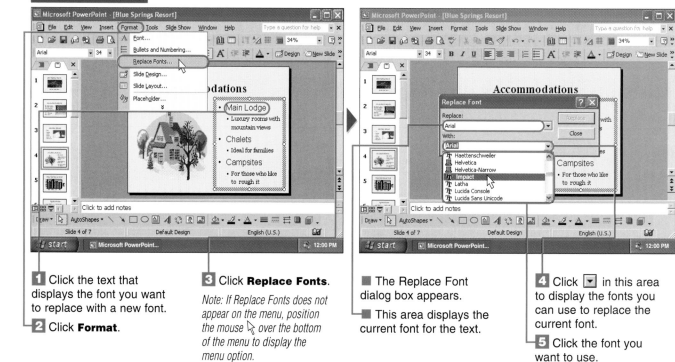

1 Click the text that displays the font you want to replace with a new font.

2 Click **Format**.

3 Click **Replace Fonts**.

Note: If Replace Fonts does not appear on the menu, position the mouse ⃟ over the bottom of the menu to display the menu option.

■ The Replace Font dialog box appears.

■ This area displays the current font for the text.

4 Click ▼ in this area to display the fonts you can use to replace the current font.

5 Click the font you want to use.

Why didn't the font in my chart change when I replaced a font in my presentation?

PowerPoint will not replace the fonts used in charts in your presentation. For information on adding charts, see page 136.

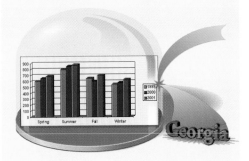

Which font should I choose for my presentation?

The font you should choose depends on the text you want to format. A serif font, such as Times New Roman or Georgia, has short lines added to the top and bottom of each character. Serif fonts can help make large amounts of text easier to read, so you may want to use a serif font for paragraphs on your slides.

A sans serif font, such as Arial or Verdana, does not have short lines added to the top and bottom of each character. Sans serif fonts are well suited to small amounts of text, such as slide titles.

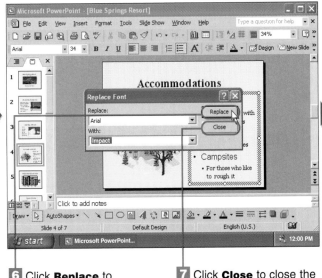

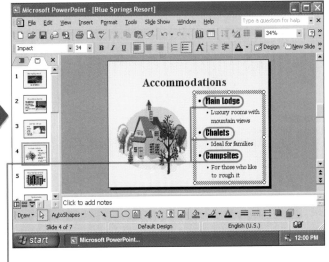

6 Click **Replace** to replace the current font with the font you selected.

7 Click **Close** to close the Replace Font dialog box.

■ The font changes throughout your presentation.

CHANGE INDENTATION OF TEXT

You can change the indentation of text to emphasize the start of a new paragraph.

Indent first line

Indent all but first line

CHANGE INDENTATION OF TEXT

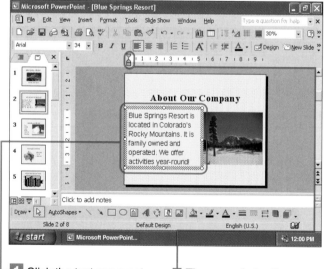

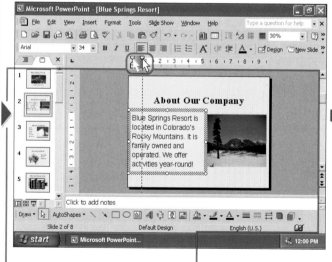

1 Click the text you want to indent. Handles (o) appear around the text.

■ These symbols allow you to indent the left edge of the text.

▽ Indent the first line
△ Indent all but the first line
□ Indent all lines

2 Position the mouse ⌐ over the indent symbol you want to use to indent the text.

3 Drag the indent symbol to a new position on the ruler.

■ A dotted line shows the new indent position.

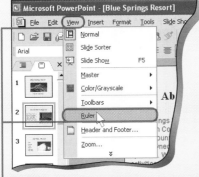

**The ruler is not displayed on my screen.
How do I display the ruler?**

1 Click **View**.

2 Click **Ruler**.

*Note: If Ruler does not appear on
the menu, position the mouse
over the bottom of the menu to
display the menu option.*

■ To once again hide the
ruler, repeat steps **1** and **2**.

How can I indent text that displays bullets?

If the text you are indenting displays bullets,
you can use the indent symbols to indent
the text and bullets or adjust the amount of
space between the bullets and the text.

▽ Indent bullets

△ Indent text for the bullets

☐ Indent both text and bullets

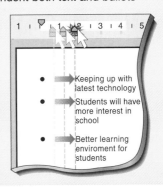

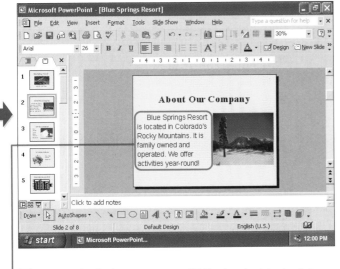

■ PowerPoint indents
the text you selected.

■ To deselect text, click
outside the selected area.

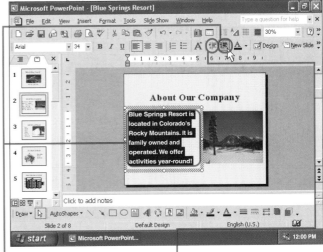

QUICKLY INDENT TEXT

1 Select the text you
want to indent. To select
text, see page 56.

2 Click 🔲 to indent
the left edge of the text.

*Note: If 🔲 is not displayed,
click ⏩ on the Formatting
toolbar to display the button.*

■ You can repeat step **2**
to further indent the text.

■ To decrease the indent,
click 🔲.

CHANGE TAB SETTINGS

You can use tabs to line up columns of text on a slide. PowerPoint offers four types of tabs for you to choose from.

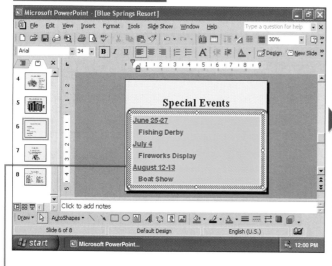

ADD A TAB

1 Click the text you want to use a new tab. Handles (o) appear around the text.

■ To add a tab to text you are about to type, click the location on your slide where you want to type the text.

2 Click this area until the type of tab you want to add appears.

- **⌞** Left tab
- **⌄** Center tab
- **⌟** Right tab
- **⌄** Decimal tab

Note: If the ruler is not displayed, see the top of page 97 to display the ruler.

Do I need to add a new tab to my slide?

Depending on where you want to move the text on your slide, you may not need to add a new tab. PowerPoint automatically places a left tab every inch across a slide. You can use and move the tabs PowerPoint set as you would any tab. If you add a new tab, PowerPoint will remove the automatic tabs that appear before the new tab.

How do I move a tab?

1 Select the text that uses the tab you want to move. To select text, see page 56.

2 Position the mouse over the tab you want to move and then drag the tab to a new location on the ruler. A dotted line shows the new location.

■ The text that uses the tab moves to the new location.

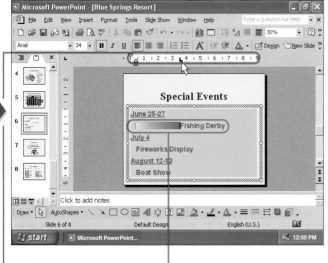

3 Click the bottom half of the ruler where you want to add the tab.

■ The new tab appears on the ruler.

USE A TAB

1 Click to the left of the first character in the line you want to move to the tab. Then press the `Tab` key.

■ The insertion point and the text that follows move to the tab you set.

REMOVE A TAB

1 Click the text that uses the tab you want to remove. Handles (o) appear around the text.

2 Position the mouse over the tab you want to remove and then drag the tab downward off the ruler.

■ The tab disappears from the ruler.

■ To move the text back to the left margin, click to the left of the first character. Then press the `Backspace` key.

CHAPTER 5

Change Appearance of Slides

Do you want to change the overall look of the slides in your presentation? Read this chapter to learn how to change the design template, color scheme and background of your slides.

Dinner Tonight!

Eleanor and Lou Whitman

PRESENTATION

CHANGE THE DESIGN TEMPLATE

PowerPoint offers many design templates that you can choose from to give the slides in your presentation a professional look.

You can change the design template for your entire presentation or for a single slide. Changing the design template for a single slide can make the slide stand out from the rest of your presentation.

CHANGE THE DESIGN TEMPLATE

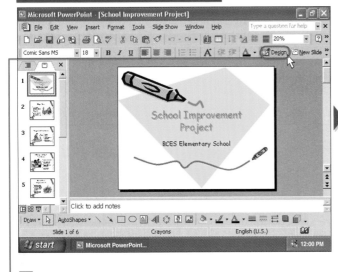

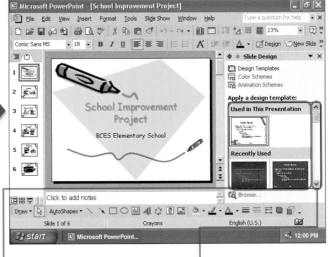

1 Click **Design** to display the Slide Design task pane.

Note: If the Design button is not displayed, click ⟩⟩ on the Formatting toolbar to display the button.

■ The Slide Design task pane appears.

■ This area displays the available design templates.

Note: The design templates are organized into three sections— Used in This Presentation, Recently Used and Available For Use.

■ You can use the scroll bar to browse through the design templates.

When I changed the design template for my presentation, why didn't some parts of my slides change?

The new design template may not affect parts of a slide you have previously formatted. For example, if you changed the font of text on a slide before changing the design template, the new design template will not affect the font of the text you changed.

Can I apply a blank design template to my slides?

PowerPoint offers a blank template in the Available For Use section of the Slide Design task pane. Using a blank design template is useful if you find it difficult to work with the content of your presentation when colors are applied to the presentation. When you are finished working with your presentation, you can change the design template to a more colorful template.

APPLY A DESIGN TEMPLATE TO ONE SLIDE

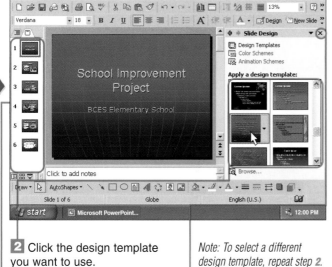

2 Click the design template you want to use.

■ All the slides in your presentation display the design template you selected.

Note: To select a different design template, repeat step 2.

3 When you finish selecting a design template, you can click ☒ to hide the Slide Design task pane.

1 Display the slide you want to apply a design template to.

2 Position the mouse ▷ over the design template you want to use. An arrow (⏷) appears.

3 Click the arrow (⏷) to display a list of options.

4 Click **Apply to Selected Slides**.

CHANGE THE COLOR SCHEME

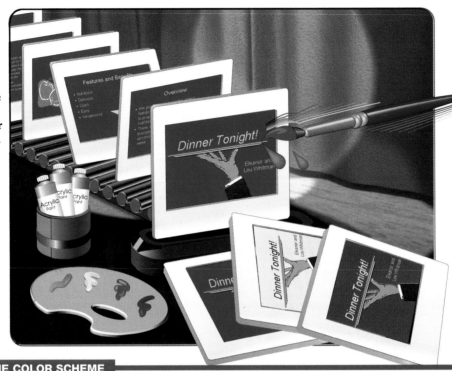

You can change the color scheme of all the slides in your presentation.

You can also change the color scheme of a single slide. Changing the color scheme for a single slide can make the slide stand out from the rest of your presentation.

Each color scheme contains a set of eight coordinated colors, including colors for the background, text, lines, shadows, titles and bullets.

CHANGE THE COLOR SCHEME

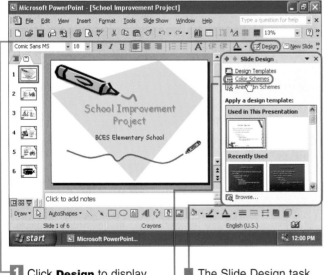

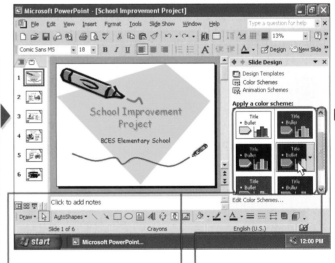

1 Click **Design** to display the Slide Design task pane.

Note: If the Design button is not displayed, click 🔅 *on the Formatting toolbar to display the button.*

■ The Slide Design task pane appears.

2 Click **Color Schemes** to display the available color schemes.

■ This area displays the available color schemes.

Note: The available color schemes depend on the current design template. For information on design templates, see page 102.

■ You can use the scroll bar to browse through the color schemes.

3 Click the color scheme you want to use.

What should I consider when changing the color scheme of slides?

When selecting a color scheme, you should consider how you will deliver the presentation. If you will be using overheads, you should choose a color scheme with a light background and dark text. If you will be using 35mm slides or delivering your presentation on a computer screen, you should choose a color scheme with a dark background and light text.

Some of the slides in my presentation did not change to the new color scheme. What is wrong?

You may have used more than one design template in your presentation. By default, PowerPoint applies the new color scheme only to slides with the same design template as the current slide. To apply the color scheme to all the slides in your presentation, perform steps **2** to **4** on page 105, selecting **Apply to All Slides** in step **4**. For more information on design templates, see page 102.

CHANGE THE COLOR SCHEME FOR ONE SLIDE

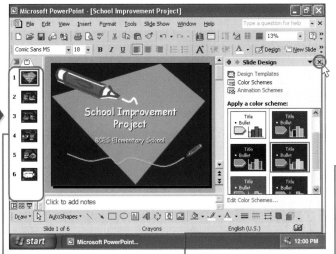

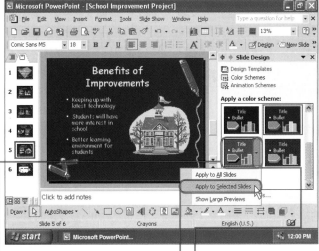

■ All the slides in your presentation display the color scheme you selected.

Note: To select a different color scheme, repeat step 3.

4 When you have finished selecting a color scheme, you can click ☒ to hide the Slide Design task pane.

1 Display the slide you want to use a different color scheme.

2 Position the mouse ⤵ over the color scheme you want to use. An arrow (▾) appears.

3 Click the arrow (▾) to display a list of options.

4 Click **Apply to Selected Slides**.

CHANGE THE SLIDE BACKGROUND

You can change the background color of your slides to make your presentation more attractive.

CHANGE BACKGROUND COLOR

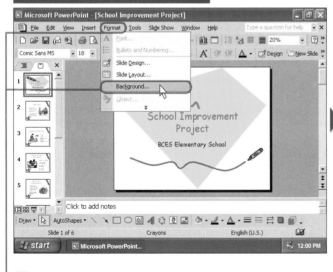

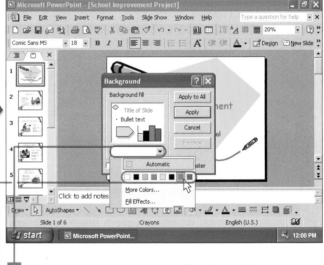

1 Click **Format**.

2 Click **Background**.

Note: If Background does not appear on the menu, position the mouse ▷ over the bottom of the menu to display the menu option.

■ The Background dialog box appears.

3 Click this area to display the available colors.

4 Click the color you want to use for the background of the slide.

Note: The available colors depend on the color scheme of the slide. For information on color schemes, see page 104.

Why didn't the entire background change?

You Previously Changed Items

The new background may not affect items you have previously changed on a slide. For example, if you previously changed the background of a text box on a slide, the text box will not be affected by the new background.

Items are on the Slide Master

The text or objects that did not change may be part of the Slide Master. To change the entire background of your slides, perform steps **1** and **2** below. Then click **Omit background graphics from master** (☐ changes to ☑) and perform step **5**. For more information on the Slide Master, see page 114.

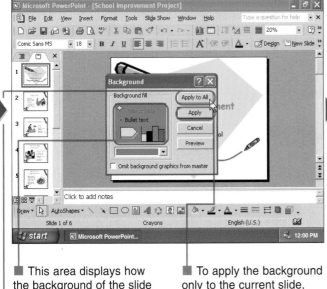

■ This area displays how the background of the slide will appear.

5 Click **Apply to All** to apply your changes to every slide in your presentation.

■ To apply the background only to the current slide, click **Apply**.

■ The slides in your presentation display the new background color.

CHANGE THE SLIDE BACKGROUND

You can apply a gradient, texture or pattern to the background of your slides.

—**1** Click **Format**.

—**2** Click **Background**.

Note: If Background does not appear on the menu, position the mouse ꝅ over the bottom of the menu to display the menu option.

■ The Background dialog box appears.

3 Click this area to apply a gradient, texture or pattern to the background of your slides.

4 Click **Fill Effects**.

■ The Fill Effects dialog box appears.

**How do I change the color of the
gradients displayed in the Fill Effects
dialog box?**

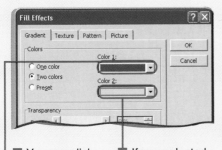

■ You can click
this area to select
a different color
for the displayed
gradients.

■ If you selected
Two colors in step **6**
below, you can click
this area to select a
different second color
for the displayed
gradients.

**Does PowerPoint offer any preset gradients
I can use?**

Yes. PowerPoint offers preset gradients, such
as Early Sunset, Ocean and Rainbow, that
you can use to quickly add a gradient to the
background of your slides.

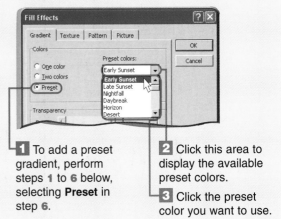

1 To add a preset
gradient, perform
steps **1** to **6** below,
selecting **Preset** in
step **6**.

2 Click this area to
display the available
preset colors.

3 Click the preset
color you want to use.

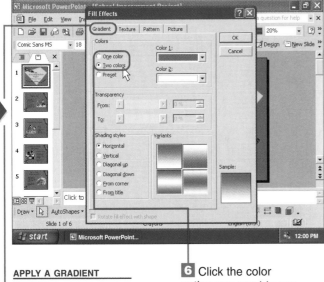

APPLY A GRADIENT

5 To apply a gradient,
click the **Gradient** tab.

6 Click the color
option you want to use
(○ changes to ⊙).

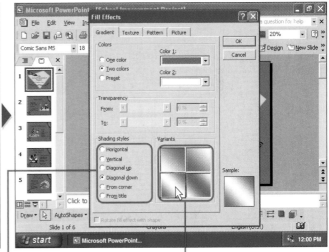

7 Click the shading
style you want to use
(○ changes to ⊙).

8 Click the way you want
the gradient to appear. Then
perform steps **13** and **14**
starting on page 110.

CONTINUED

109

CHANGE THE SLIDE BACKGROUND

You can choose to display a background you selected on every slide in your presentation or on only one slide.

Displaying a different background on one slide can help emphasize a slide or introduce a new part of your presentation.

APPLY A GRADIENT, TEXTURE OR PATTERN (CONTINUED)

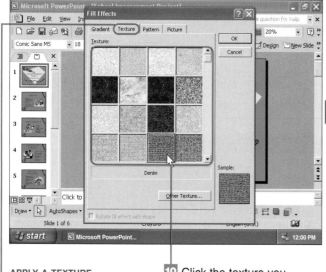

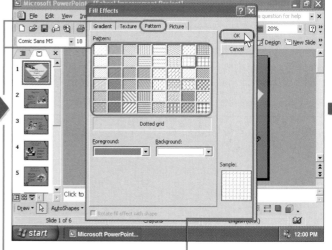

APPLY A TEXTURE

9 To apply a texture, click the **Texture** tab.

10 Click the texture you want to use. Then perform steps **13** and **14**.

APPLY A PATTERN

11 To apply a pattern, click the **Pattern** tab.

12 Click the pattern you want to use. Then perform steps **13** and **14**.

CONFIRM YOUR CHANGES

13 Click **OK** to confirm your changes.

What slide background should I choose?

When selecting a slide background, make sure the gradient, texture or pattern you choose does not make the text on the slides difficult to read. You may need to change the color of the text on the slides to make the text easier to read. To change the color of text, see page 81.

How do I change the color of the patterns displayed in the Fill Effects dialog box?

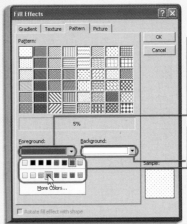

1 To change the foreground color of the patterns, click this area to display the available colors.

2 Click the color you want to use.

■ To change the background color of the patterns, repeat steps **1** and **2** in this area.

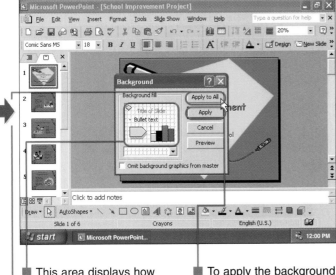

■ This area displays how the slide will appear.

14 Click **Apply to All** to apply your changes to every slide in your presentation.

■ To apply the background only to the current slide, click **Apply**.

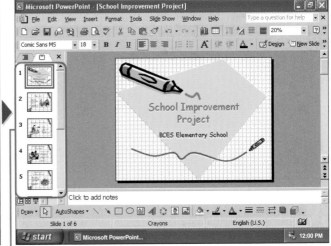

■ The slides in your presentation display the new background.

Note: If the entire slide background does not change, see the top of page 107.

CHANGE A HEADER OR FOOTER

You can display specific information on every slide in your presentation. For example, you may want to display your company name on each slide.

You can display the date and time, slide number and footer text on each slide.

CHANGE A HEADER OR FOOTER

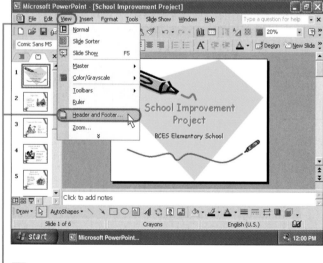

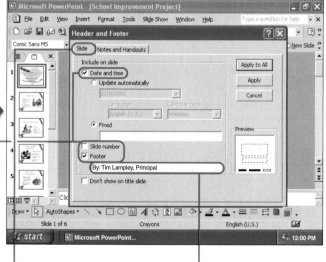

■1 Click **View**.

■2 Click **Header and Footer**.

■ The Header and Footer dialog box appears.

■3 Click the **Slide** tab.

■4 Each item that displays a check mark (✔) will appear on every slide in your presentation. Click an item to add (☑) or remove (☐) a check mark.

■5 If you selected **Footer** in step **4**, click this area and then type the footer text you want to appear on every slide.

112

Why do my slides already display header or footer information?

If you used the AutoContent Wizard to create your presentation, PowerPoint may have automatically added header or footer information to your slides for you. For information on using the AutoContent Wizard, see page 18.

Can I change the header and footer displayed on my notes and handouts?

Yes. Perform steps **1** to **7** below, except click the **Notes and Handouts** tab in step **3**. Then click **Apply to All** to apply the changes to all your notes and handouts.

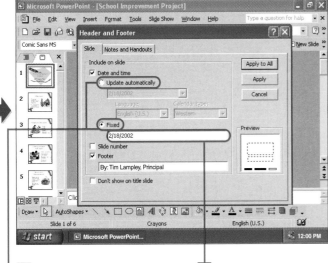

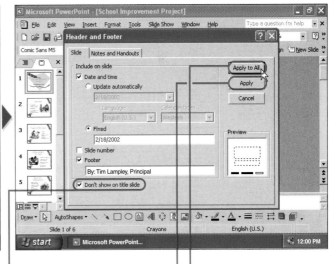

6 If you selected **Date and time** in step **4**, click one of the following options (○ changes to ⊙).

Update automatically
Display the current date

Fixed
Display a date you specify

7 If you selected **Fixed** in step **6**, type the date you want to display on your slides.

8 If you do not want the information you specified to appear on the title slide, click this option (☐ changes to ☑).

9 Click **Apply to All** to apply your changes to every slide in your presentation.

■ To apply your changes to only the current slide, click **Apply**.

USING THE SLIDE MASTER VIEW

You can use the Slide Master view to change the appearance of all the slides in your presentation at once.

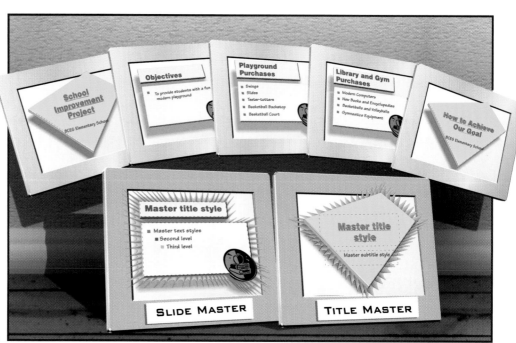

The Slide Master view can display a Slide Master or a Title Master for your presentation. A Slide Master allows you to change the appearance of all the slides in your presentation that are not title slides. A Title Master allows you to change the appearance of the title slides in your presentation.

USING THE SLIDE MASTER VIEW

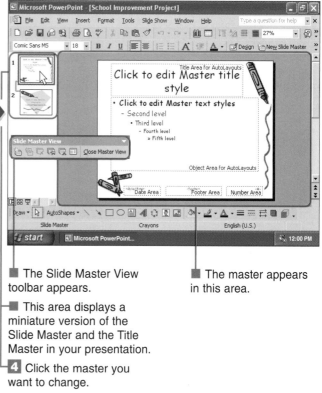

1 Click **View**.

2 Click **Master**.

3 Click **Slide Master**.

■ The Slide Master View toolbar appears.

■ This area displays a miniature version of the Slide Master and the Title Master in your presentation.

4 Click the master you want to change.

■ The master appears in this area.

Can I use the Slide Master view to add my company logo to every slide in my presentation?

Yes. You can add an object, such as a picture, clip art image or AutoShape, to the Slide Master as you would add an object to any slide in your presentation. To add an object to a slide, see pages 120 to 129. If there are multiple masters in your presentation, you must add the logo to all the masters.

Why do multiple sets of Slide and Title Masters appear in the Slide Master view?

PowerPoint displays a Slide Master and a Title Master for each design template you used in your presentation. For information on design templates, see page 102.

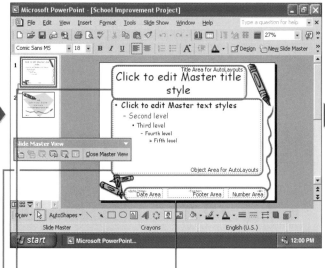

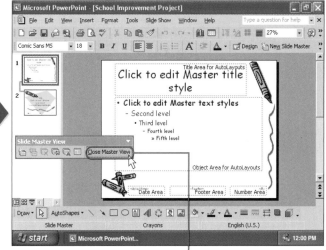

■ Changing the appearance of this text will change the appearance of the title on each slide.

■ Changing the appearance of this text will change the appearance of the points on each slide.

Note: To change the appearance of text, see pages 78 to 89.

■ These areas display the date, footer text and slide number on each slide. To change this information, see page 112.

■ You can move or resize a placeholder on a master as you would move or resize any object on a slide. To move or resize an object, see page 170.

Note: The available placeholders depend on the master you selected in step 4.

5 When you finish making changes to the master, click **Close Master View**.

CREATE A DESIGN TEMPLATE

You can create a design template that stores the formatting and color scheme you use most often. This saves you from having to recreate the design for future presentations.

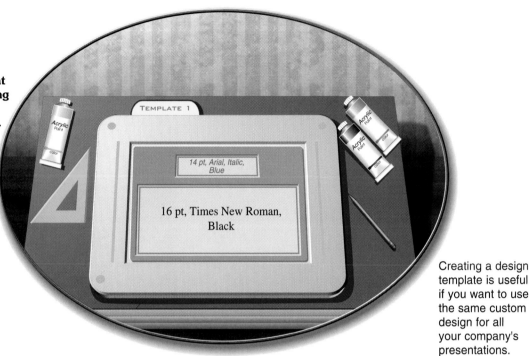

Creating a design template is useful if you want to use the same custom design for all your company's presentations.

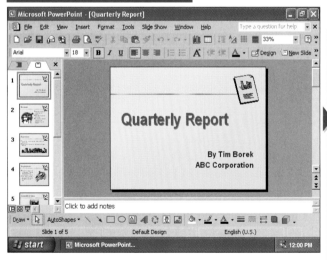

1 Open the presentation you want to use as the basis for the design template. To open a presentation, see page 28.

2 Click **File**.

3 Click **Save As**.

■ The Save As dialog box appears.

How do I use a design template I created?

The design template you created will be available in the Slide Design task pane the next time you start PowerPoint. You can apply the design template to your entire presentation or to a single slide. For more information, see page 102.

Why didn't PowerPoint save all the formatting in my presentation as part of the design template?

PowerPoint will only save the formatting that is displayed on the Slide Master and the Title Master as part of the design template. Before creating the design template, you should make sure the formatting you want the design template to include is displayed on the masters. For information on using the Slide Master view, see page 114.

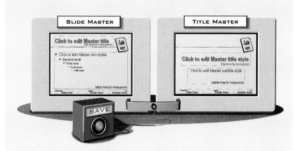

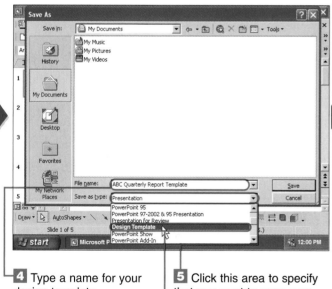

4 Type a name for your design template.

Note: The name cannot contain the * : ? > < | or " characters.

5 Click this area to specify that you want to save your presentation as a design template.

6 Click **Design Template**.

■ This area indicates that PowerPoint will store your presentation in the Templates folder.

7 Click **Save** to save your presentation as a design template.

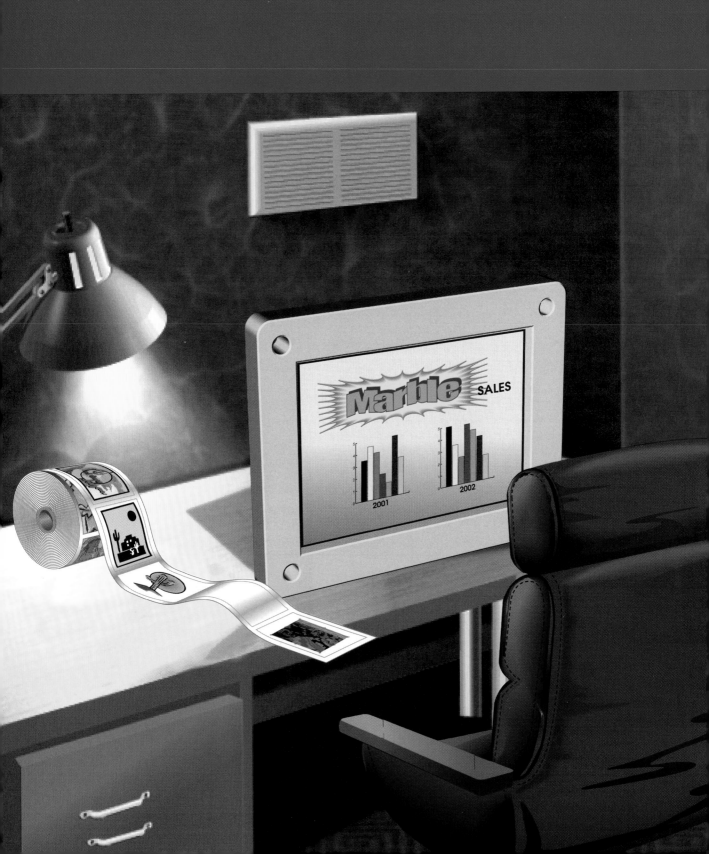

CHAPTER 6

Add Simple Objects

Would you like to use objects, such as AutoShapes and clip art images, to enhance the appearance of your slides? This chapter shows you how.

ADD AN AUTOSHAPE

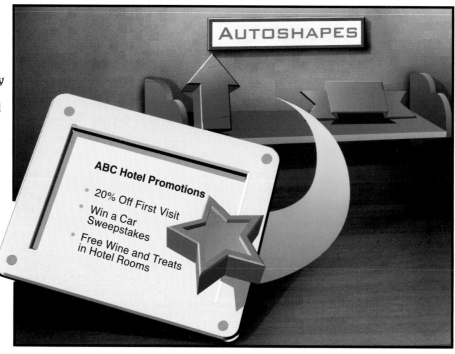

PowerPoint provides many ready-made shapes, called AutoShapes, that you can add to your slides.

PowerPoint offers several types of AutoShapes, such as lines, arrows, stars and banners.

ADD AN AUTOSHAPE

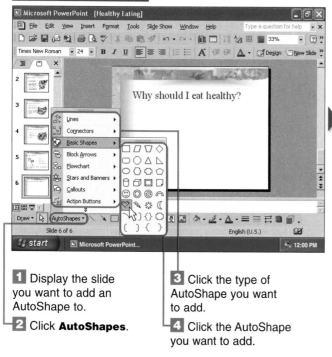

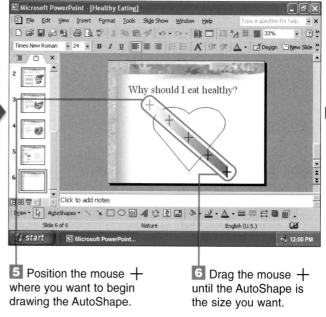

1 Display the slide you want to add an AutoShape to.

2 Click **AutoShapes**.

3 Click the type of AutoShape you want to add.

4 Click the AutoShape you want to add.

5 Position the mouse ✛ where you want to begin drawing the AutoShape.

6 Drag the mouse ✛ until the AutoShape is the size you want.

Can I add text to an AutoShape?

You can add text to most AutoShapes. This is particularly useful for AutoShapes such as banners and callouts. To add text to an AutoShape, click the AutoShape and then type the text you want the AutoShape to display. To change the size of the text, see page 79.

 Why do green and yellow handles appear on some AutoShapes?

You can use the green and yellow handles to change the appearance of an AutoShape.

To rotate an AutoShape, position the mouse pointer over the green handle (●) and then drag the mouse to a new position. For more information on rotating objects, see page 182.

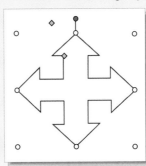

To change the design of an AutoShape, position the mouse pointer over the yellow handle (◇) and then drag the mouse until the shape displays the design you want.

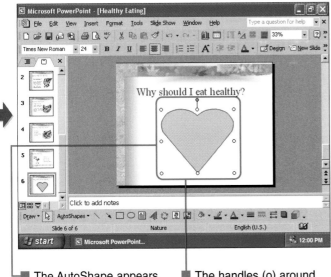

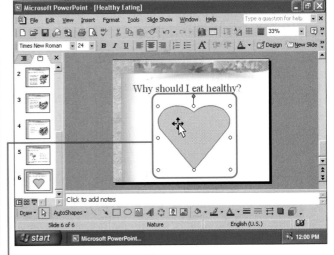

■ The AutoShape appears on the slide.

Note: To change the color of an AutoShape, see page 174.

■ The handles (o) around the AutoShape allow you to change the size of the AutoShape. To move or resize an AutoShape, see page 170.

■ To deselect an AutoShape, click outside the AutoShape.

DELETE AN AUTOSHAPE

1 Click the AutoShape you want to delete.

2 Press the Delete key to remove the AutoShape from the slide.

ADD A TEXT BOX

You can add a text box to a slide to include additional information in your presentation.

You can edit the text in a text box as you would edit any text on a slide.

ADD A TEXT BOX

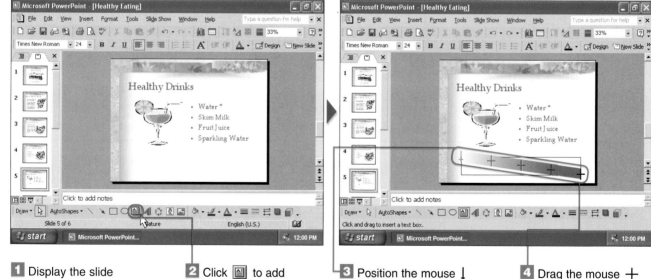

1 Display the slide you want to add a text box to.

2 Click 📄 to add a text box.

3 Position the mouse ↓ where you want to begin drawing the text box.

4 Drag the mouse ✛ until the text box is the size you want.

Can I format the text in a text box?

Yes. You can format the text in a text box as you would format any text on a slide. For example, you can bold, italicize and change the font of text in a text box. To format text, see pages 78 to 84.

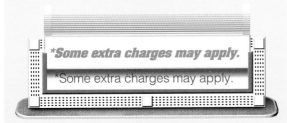

Why doesn't the text in the text box I added appear in the outline of my presentation?

The text in a text box you added will not appear in the outline of your presentation. To have the text appear in the outline, you must enter the text in a placeholder. To change the layout of a slide to one that includes a text placeholder, see page 46.

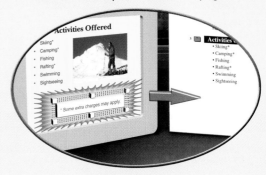

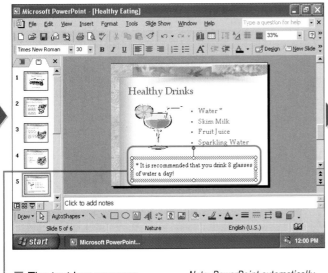

■ The text box appears on the slide.

5 Type the text you want the text box to display.

Note: PowerPoint automatically adjusts the height of the text box to accommodate the text you type.

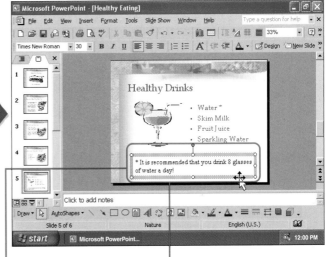

■ The handles (o) around the text box allow you to change the size of the text box. To move or resize a text box, see page 170.

■ To deselect the text box, click outside the text box.

DELETE A TEXT BOX

1 Click the text box you want to delete. Handles (o) appear around the text box.

2 Click an edge of the text box.

3 Press the Delete key to delete the text box.

ADD WORDART

You can add WordArt to a slide in your presentation to display a decorative title or draw attention to important information.

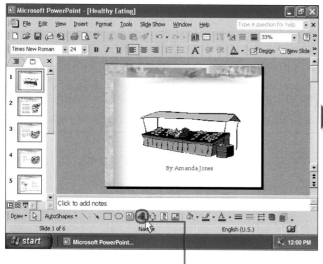

1 Display the slide you want to add WordArt to.

2 Click to add WordArt.

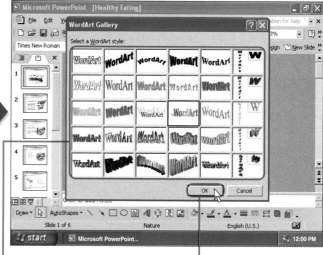

■ The WordArt Gallery dialog box appears.

3 Click the WordArt style you want to use.

4 Click **OK** to confirm your selection.

124

How do I edit WordArt text?

To edit WordArt text, double-click the WordArt to redisplay the Edit WordArt Text dialog box. Then perform steps 5 and 6 below to specify the new text you want the WordArt to display.

When I add WordArt to a slide, why does the WordArt toolbar appear?

The WordArt toolbar contains buttons that allow you to change the appearance of WordArt. For example, you can click [Aa] to display all the letters in the WordArt at the same height.

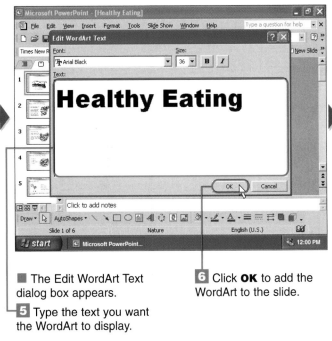

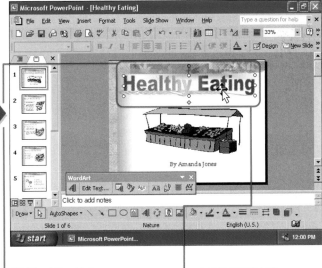

■ The Edit WordArt Text dialog box appears.

5 Type the text you want the WordArt to display.

6 Click **OK** to add the WordArt to the slide.

■ The WordArt appears on the slide.

■ The handles (o) around the WordArt allow you to change the size of the WordArt. To move or resize WordArt, see page 170.

■ To deselect WordArt, click outside the WordArt.

DELETE WORDART

1 Click the WordArt you want to delete and then press the Delete key.

ADD A CLIP ART IMAGE

You can add a professionally-designed clip art image to a slide. Clip art images can help illustrate concepts and make your presentation more interesting and entertaining.

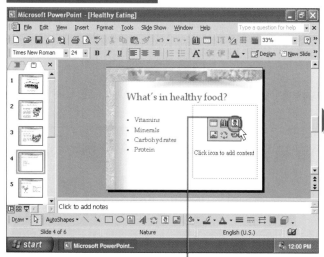

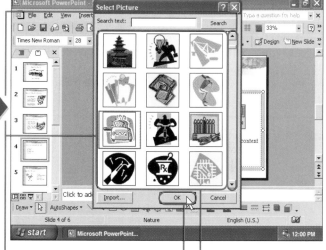

1 Display the slide you want to add a clip art image to.

2 Change the layout of the slide to one that includes a placeholder for a clip art image. To change the slide layout, see page 46.

3 Click the clip art icon ( ) to add a clip art image.

Note: Depending on the layout you chose in step 2, you may need to double-click the placeholder to add a clip art image.

■ The Select Picture dialog box appears.

■ This area displays the clip art images you can add to your slide.

■ You can use the scroll bar to browse through the clip art images.

4 Click the clip art image you want to add to your slide.

5 Click **OK** to add the clip art image to your slide.

Can I search for clip art images?

You can search for clip art images by specifying one or more words of interest in the Select Picture dialog box.

1 In the Select Picture dialog box, click this area and type a word that describes the clip art image you want to search for. Then press the **Enter** key.

■ The dialog box will display the clip art images that match the words you specify.

Where can I obtain more clip art images?

You can buy collections of clip art images at computer stores. Many Web sites, such as www.clipartconnection.com and www.noeticart.com, also offer clip art images you can use on your slides.

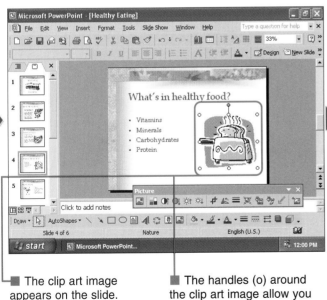

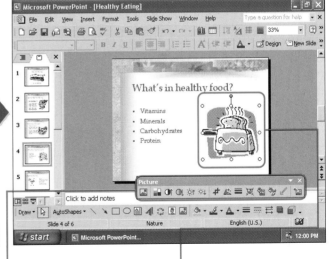

■ The clip art image appears on the slide.

■ The handles (o) around the clip art image allow you to change the size of the image. To move or resize a clip art image, see page 170.

■ The Picture toolbar also appears, displaying buttons that allow you to change the clip art image.

■ To deselect a clip art image, click outside the image.

DELETE A CLIP ART IMAGE

1 Click the clip art image you want to delete and then press the **Delete** key.

ADD A PICTURE

You can add a picture stored on your computer to a slide in your presentation.

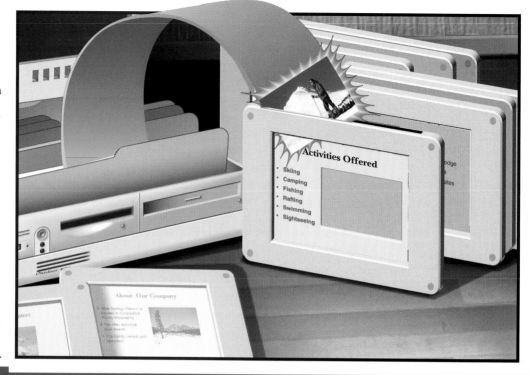

Adding a picture is useful when you want to display your company logo or a picture of your products on a slide.

ADD A PICTURE

1 Display the slide you want to add a picture to.

2 Change the layout of the slide to one that includes a placeholder for a picture. To change the slide layout, see page 46.

3 Click the picture icon ( ) to add a picture to the slide.

■ The Insert Picture dialog box appears.

■ This area shows the location of the displayed pictures. You can click this area to change the location.

■ This area allows you to access pictures in commonly used locations. You can click a location to display the pictures stored in the location.

Note: For information on the commonly used locations, see the top of page 27.

128

Where can I obtain pictures?

There are many places that offer pictures you can use on your slides, such as Web sites and computer stores. You can also use a scanner to scan existing pictures into your computer or create your own pictures using an image editing program, such as Jasc Paint Shop Pro.

Why did the Picture toolbar appear when I added a picture to a slide?

The Picture toolbar contains buttons that allow you to change the appearance of a picture. For example, you can click [icon] or [icon] to increase or decrease the brightness of a picture. If the Picture toolbar does not appear, see page 51 to display the toolbar.

4 Click the picture you want to add to the slide.

5 Click **Insert** to add the picture to the slide.

■ The picture appears on the slide.

■ The handles (o) around the picture allow you to change the size of the picture. To move or resize a picture, see page 170.

■ To deselect the picture, click outside the picture.

DELETE A PICTURE

1 Click the picture you want to delete and then press the Delete key.

CREATE A PHOTO ALBUM

You can create a photo album to neatly display several pictures in a presentation.

When you create a photo album, PowerPoint creates a new presentation to store the photo album.

CREATE A PHOTO ALBUM

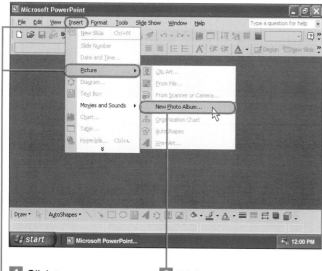

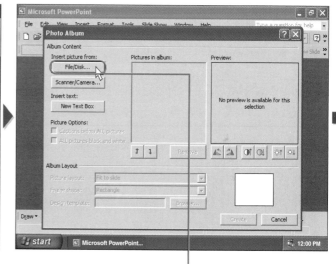

1 Click **Insert**.

2 Click **Picture**.

3 Click **New Photo Album**.

Note: If New Photo Album does not appear on the menu, position the mouse ⌖ over the bottom of the menu to display the menu option.

■ The Photo Album dialog box appears.

4 Click **File/Disk** to locate the pictures on your computer that you want to add to the photo album.

130

How can I remove a picture from a photo album?

If you accidentally included a picture in the photo album you are creating, you can remove the picture.

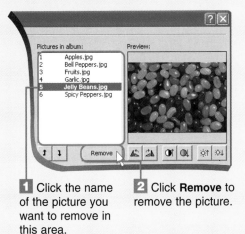

1 Click the name of the picture you want to remove in this area.

2 Click **Remove** to remove the picture.

A preview of a picture is displayed on its side in the Photo Album dialog box. What should I do?

A picture you have scanned and saved on your computer may be displayed on its side or upside down. You can rotate the picture so it will appear properly in the photo album.

1 Click the name of the picture you want to rotate in this area.

2 Click one of the following buttons.

⬛ Rotate counterclockwise
⬛ Rotate clockwise

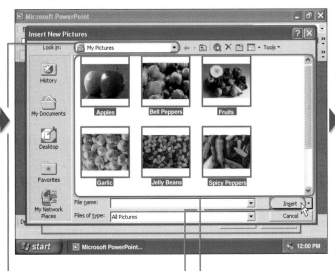

■ The Insert New Pictures dialog box appears.

■ This area shows the location of the displayed files. You can click this area to change the location.

5 Press and hold down the **Ctrl** key as you click each picture you want to add to the photo album.

6 Click **Insert** to add the pictures to the photo album.

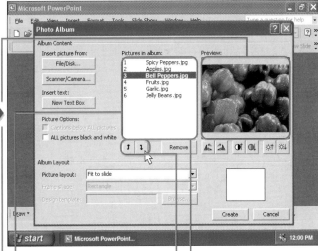

■ This area lists the names of the pictures you selected. The numbers indicate the order the pictures will appear in the photo album.

■ This area displays a preview of the picture that is currently highlighted in the list.

7 To change the order of the pictures, click a picture you want to move.

8 Click ⬆ or ⬇ to move the picture up or down in the list.

CONTINUED ▶

131

CREATE A PHOTO ALBUM

When creating a photo album, you can select the way you want to display the pictures. PowerPoint offers several ways you can display one, two or four pictures on each slide. For example, you can choose Fit to Slide to have one picture fill the entire slide or you can display the pictures without a title on the slide.

ONE PICTURE

TWO PICTURES

FOUR PICTURES

CREATE A PHOTO ALBUM (CONTINUED)

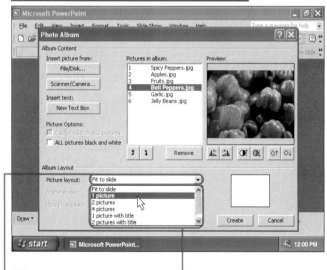

9 To select the way you want to display the pictures on each slide, click this area.

10 Click the way you want to display the pictures.

11 To select a frame shape for the pictures on each slide, click this area.

12 Click the frame shape you want to use.

*Note: This option is not available if you selected **Fit to slide** in step 10.*

■ This area displays a preview of how the picture(s) will appear on each slide.

How do I make changes to a photo album?

To avoid unexpected changes to your photo album, you should only make changes to the photo album using the Format Photo Album dialog box.

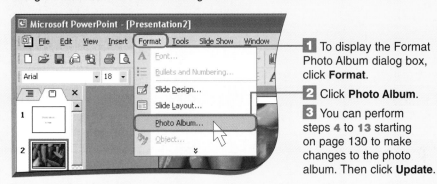

1 To display the Format Photo Album dialog box, click **Format**.

2 Click **Photo Album**.

3 You can perform steps **4** to **13** starting on page 130 to make changes to the photo album. Then click **Update**.

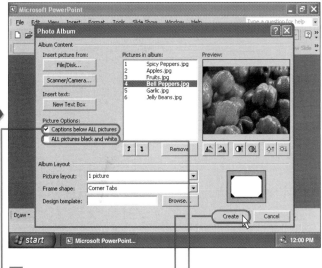

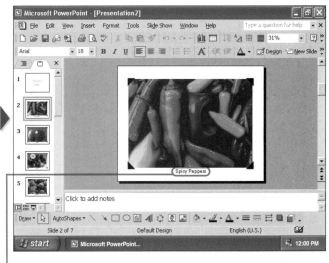

13 To have PowerPoint include a caption below each picture, click this option (☐ changes to ☑).

*Note: This option is not available if you selected **Fit to slide** in step 10.*

■ You can click this option to display all the pictures in black and white (☐ changes to ☑).

14 Click **Create** to create the photo album.

■ PowerPoint creates the photo album.

■ If you selected to display a caption below each picture in step **13**, a text box appears below each picture displaying the name of the picture. You can edit the text in these text boxes as you would edit any text box. For more information, see page 122.

■ You can save the photo album as you would save any presentation. To save a presentation, see page 26.

133

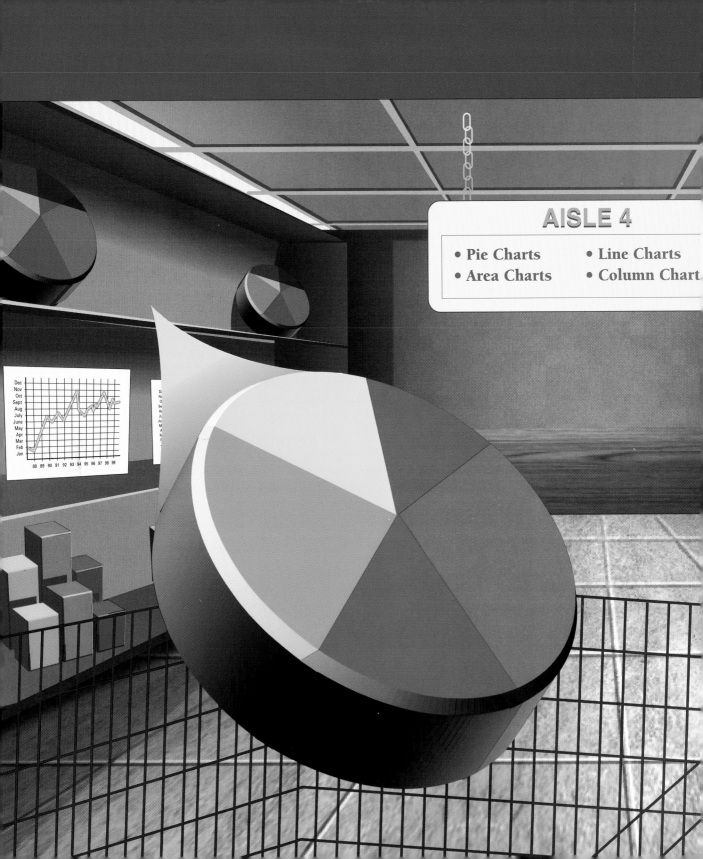

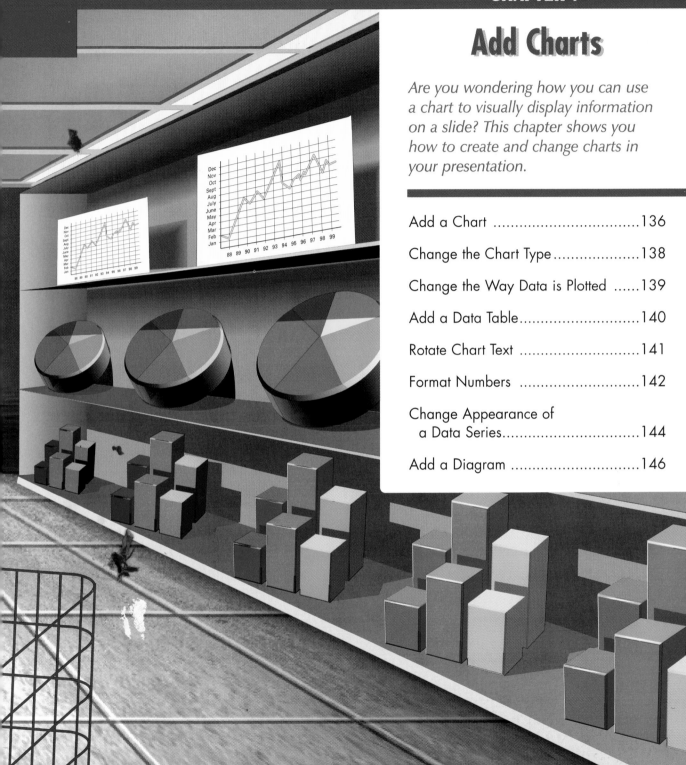

CHAPTER 7

Add Charts

Are you wondering how you can use a chart to visually display information on a slide? This chapter shows you how to create and change charts in your presentation.

ADD A CHART

You can add a
chart to a slide
to show trends
and compare
data.

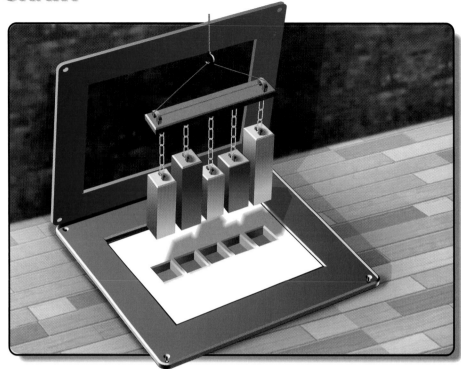

A chart is more
appealing and
often easier to
understand than
a list of numbers.

ADD A CHART

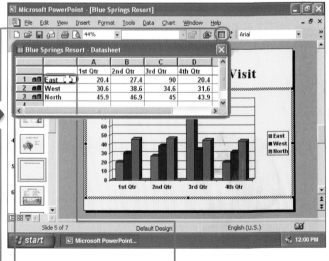

1 Display the slide you
want to add a chart to.

2 Change the layout
of the slide to one that
includes a placeholder
for a chart. To change the
slide layout, see page 46.

3 Click the chart icon (📊)
to add a chart.

*Note: Depending on the layout
you chose in step 2, you may
need to double-click the
placeholder to add a chart.*

■ A datasheet appears,
displaying sample data to
show you where to enter
information.

■ If the datasheet does
not appear, click 📊 to
display the datasheet.

*Note: If 📊 is not displayed,
click ⯮ on the Standard toolbar
to display the button.*

4 To replace the data
in a cell, click the cell.
A thick border appears
around the cell.

How do I change the data displayed in a chart?

Double-click the chart to activate the chart and display the datasheet. You can then perform steps 4 to 7 below to change the data displayed in the chart.

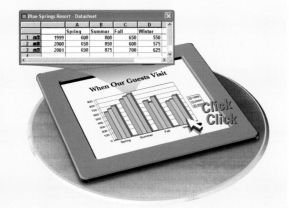

How can I add a chart without changing the slide layout?

You can click the Insert Chart button (📊) and then perform steps 4 to 7 below to add a chart to a slide without first changing the layout of the slide.

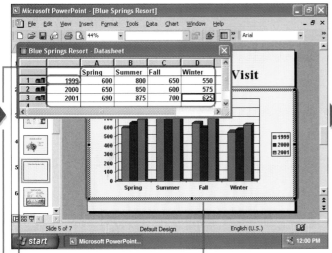

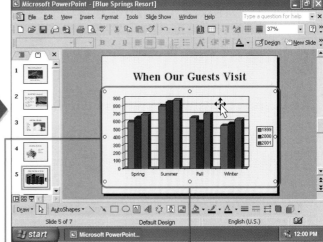

5 Type your data and then press the **Enter** key.

Note: To remove data from a cell and leave the cell empty, click the cell and then press the **Delete** *key.*

6 Repeat steps 4 and 5 until you finish entering all your data.

■ As you enter data, PowerPoint updates the chart on the slide.

7 When you finish entering data for the chart, click a blank area on your screen.

■ The datasheet disappears and you can clearly view the chart on the slide.

■ The handles (o) around the chart allow you to change the size of the chart. To move or resize a chart, see page 170.

DELETE A CHART

1 Click the chart you want to delete and then press the **Delete** key.

137

CHANGE THE CHART TYPE

After you create a chart, you can change the chart type to present your data more effectively.

The type of chart you should use depends on your data. For example, area, column and line charts are ideal for showing changes to values over time. Pie charts are ideal for showing percentages.

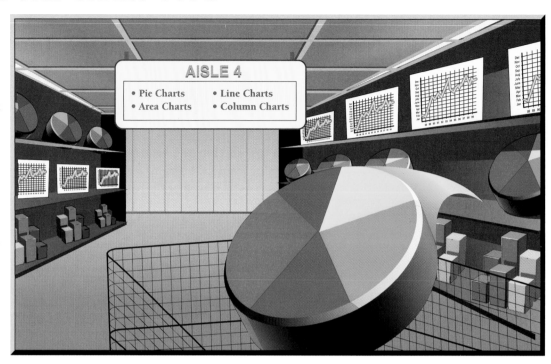

CHANGE THE CHART TYPE

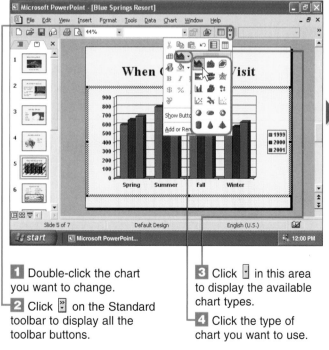

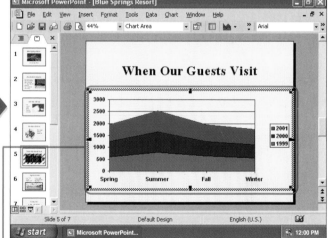

1 Double-click the chart you want to change.

2 Click 🔽 on the Standard toolbar to display all the toolbar buttons.

3 Click 🔽 in this area to display the available chart types.

4 Click the type of chart you want to use.

■ The chart displays the chart type you selected.

■ To deselect the chart, click outside the chart.

You can change
the way PowerPoint
plots the data in a
chart. This allows
you to emphasize
different information
in the chart.

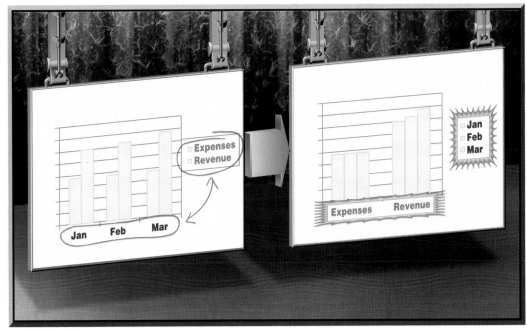

CHANGE THE WAY DATA IS PLOTTED

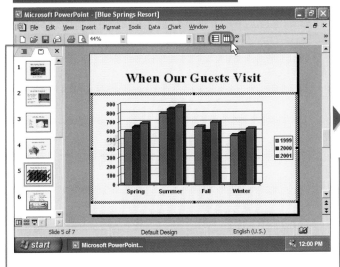

1 Double-click the chart
you want to change.

2 Click one of the
following buttons.

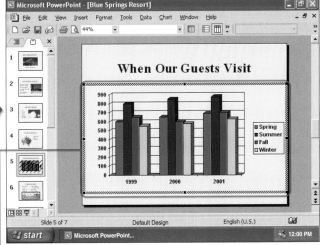

*Note: If the button you want is
not displayed, click* ** on the
*Standard toolbar to display the
button.*

■ The chart displays
the change.

■ To deselect the chart,
click outside the chart.

Plot data by row

Plot data by column

ADD A DATA TABLE

The datasheet is not displayed during a slide show or when you print your presentation. If you want to display or print the information from the datasheet, you must add a data table to your chart.

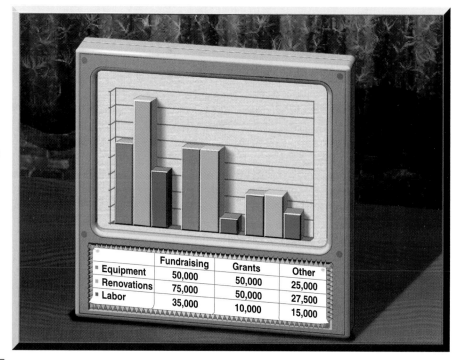

You cannot add a data table to some types of charts.

ADD A DATA TABLE

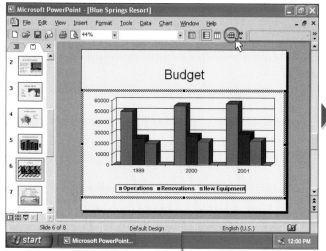

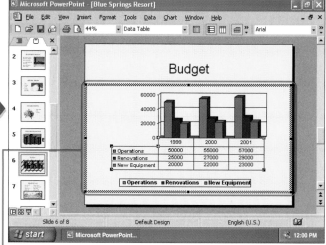

1 Double-click the chart you want to change.

2 Click 🔳 to add a data table to the chart.

Note: If 🔳 is not displayed, click ⏵ on the Standard toolbar to display the button.

■ The chart displays the data table.

■ To deselect the chart, click outside the chart.

■ To remove a data table from a chart, repeat steps **1** and **2**.

ROTATE CHART TEXT

You can rotate text on a chart axis to improve the appearance of the chart.

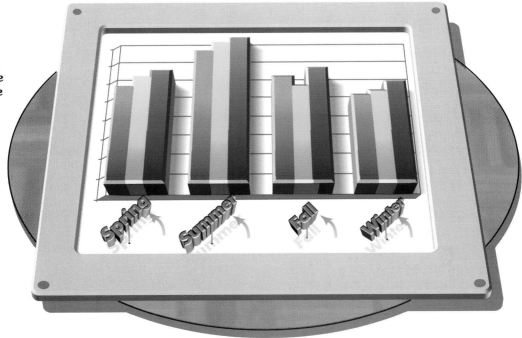

ROTATE CHART TEXT

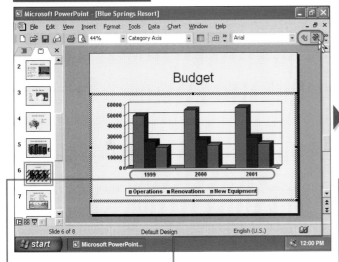

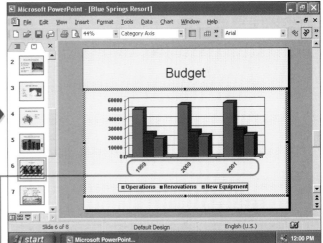

1 Double-click the chart you want to change.

2 Click the text you want to rotate.

3 Click one of the following buttons.

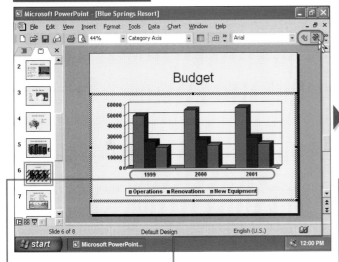 Rotate text downward

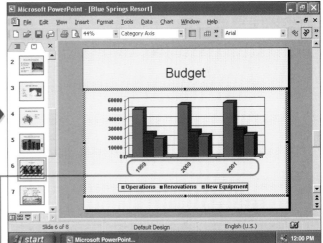 Rotate text upward

Note: If the button you want is not displayed, click ☒ on the Formatting toolbar to display the button.

■ PowerPoint rotates the text in the chart.

■ To deselect the text, click outside the chart.

■ To return the text to its original position, repeat steps **1** to **3**.

FORMAT NUMBERS

You can change the appearance of numbers in a chart without retyping the numbers.

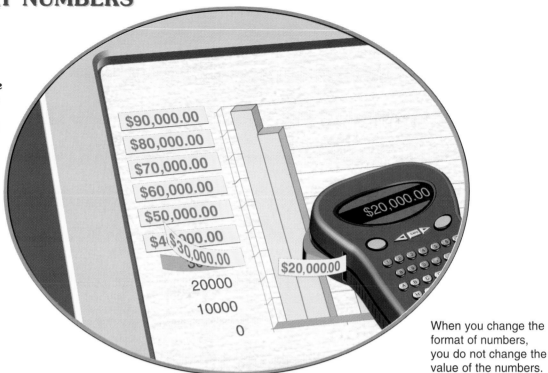

When you change the format of numbers, you do not change the value of the numbers.

CHANGE THE NUMBER STYLE

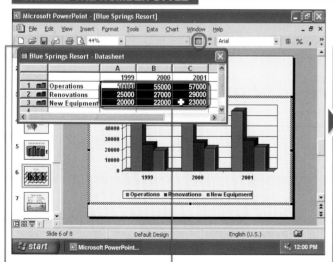

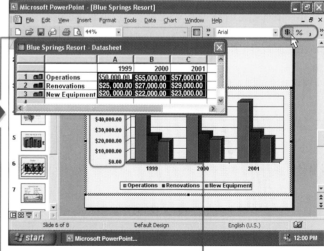

1 Double-click the chart you want to change.

■ If the datasheet does not appear, click 🔲 to display the datasheet.

Note: If 🔲 is not displayed, click ⯈⯈ on the Standard toolbar to display the button.

2 To select the numbers you want to change, drag the mouse ⊕ over the cells containing the numbers.

3 Click one of the following buttons.

$	Currency
%	Percent
,	Comma

Note: If the button you want is not displayed, click ⯈⯈ on the Formatting toolbar to display the button.

■ The numbers in the chart display the new style.

■ To deselect the chart, click outside the chart.

Why do number signs (#) appear in the datasheet?

Number signs (#) appear in the datasheet when a number is too long to fit in a cell.

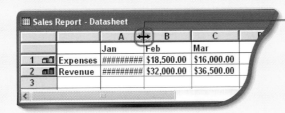

■ To change the width of a column to display the number, position the mouse ⬚ over the right edge of the column heading (⬚ changes to ↔). Then double-click to quickly change the column width.

ADD OR REMOVE A DECIMAL PLACE

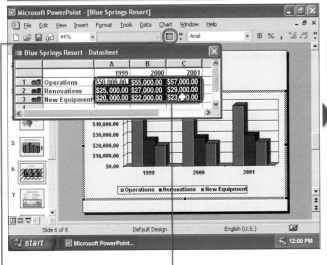

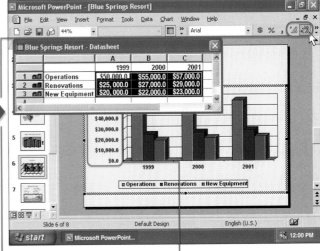

1 Double-click the chart you want to change.

■ If the datasheet does not appear, click 📱 to display the datasheet.

Note: If 📱 is not displayed, click » on the Standard toolbar to display the button.

2 To select the numbers you want to change, drag the mouse ⬚ over the cells containing the numbers.

3 Click one of the following buttons.

🔢 Add decimal place

🔢 Remove decimal place

Note: If the button you want is not displayed, click » on the Formatting toolbar to display the button.

■ The number of decimal places displayed in the chart increases or decreases.

■ To deselect the chart, click outside the chart.

CHANGE APPEARANCE OF A DATA SERIES

You can change the color of a data series in a chart. You can also add a pattern to a data series.

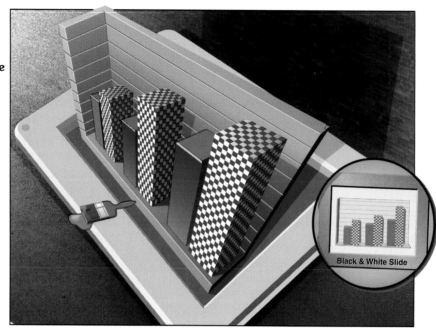

Black & White Slide

If you will print your chart on a black-and-white printer, adding a pattern to a data series may make it easier to identify the data series in the chart.

When you change the appearance of a data series, PowerPoint automatically updates the chart legend.

CHANGE COLOR OF A DATA SERIES

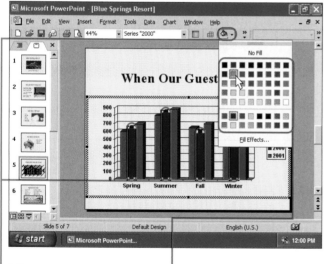

1 Double-click the chart you want to change.

2 Click the data series you want to change. Handles (■) appear on the data series.

3 Click in this area to display the available colors.

Note: If ▒ ▾ is not displayed, click ▹▹ on the Standard toolbar to display the button.

4 Click the color you want to use.

■ The data series displays the color you selected.

ADD A PATTERN TO A DATA SERIES

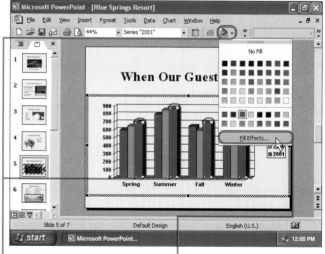

1 Double-click the chart you want to change.

2 Click the data series you want to change. Handles (■) appear on the data series.

3 Click in this area.

Note: If ▒ ▾ is not displayed, click ▹▹ on the Standard toolbar to display the button.

4 Click **Fill Effects**.

■ The Fill Effects dialog box appears.

Can I change the appearance of other parts of a chart?

You can change the appearance of other parts of a chart, such as the background of the chart or the chart legend.

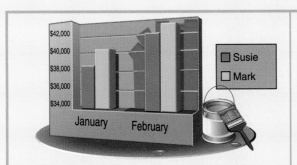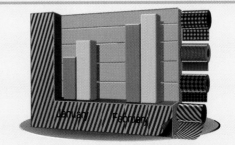

To change the color of part of a chart, perform steps **1** to **4** on page 144, except click the part of the chart you want to change in step **2**.

To add a pattern to part of a chart, perform steps **1** to **7** starting on page 144, except click the part of the chart you want to change in step **2**.

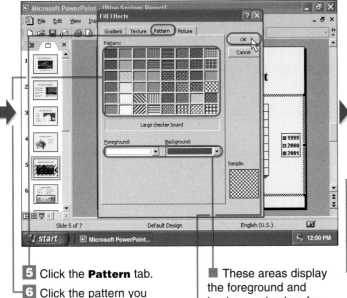

5 Click the **Pattern** tab.

6 Click the pattern you want to use.

■ These areas display the foreground and background colors for the current patterns. You can click an area to select a different color.

7 Click **OK** to confirm your changes.

■ The data series displays the pattern you selected.

■ To deselect the data series, click outside the chart.

ADD A DIAGRAM

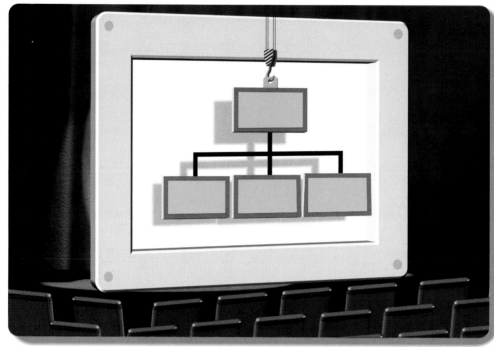

You can add a diagram to a slide to illustrate a concept or idea.

PowerPoint provides several types of diagrams for you to choose from.

ADD A DIAGRAM

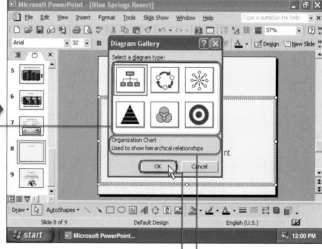

1 Display the slide you want to add a diagram to.

2 Change the layout of the slide to one that includes a placeholder for a diagram. To change the slide layout, see page 46.

3 Click the diagram icon (⟳) to add a diagram to the slide.

Note: Depending on the layout you chose, you may need to double-click the placeholder to add a diagram.

■ The Diagram Gallery dialog box appears.

4 Click the type of diagram you want to add to the slide.

Note: For information on the types of diagrams, see the top of page 147.

■ This area displays a description of the diagram you selected.

5 Click **OK** to add the diagram to your slide.

What types of diagrams can I add to my slides?

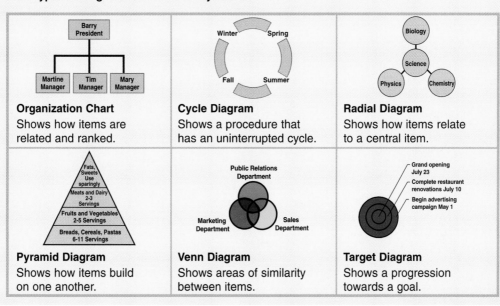

Organization Chart
Shows how items are related and ranked.

Cycle Diagram
Shows a procedure that has an uninterrupted cycle.

Radial Diagram
Shows how items relate to a central item.

Pyramid Diagram
Shows how items build on one another.

Venn Diagram
Shows areas of similarity between items.

Target Diagram
Shows a progression towards a goal.

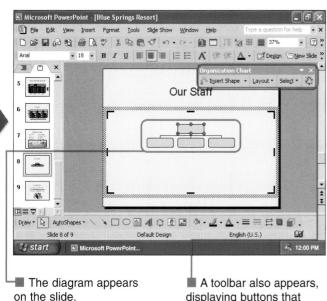

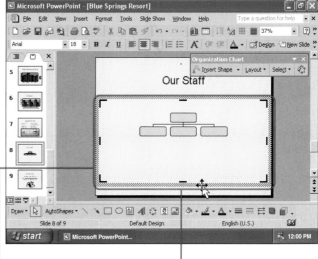

■ The diagram appears on the slide.

Note: To customize the diagram, see pages 148 to 151.

■ A toolbar also appears, displaying buttons that allow you to change the diagram.

■ To deselect a diagram, click outside the diagram.

DELETE A DIAGRAM

1 Click the diagram you want to delete. A border appears around the diagram.

2 Click the border and then press the Delete key.

■ The diagram disappears from the slide.

CONTINUED

ADD A DIAGRAM

You can add text to a diagram to provide descriptions for the shapes in the diagram.

ADD TEXT TO A DIAGRAM

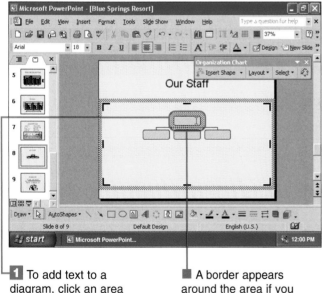

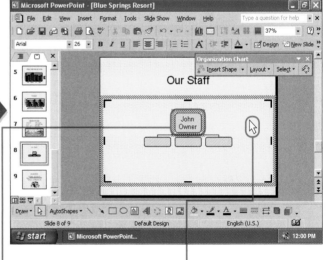

1 To add text to a diagram, click an area where you want to add text.

■ A border appears around the area if you can add text to the area.

2 Type the text you want to add.

Note: In this example, the size of text was increased to make the text easier to read. To change the size of text, see page 79.

3 When you finish typing the text, click outside the text area.

■ You can repeat steps **1** to **3** for each area of text you want to add.

You can add a new shape to a diagram to include additional information in the diagram.

When adding a new shape to an organization chart, there are three types of shapes you can choose from—subordinate, coworker or assistant.

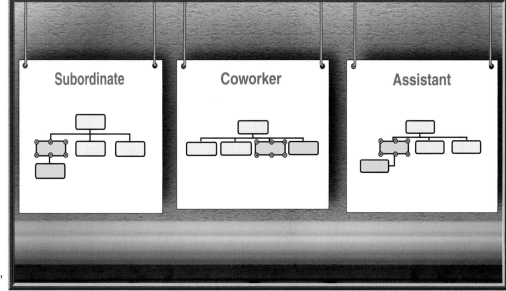

Subordinate   Coworker   Assistant

ADD A SHAPE

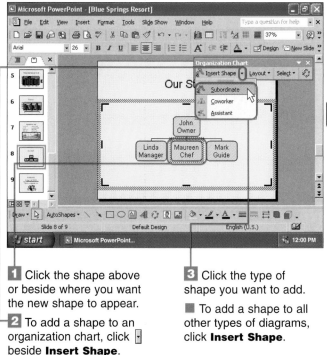

1 Click the shape above or beside where you want the new shape to appear.

2 To add a shape to an organization chart, click ⋅ beside **Insert Shape**.

3 Click the type of shape you want to add.

■ To add a shape to all other types of diagrams, click **Insert Shape**.

■ A new shape appears in the diagram.

■ You can add text to the text area for the new shape.

DELETE A SHAPE

1 Click an edge of the shape you want to delete. Handles (⊗) appear around the shape.

2 Press the Delete key to delete the shape.

149

ADD A DIAGRAM

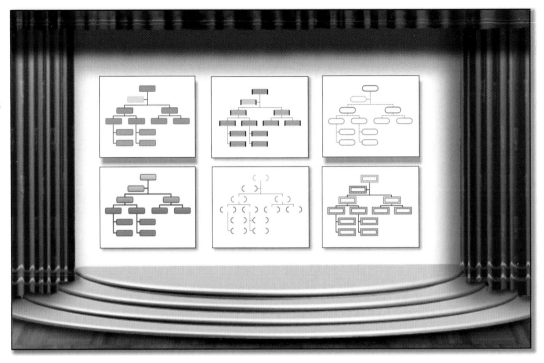

PowerPoint offers
many ready-to-use
styles that you can
choose from to
give a diagram a
new appearance.

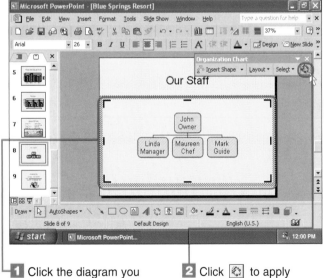

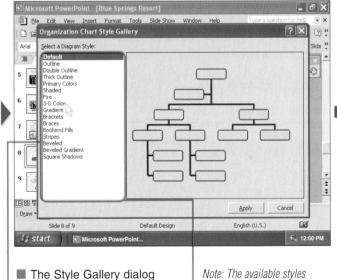

1 Click the diagram you
want to apply a style to.
A border appears around
the diagram.

2 Click 🖼 to apply
a style to the diagram.

■ The Style Gallery dialog
box appears.

■ This area displays a list
of the available styles.

*Note: The available styles
depend on the type of diagram
you selected in step 1.*

3 Click the style you
want to use.

150

Can I change the color of only one shape instead of applying a style to the entire diagram?

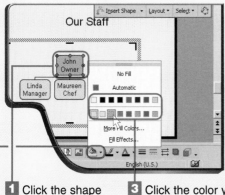

1 Click the shape you want to change to a different color.

2 Click **▾** in this area to display the available colors.

3 Click the color you want to use.

Note: The available colors depend on the color scheme of the slide. For information on color schemes, see page 104.

Can I change the color of the text in a diagram?

Yes. You can change the color of text in a diagram as you would change the color of any text on a slide. To change the color of text, see page 81.

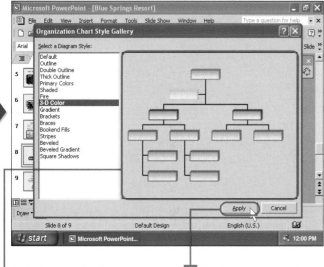

■ This area displays a preview of the style you selected.

Note: You can repeat step 3 to view a preview of a different style.

4 Click **Apply** to apply the style to the diagram.

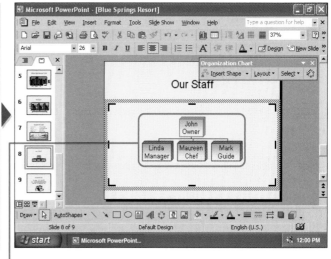

■ The diagram displays the new style.

■ To return to the original diagram style, repeat steps 1 to 4, selecting **Default** in step 3.

CHAPTER 8

Add Tables

Do you want to use a table to organize information on a slide? In this chapter, you will learn how to create and work with tables.

ADD A TABLE

You can add a table
to neatly display
information on a
slide. Tables can
help you organize
lists of information,
such as a schedule
of events or a price
list.

ADD A TABLE

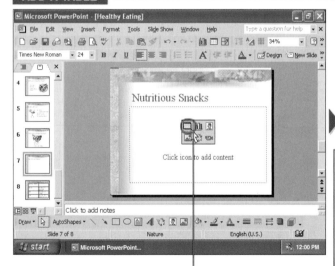

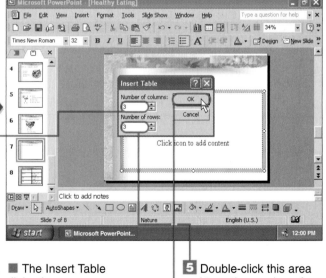

1 Display the slide you
want to add a table to.

2 Change the layout
of the slide to one that
includes a placeholder
for a table. To change the
slide layout, see page 46.

3 Click the table
icon (▦) to add a
table to the slide.

*Note: Depending on the
layout you chose, you may
need to double-click the
placeholder to add a table.*

■ The Insert Table
dialog box appears.

4 Type the number of
columns you want the
table to include.

5 Double-click this area
and type the number of
rows you want the table
to include.

6 Click **OK** to create
the table.

What are the parts of a table?

A table consists of rows, columns and cells.

Row

Column

Cell

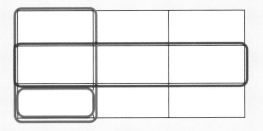

Can I change the appearance of text in a table?

Yes. You can format text in a table as you would format any text on a slide. For example, you can change the font, size, color and alignment of text in a table. To format text, see pages 78 to 99.

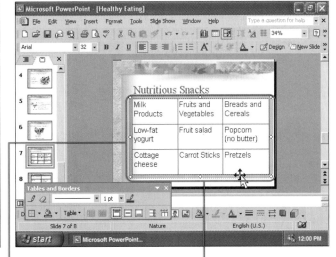

Pianist	Age	Song
Kate Roberts	12	Mary Had a Little Lamb
Morgan Brown	10	Twinkle, Twinkle, Little Star
Patrick O'Reilly	12	On Top of Old Smokey

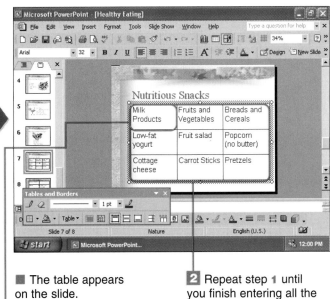

■ The table appears on the slide.

ENTER TEXT INTO A TABLE

1 Click the cell in the table where you want to enter text. Then type the text.

2 Repeat step 1 until you finish entering all the text you want the table to display.

■ When you finish entering text in the table, click outside the table.

DELETE A TABLE

1 Click in the table you want to delete. Handles (o) appear around the table.

2 Click an edge of the table.

3 Press the Delete key to delete the table.

CHANGE ROW HEIGHT OR COLUMN WIDTH

You can change the height of rows and the width of columns to improve the layout of your table.

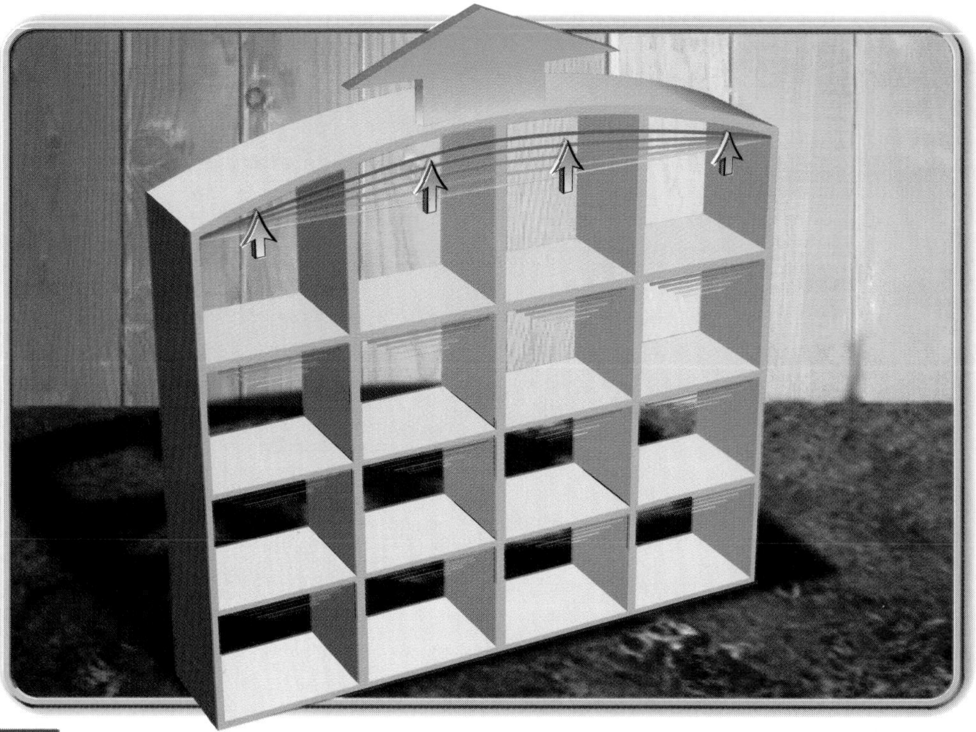

CHANGE ROW HEIGHT

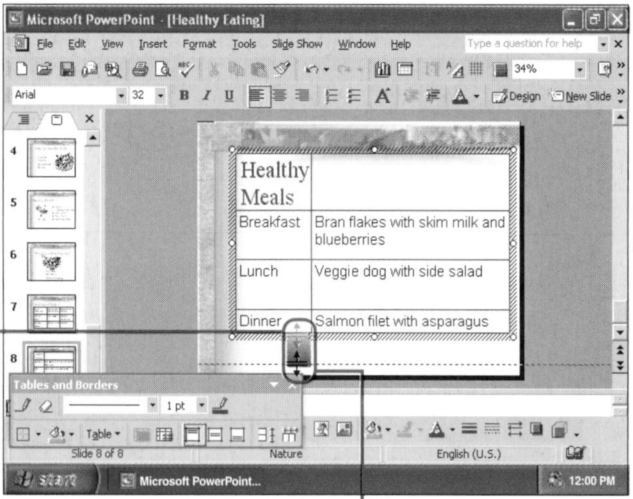

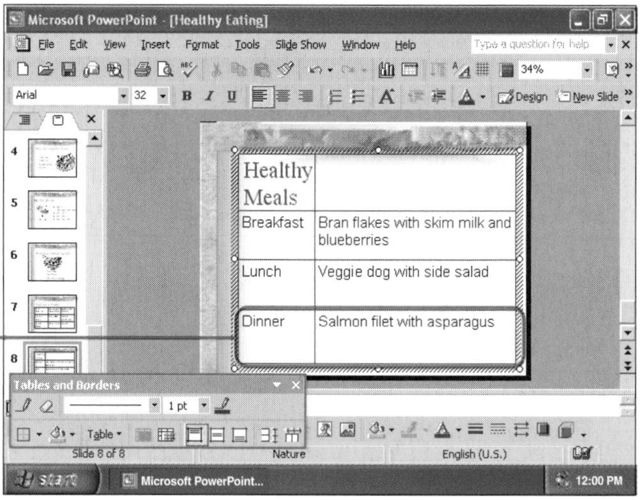

1 Position the mouse I over the bottom edge of the row you want to change to a new height (I changes to ‡).

2 Drag the row edge to a new position.

■ A dotted line shows the new position.

■ The row displays the new height.

■ To deselect the table, click outside the table.

Can PowerPoint automatically adjust a row height?

Yes. When you enter text into a table, PowerPoint automatically increases the row height to accommodate the text you type.

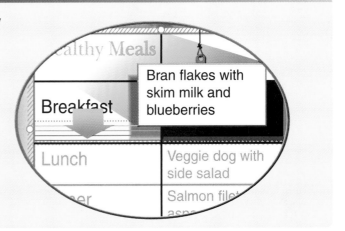

CHANGE COLUMN WIDTH

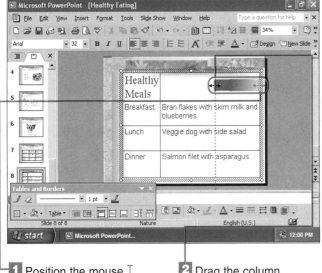

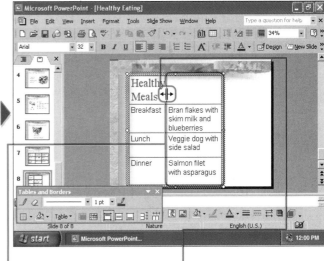

1 Position the mouse I over the right edge of the column you want to change to a new width (I changes to ←‖→).

2 Drag the column edge to a new position.

■ A dotted line shows the new position.

■ The column displays the new width.

■ To deselect the table, click outside the table.

FIT LONGEST ITEM

1 To quickly change a column width to fit the longest item in the column, double-click the right edge of the column.

ADD A ROW OR COLUMN

You can add a row or column to your table to insert additional information.

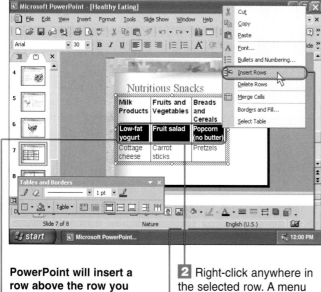

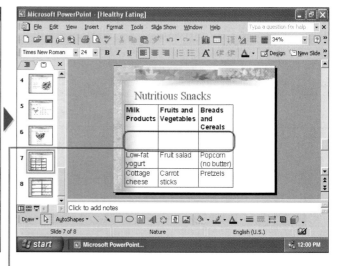

PowerPoint will insert a row above the row you select.

1 To select a row, drag the mouse I over all the cells in the row.

2 Right-click anywhere in the selected row. A menu appears.

3 Click **Insert Rows**.

■ The new row appears in your table and all the rows that follow shift downward.

■ To deselect the table, click outside the table.

How do I add a row to the bottom of a table?

To add a row to the bottom of a table, click the bottom right cell in the table. Then press the Tab key.

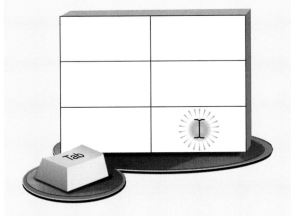

After adding a row or column, my table no longer fits on the slide. What should I do?

You may need to move or resize the table to fit the table on the slide. To move or resize a table, see page 170.

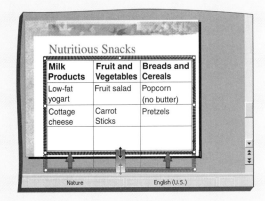

ADD A COLUMN

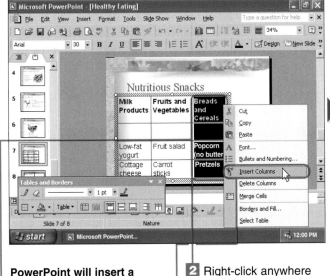

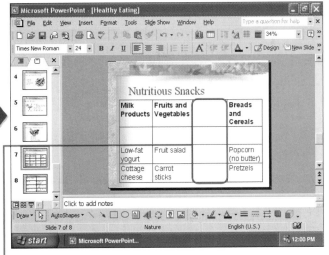

PowerPoint will insert a column to the left of the column you select.

1 To select a column, drag the mouse I over all the cells in the column.

2 Right-click anywhere in the selected column. A menu appears.

3 Click **Insert Columns**.

■ The new column appears in your table and all the columns that follow shift to the right.

■ To deselect the table, click outside the table.

DELETE A ROW OR COLUMN

You can delete a row or column you no longer need from your table.

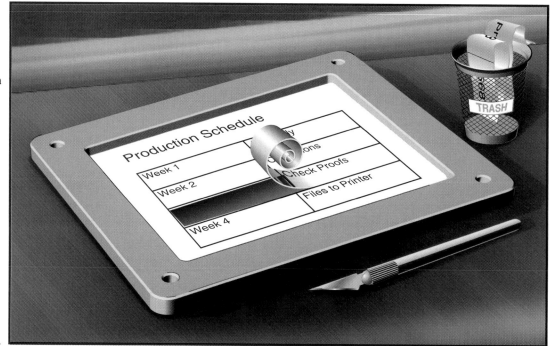

Deleting a row or column will also delete all the information in the row or column.

DELETE A ROW

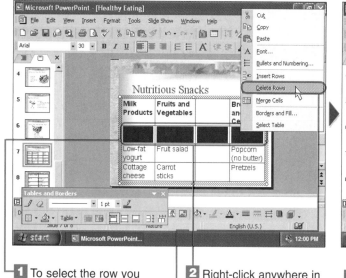

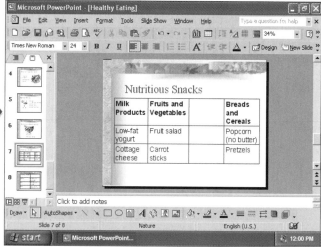

1 To select the row you want to delete, drag the mouse I over all the cells in the row.

2 Right-click anywhere in the selected row. A menu appears.

3 Click **Delete Rows**.

■ The row disappears from your table and all the rows that follow shift upward.

■ To deselect the table, click outside the table.

Can I delete the information in a row or column without removing the row or column from my table?

Yes. To select the cells in your table that contain the information you want to delete, drag the mouse I over the cells until you highlight the cells. Then press the Delete key to remove the information.

How can I restore a row or column I accidentally deleted?

If you accidentally deleted a row or column, you can click the Undo button (↺) to immediately restore the row or column to your table. For more information on the Undo feature, see page 59.

DELETE A COLUMN

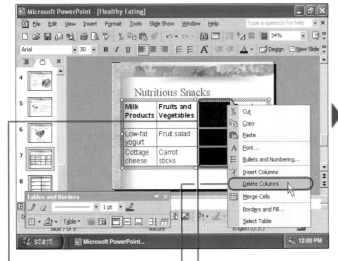

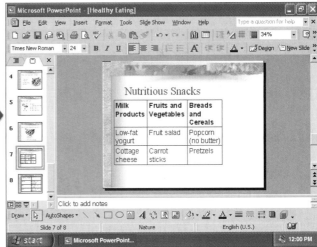

1 To select the column you want to delete, drag the mouse I over all the cells in the column.

2 Right-click anywhere in the selected column. A menu appears.

3 Click **Delete Columns**.

■ The column disappears from your table and all the columns that follow shift to the left.

■ To deselect the table, click outside the table.

COMBINE CELLS

You can combine two or more cells in your table to create one large cell. Combining cells is useful when you want to display a title across the top or down the side of your table.

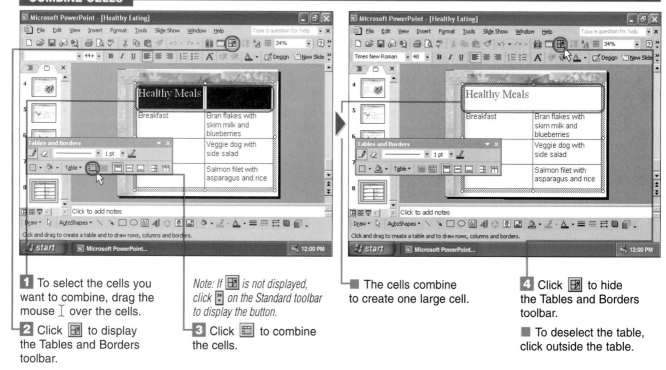

1 To select the cells you want to combine, drag the mouse I over the cells.

2 Click ▦ to display the Tables and Borders toolbar.

Note: If ▦ is not displayed, click ›› on the Standard toolbar to display the button.

3 Click ▦ to combine the cells.

■ The cells combine to create one large cell.

4 Click ▦ to hide the Tables and Borders toolbar.

■ To deselect the table, click outside the table.

162

You can split
one cell in your
table into two
smaller cells.

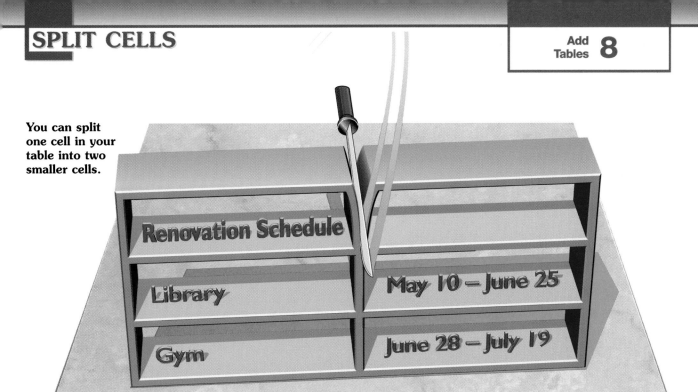

SPLIT CELLS

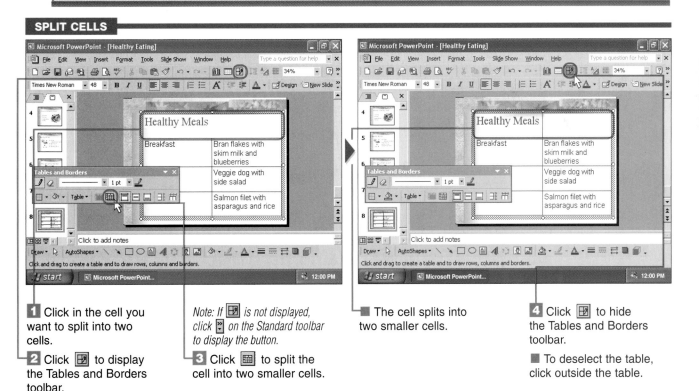

1 Click in the cell you
want to split into two
cells.

2 Click 🖾 to display
the Tables and Borders
toolbar.

*Note: If 🖾 is not displayed,
click 🔀 on the Standard toolbar
to display the button.*

3 Click 🎛 to split the
cell into two smaller cells.

■ The cell splits into
two smaller cells.

4 Click 🖾 to hide
the Tables and Borders
toolbar.

■ To deselect the table,
click outside the table.

ADD COLOR TO CELLS

You can add color to cells to make the cells stand out in your table.

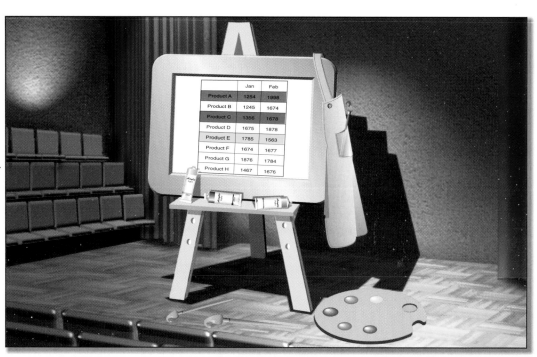

Changing the color for specific cells in your table can help you emphasize important information in the table.

The colors available for the cells in your table depend on the color scheme of the slide. For information on color schemes, see page 104.

ADD COLOR TO CELLS

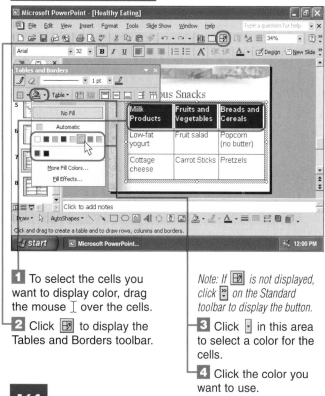

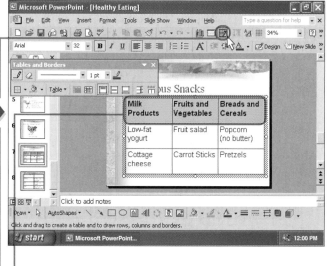

1 To select the cells you want to display color, drag the mouse I over the cells.

2 Click 📝 to display the Tables and Borders toolbar.

Note: If 📝 is not displayed, click 🔽 on the Standard toolbar to display the button.

3 Click ⊡ in this area to select a color for the cells.

4 Click the color you want to use.

■ The cells appear in the color you selected.

5 Click 📝 to hide the Tables and Borders toolbar.

■ To deselect the table, click outside the table.

■ To remove color from cells, repeat steps **1** to **5**, selecting **No Fill** in step **4**.

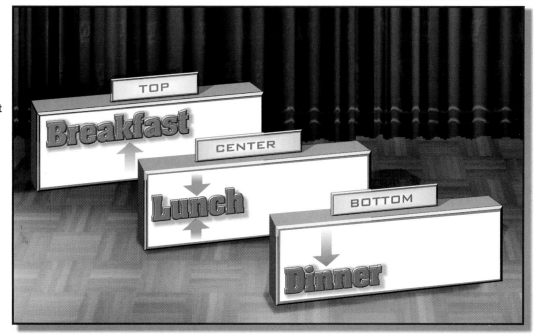

You can enhance the appearance of your table by changing the vertical alignment of text in cells.

When you enter text into a cell, PowerPoint automatically aligns the text at the top of the cell.

VERTICALLY ALIGN TEXT IN CELLS

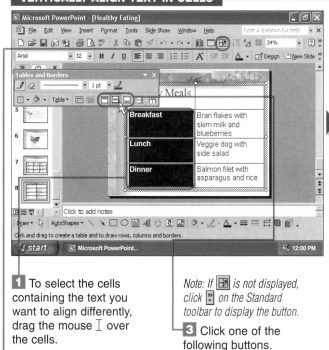

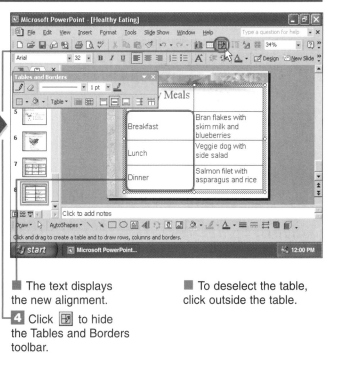

1 To select the cells containing the text you want to align differently, drag the mouse I over the cells.

2 Click 🔳 to display the Tables and Borders toolbar.

Note: If 🔳 is not displayed, click ⟩⟩ on the Standard toolbar to display the button.

3 Click one of the following buttons.

⬛ Align top

⬛ Center vertically

⬛ Align bottom

■ The text displays the new alignment.

4 Click 🔳 to hide the Tables and Borders toolbar.

■ To deselect the table, click outside the table.

CHANGE TABLE BORDERS

You can change the borders in your table to enhance the appearance of the slide in your presentation.

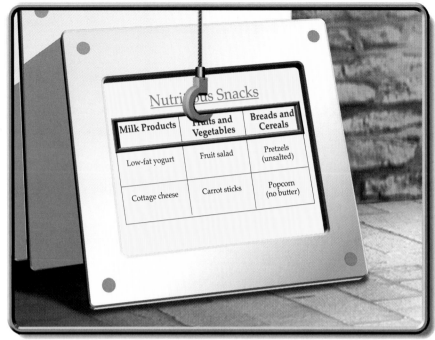

Changing the border for specific cells in your table can help you emphasize important information or divide your table into sections.

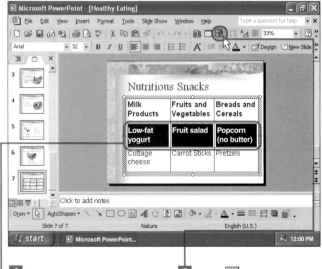

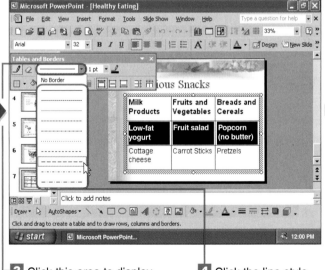

1 To select the cells where you want to change the border, drag the mouse I over the cells.

2 Click ⊞ to display the Tables and Borders toolbar.

Note: If ⊞ is not displayed, click » on the Standard toolbar to display the button.

3 Click this area to display a list of the available line styles for the border.

4 Click the line style you want to use.

166

How do I change the line thickness for a border?

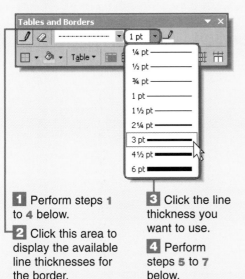

1 Perform steps **1** to **4** below.

2 Click this area to display the available line thicknesses for the border.

3 Click the line thickness you want to use.

4 Perform steps **5** to **7** below.

Can I change the color of a table border?

Yes. Perform steps **1** to **4** below. Click  and select the border color you want to use. Then perform steps **5** to **7** below. The available border colors depend on the color scheme of the slide. For information on color schemes, see page 104.

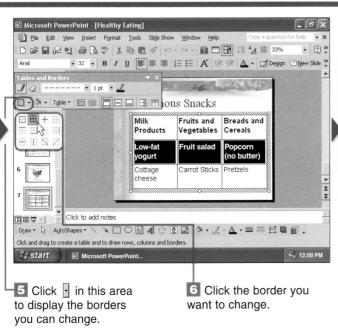

5 Click · in this area to display the borders you can change.

6 Click the border you want to change.

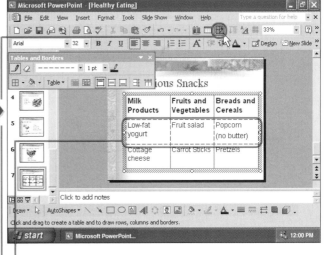

■ The cells you selected display the new border.

7 Click 🔳 to hide the Tables and Borders toolbar.

■ To deselect the table, click outside the table.

■ To delete a border from your table, perform steps **1** and **2**. Then perform steps **5** to **7**, selecting 🔳 in step **6**.

CHAPTER 9

Work With Objects

Would you like to customize the objects on your slides? Read this chapter to learn how to change the size or color of an object, how to make an object 3-D and how to display a grid that can help you arrange objects on your slides.

MOVE OR RESIZE AN OBJECT

You can change the location and size of an object on a slide.

PowerPoint allows you to move and resize objects such as AutoShapes, WordArt, pictures, clip art images, charts and tables.

MOVE AN OBJECT

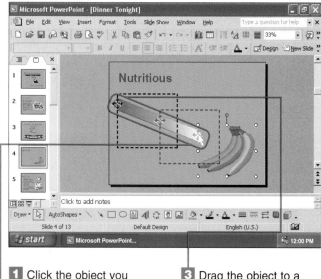

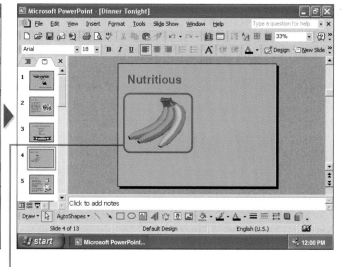

1 Click the object you want to move. Handles (o) appear around the object.

2 Position the mouse ⃗ over an edge of the object (⃗ changes to ✛).

3 Drag the object to a new location on the slide.

■ A dashed line indicates where the object will appear.

■ The object appears in the new location.

■ To deselect the object, click outside the object.

170

How can I change the way an object is moved or resized?

Move Only Horizontally or Vertically

To move an object only horizontally or vertically on a slide, press and hold down the Shift key as you move the object.

Maintain Object's Center When Resizing

To keep the center of an object in the same place while resizing the object, press and hold down the Ctrl key as you resize the object.

RESIZE AN OBJECT

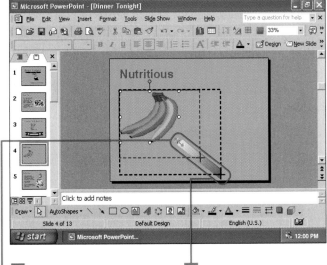

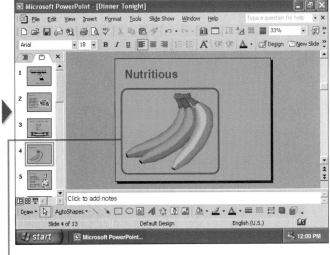

1 Click the object you want to resize. Handles (o) appear around the object.

2 Position the mouse over one of the handles (changes to ↖, ↗, ↔ or ↕).

3 Drag the handle until the object is the size you want.

■ A dashed line shows the new size.

■ The object appears in the new size.

■ To deselect the object, click outside the object.

171

DELETE AN OBJECT

You can delete
an object you no
longer want to
appear on a slide.

You can delete
an object such as
a clip art image,
picture or text box.

DELETE AN OBJECT

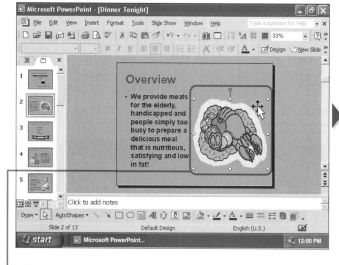

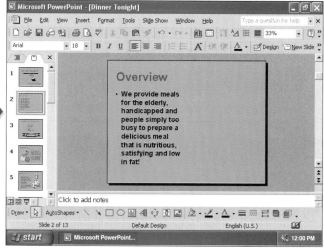

1 Click the object you
want to delete. Handles (o)
appear around the object.

2 Press the Delete key
to delete the object.

■ You may need to press
the Delete key again to
remove the placeholder
for the object from the slide.

■ The object disappears
from the slide.

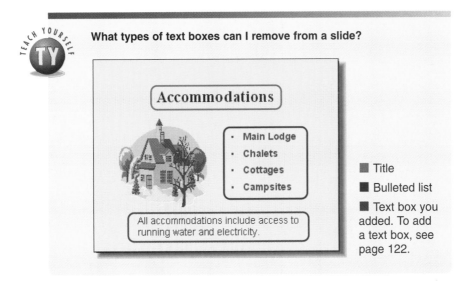

What types of text boxes can I remove from a slide?

Accommodations

· Main Lodge
· Chalets
· Cottages
· Campsites

All accommodations include access to running water and electricity.

■ Title
■ Bulleted list
■ Text box you added. To add a text box, see page 122.

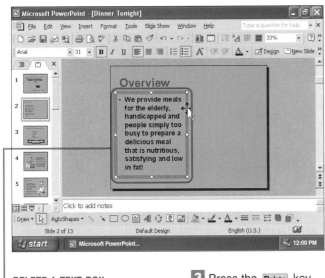

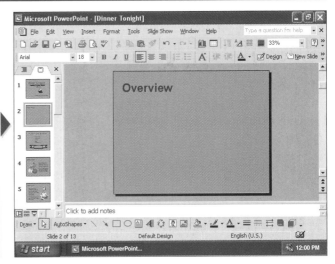

DELETE A TEXT BOX, TABLE OR DIAGRAM

1 Click the item you want to delete. Handles (o) appear around the item.

2 Click an edge of the item.

3 Press the Delete key to delete the text box, table or diagram.

■ You may need to press the Delete key again to remove the placeholder for the item from the slide.

■ The text box, table or diagram disappears from the slide.

CHANGE OBJECT COLOR

You can change the color of an object on a slide to better suit the design of the slide.

PowerPoint allows you to change the color of objects such as WordArt and charts. You can also change the color of most AutoShapes and some clip art images.

CHANGE OBJECT COLOR

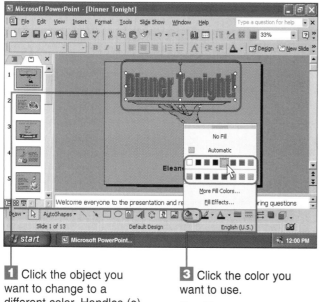

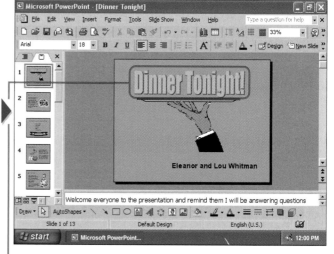

1 Click the object you want to change to a different color. Handles (o) appear around the object.

2 Click ⋮ in this area to display the available colors.

3 Click the color you want to use.

Note: The available colors depend on the color scheme of the slide. For information on color schemes, see page 104.

■ The object appears in the color you selected.

■ To deselect the object, click outside the object.

■ To return the object to the default color, repeat steps **1** to **3**, selecting **Automatic** in step **3**.

CHANGE LINE COLOR

You can change
the color of the
line surrounding
an object on a
slide.

You can change
the line color
for objects such
as text boxes,
pictures, charts
and AutoShapes.

CHANGE LINE COLOR

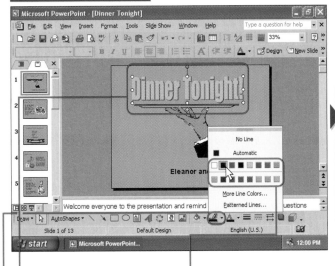

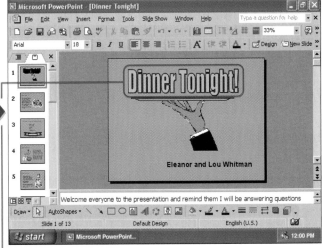

1 Click the object you
want to change the line
color for. Handles (o)
appear around the object.

2 Click ▪ in this area to
display the available line
colors.

3 Click the color you
want to use.

*Note: The available colors
depend on the color scheme of
the slide. For information on
color schemes, see page 104.*

■ The line surrounding
the object appears in the
color you selected.

■ To deselect the object,
click outside the object.

DELETE A LINE

1 To delete a line
surrounding an object,
repeat steps **1** to **3**,
selecting **No Line** in
step **3**.

CHANGE LINE THICKNESS

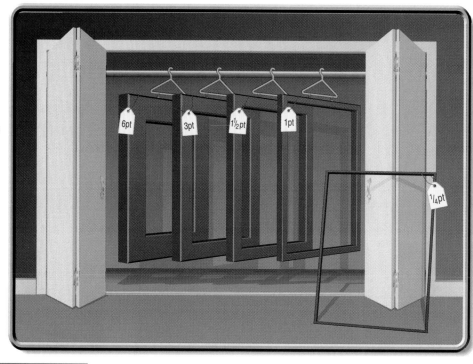

You can emphasize an object by changing the thickness of the line surrounding the object.

You can change the line thickness for objects such as text boxes, pictures, charts and AutoShapes.

CHANGE LINE THICKNESS

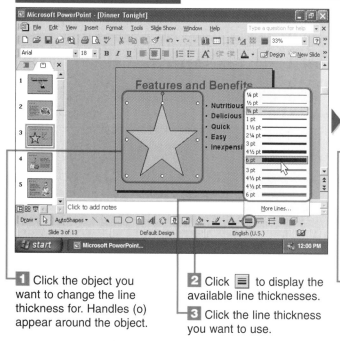

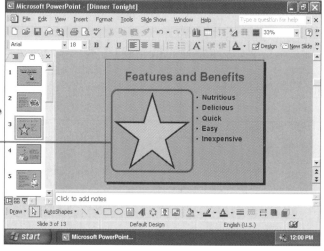

1 Click the object you want to change the line thickness for. Handles (o) appear around the object.

2 Click ≣ to display the available line thicknesses.

3 Click the line thickness you want to use.

■ The line surrounding the object displays the new thickness.

■ To deselect the object, click outside the object.

Note: To delete the line surrounding an object, see page 175.

176

You can change the line surrounding an object to a dashed or dotted line.

CHANGE LINE STYLE

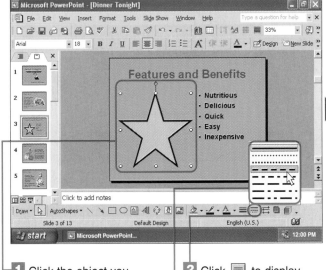

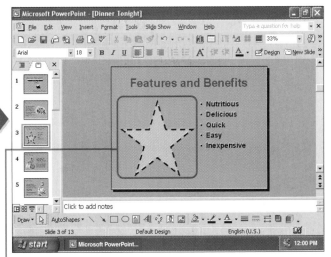

1 Click the object you want to change the line style for. Handles (o) appear around the object.

2 Click to display the available line styles.

3 Click the line style you want to use.

■ The line surrounding the object displays the line style.

■ To deselect the object, click outside the object.

Note: To delete the line surrounding an object, see page 175.

ADD A TEXTURE OR PATTERN

You can add a texture or pattern to an object on a slide to enhance the appearance of the object.

PowerPoint allows you to add a texture or pattern to several types of objects, including AutoShapes, WordArt and text boxes.

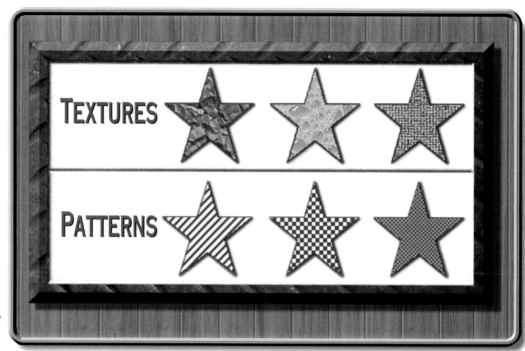

ADD A TEXTURE OR PATTERN

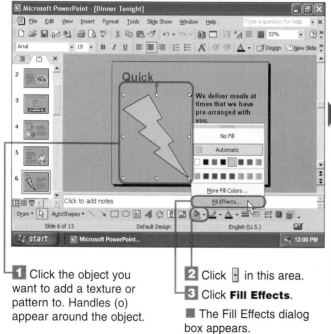

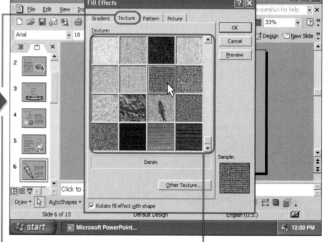

1 Click the object you want to add a texture or pattern to. Handles (o) appear around the object.

2 Click ⬇ in this area.

3 Click **Fill Effects**.

■ The Fill Effects dialog box appears.

ADD A TEXTURE

4 To add a texture, click the **Texture** tab.

5 Click the texture you want to add. Then skip to step **8**.

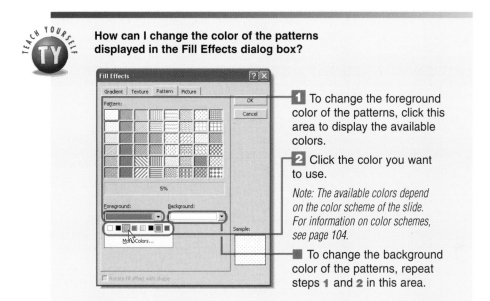

How can I change the color of the patterns displayed in the Fill Effects dialog box?

1 To change the foreground color of the patterns, click this area to display the available colors.

2 Click the color you want to use.

Note: The available colors depend on the color scheme of the slide. For information on color schemes, see page 104.

■ To change the background color of the patterns, repeat steps **1** and **2** in this area.

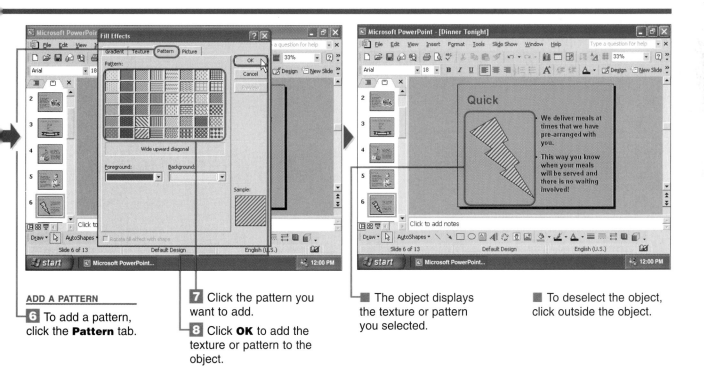

ADD A PATTERN

6 To add a pattern, click the **Pattern** tab.

7 Click the pattern you want to add.

8 Click **OK** to add the texture or pattern to the object.

■ The object displays the texture or pattern you selected.

■ To deselect the object, click outside the object.

ADD A SHADOW TO AN OBJECT

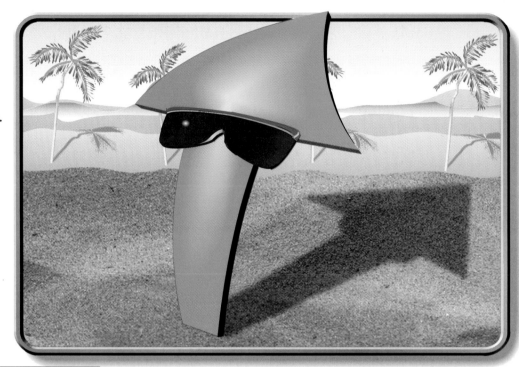

You can add a shadow to add depth to an object on a slide.

ADD A SHADOW TO AN OBJECT

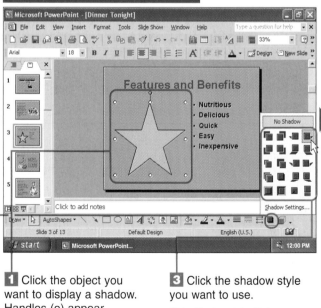

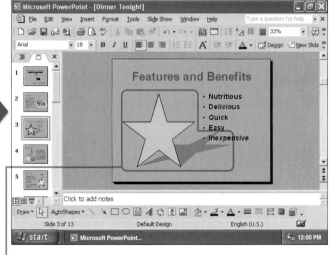

1 Click the object you want to display a shadow. Handles (o) appear around the object.

2 Click ▣ to display the available shadow styles.

3 Click the shadow style you want to use.

Note: Shadow styles that appear dimmed are not available for the object you selected.

■ The object displays the shadow.

■ To deselect the object, click outside the object.

REMOVE A SHADOW

1 To remove a shadow from an object, repeat steps **1** to **3**, selecting **No Shadow** in step **3**.

MAKE AN OBJECT 3-D

You can make an object on a slide appear three-dimensional.

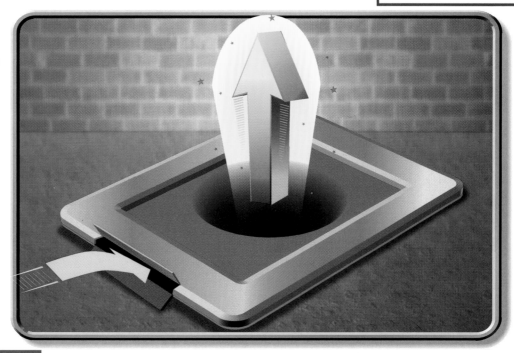

MAKE AN OBJECT 3-D

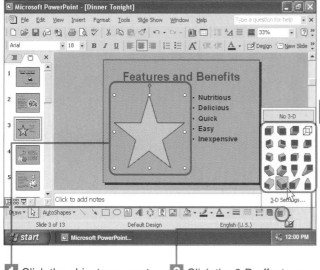

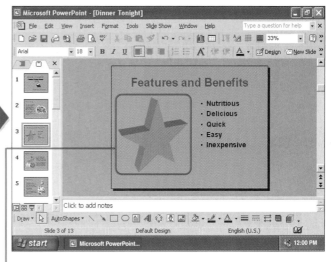

1 Click the object you want to appear three-dimensional. Handles (o) appear around the object.

2 Click 🔲 to select a 3-D effect.

3 Click the 3-D effect you want to use.

Note: If the 3-D effects are dimmed, you cannot make the object you selected three-dimensional.

■ The object displays the 3-D effect.

■ To deselect the object, click outside the object.

REMOVE A 3-D EFFECT

1 To remove a 3-D effect from an object, repeat steps **1** to **3**, selecting **No 3-D** in step **3**.

ROTATE AN OBJECT

You can rotate
an object on a
slide in your
presentation.

Objects you can
rotate include text
boxes, WordArt,
pictures and
AutoShapes.

ROTATE AN OBJECT

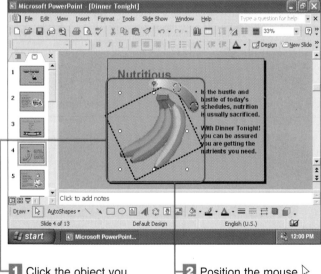

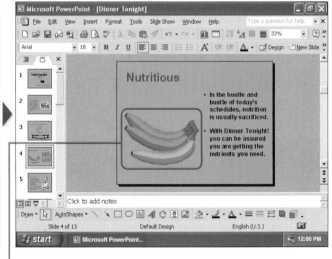

1 Click the object you
want to rotate. Handles (o)
appear around the object.

2 Position the mouse ⃗
over the green dot
(⃗ changes to ↻).

3 Drag the mouse ⟨⟩
in the direction you want
to rotate the object.

■ The object appears
in the new position.

■ To deselect an object,
click outside the object.

DISPLAY THE GRID

You can display a grid on the slides in your presentation. The grid can help you more precisely position objects on your slides.

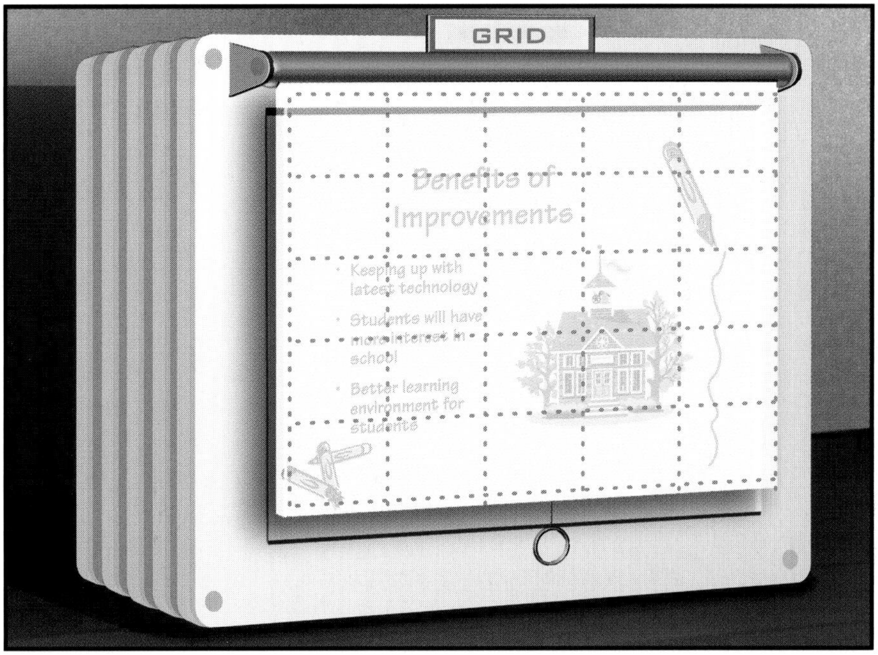

When you add, move or resize an object on a slide, PowerPoint will automatically snap the object to the grid. PowerPoint will snap objects to the grid even when the grid is not displayed.

DISPLAY THE GRID

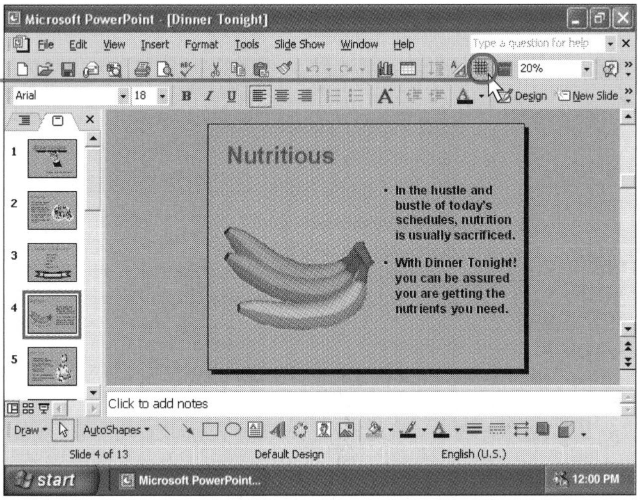

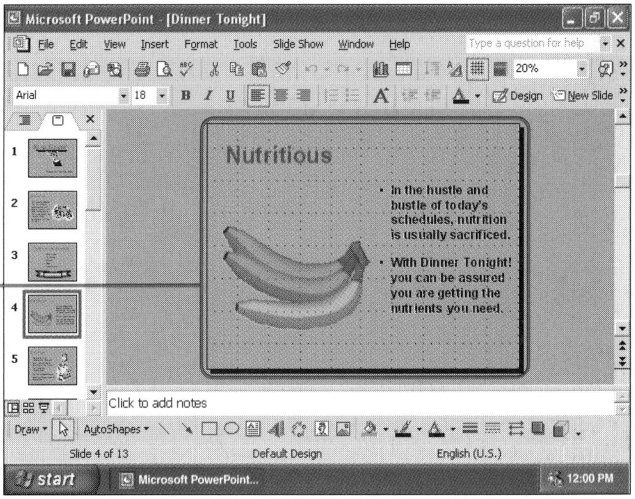

1 Click ▦ to display the grid on the slides in your presentation.

Note: If ▦ is not displayed, click » on the Standard toolbar to display the button.

■ The grid appears on the slide in this area.

Note: The grid will not appear on the slides during a slide show or when you print the presentation.

■ You can repeat step **1** to hide the grid at any time.

Note: If you want to be able to position an object on a slide without having PowerPoint snap the object to the grid, press and hold down the **Alt** *key as you add, move or resize the object.*

CHAPTER 10

Add Multimedia

Are you interested in adding multimedia, such as sounds and movies, to your slides? This chapter shows you how.

ADD A SOUND

You can add a sound to a slide in your presentation. This can help make your presentation more interesting and entertaining.

PowerPoint comes with a Clip Organizer, which offers many sounds that you can choose from.

ADD A SOUND FROM THE CLIP ORGANIZER

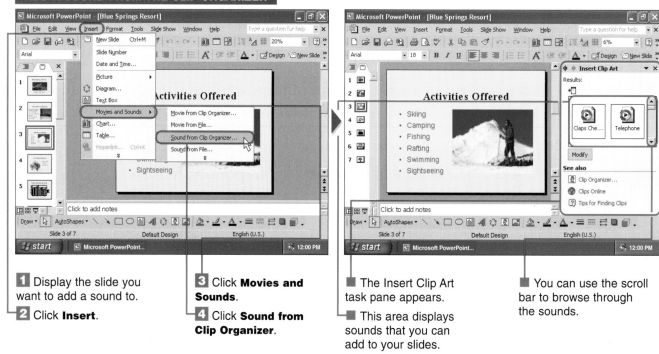

1 Display the slide you want to add a sound to.

2 Click **Insert**.

3 Click **Movies and Sounds**.

4 Click **Sound from Clip Organizer**.

■ The Insert Clip Art task pane appears.

■ This area displays sounds that you can add to your slides.

■ You can use the scroll bar to browse through the sounds.

What do I need to play sounds on my computer?

You need a sound card and speakers to play sounds on your computer. Make sure your speakers are properly connected and turned on before you begin adding sounds to slides.

 Where can I find more sounds?

If your computer is connected to the Internet, you can visit Microsoft's Design Gallery Live Web site to search for additional sounds. In the Insert Clip Art task pane, click **Clips Online** to connect to the Web site.

5 Position the mouse over the sound you want to preview. An arrow appears.

6 Click the arrow to display a list of options.

7 Click **Preview/Properties** to preview the sound.

■ The Preview/Properties dialog box appears and the sound plays.

■ To stop the sound at any time, click ■.

■ You can click ▶ to play the sound again.

8 When you finish previewing the sound, click **Close** to close the dialog box.

CONTINUED

ADD A SOUND

When you add a
sound to a slide,
you can specify
how you want
the sound to
play during a
slide show.

You can have
a sound play
automatically
when the slide
is displayed
or only when
you click the
speaker icon
on the slide.

ADD A SOUND FROM THE CLIP ORGANIZER (CONTINUED)

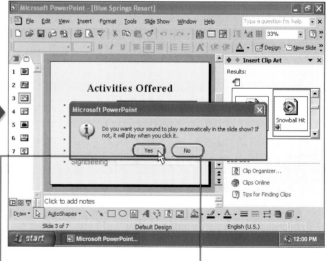

9 Click the sound you
want to add to the slide.

■ A dialog box appears,
asking how you want the
sound to play during the
slide show.

10 To have the sound play
automatically when the
slide is displayed, click **Yes**.

■ To have the sound
play when you click
the speaker icon on
the slide, click **No**.

Can I hide the speaker icon () on a slide?

If you chose to have a sound play automatically when the slide is displayed during a slide show, you may want to hide the speaker icon from view during your slide show. To hide the speaker icon, display the slide in the Normal view and then move the icon to a location off the slide. For information on the views, see page 42. To move a speaker icon, see page 170.

How do I remove a sound I added to a slide in my presentation?

To remove a sound from a slide, you must delete the speaker icon () from the slide. Display the slide in the Normal view and then click the speaker icon. Press the Delete key to remove the sound from the slide. For information on the views, see page 42.

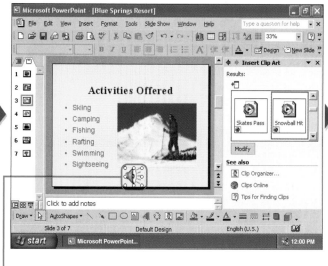

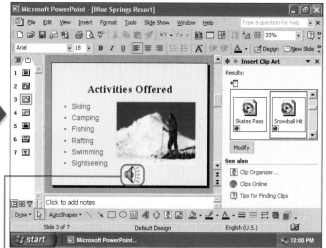

■ A speaker icon () appears. The handles (o) around the icon let you resize the icon. To move or resize the icon, see page 170.

11 To hide the handles, click outside the icon.

■ To play the sound in the Normal view, double-click the speaker icon ().

Note: To view a slide show, see page 266.

ADD A SOUND

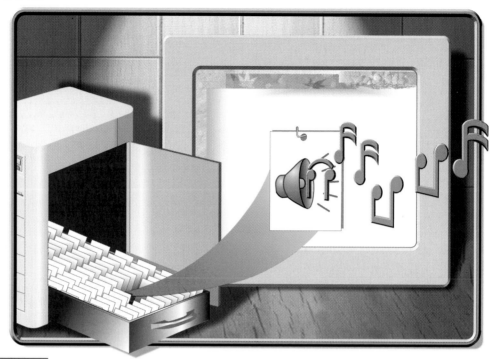

You can add a sound stored on your computer to a slide in your presentation.

Adding a sound is useful if you want to add a theme song, advertising jingle or clip from a famous speech.

ADD A SOUND FROM A FILE

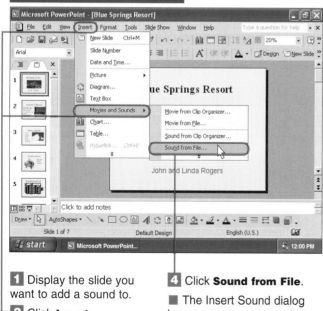

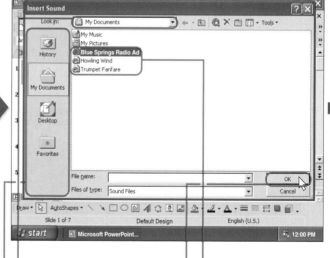

1 Display the slide you want to add a sound to.

2 Click **Insert**.

3 Click **Movies and Sounds**.

4 Click **Sound from File**.

■ The Insert Sound dialog box appears.

■ This area shows the location of the displayed sounds. You can click this area to change the location.

■ This area allows you to access sounds stored in commonly used locations. You can click a location to display the sounds stored in the location.

5 Click the name of the sound you want to add.

6 Click **OK** to add the sound to the slide.

Where can I get sounds that I can use in my presentation?

Many computer stores sell CD-ROM discs that contain collections of sounds. There are also Web sites on the Internet that offer free sounds. You can find sounds at the following Web sites.

www.favewavs.com
www.wavlist.com
www.wavcentral.com

I e-mailed my presentation to another computer and now the sound I added will not play. What is wrong?

If the sound file you added to the slide is over 100 KB in size, PowerPoint will only provide a link to the sound rather than embedding the sound on the slide. You must e-mail the sound file with the presentation to be able to play the sound on the other computer.

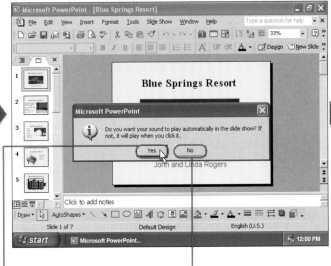

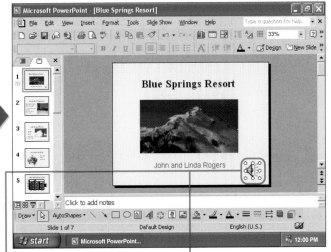

■ A dialog box appears, asking how you want the sound to play during the slide show.

7 To have the sound play automatically when the slide is displayed, click **Yes**.

■ To have the sound play when you click the speaker icon on the slide, click **No**.

■ A speaker icon (🔊) appears. The handles (o) around the icon let you resize the icon. To move or resize the icon, see page 170.

8 To hide the handles, click outside the icon.

■ To play the sound in the Normal view, double-click the speaker icon.

Note: To view a slide show, see page 266.

■ To delete the sound from the slide, see the top of page 189.

ADD A MOVIE

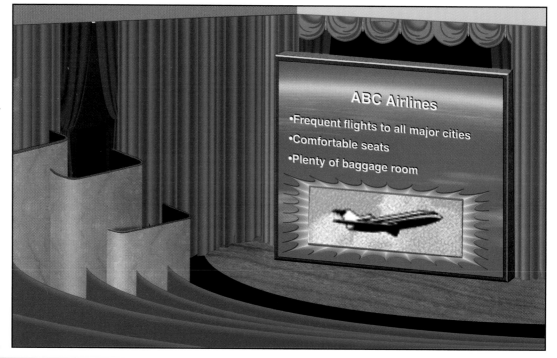

You can add a movie to a slide to add interest to your presentation.

PowerPoint provides a Clip Organizer, which offers many movies that you can choose from.

ADD A MOVIE FROM THE CLIP ORGANIZER

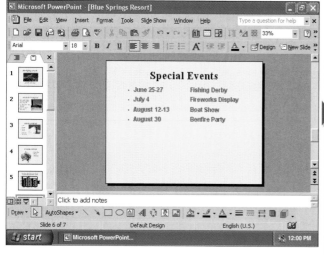

1 Display the slide you want to add a movie to.

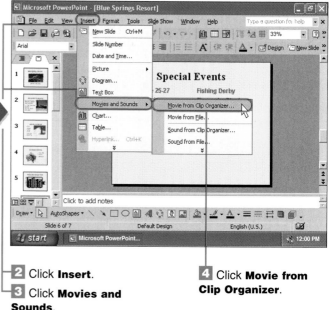

2 Click **Insert**.

3 Click **Movies and Sounds**.

4 Click **Movie from Clip Organizer**.

What types of movies does the Clip Organizer offer?

Most of the movies available in the Clip Organizer are animated GIF files, which consist of a series of images that appear one after another to give the appearance of motion. Animated GIF files have the .gif extension.

Where can I find more animated GIF files?

If your computer is connected to the Internet, you can visit Microsoft's Design Gallery Live Web site to search for additional animated GIF files. In the Insert Clip Art task pane, click **Clips Online** to connect to the Web site.

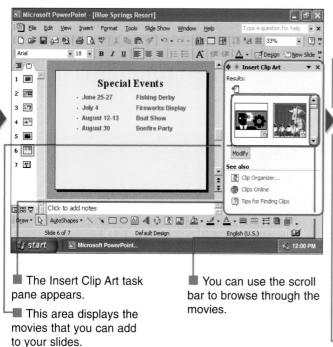

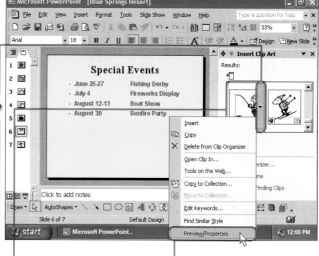

■ The Insert Clip Art task pane appears.

■ This area displays the movies that you can add to your slides.

■ You can use the scroll bar to browse through the movies.

5 Position the mouse ⬚ over the movie you want to preview. An arrow (⬚) appears.

6 Click the arrow to display a list of options.

7 Click **Preview/Properties** to preview the movie.

CONTINUED

ADD A MOVIE

When adding a movie to a slide from the Clip Organizer, you can view information about the movie, such as the file name, the file type and the size of the movie.

Name: Finance.gif
Type: GIF Image
Size: 20 KB

ADD A MOVIE FROM THE CLIP ORGANIZER (CONTINUED)

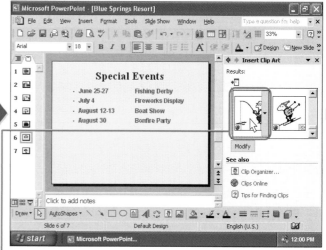

■ The Preview/Properties dialog box appears.

■ The movie plays in this area.

■ This area displays information about the movie, such as the name and type of movie.

8 When you finish previewing the movie, click **Close** to close the dialog box.

9 Click the movie you want to add to the slide.

Why did this dialog box appear when I selected the movie I wanted to add to the slide?

If you chose to add a movie that is not an animated GIF file in step 9 below, this dialog box appears, asking how you want the movie to play during the slide show.

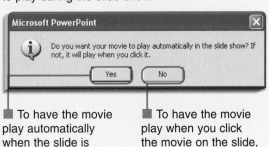

■ To have the movie play automatically when the slide is displayed, click **Yes**.

■ To have the movie play when you click the movie on the slide, click **No**.

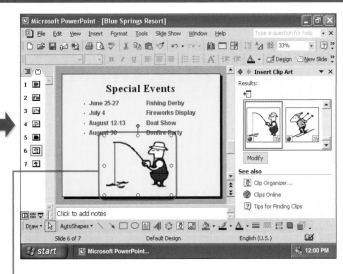

■ The first frame in the movie appears on the slide. The handles (o) around the movie let you resize the movie. To move or resize a movie, see page 170.

10 To hide the handles, click outside the movie.

■ The movie will play automatically when the slide is displayed during the slide show.

Note: To view a slide show, see page 266.

DELETE A MOVIE

1 Click the movie on the slide in the Normal view. For information on the views, see page 42.

2 Press the Delete key to remove the movie from the slide.

■ You may need to press the Delete key again to remove the placeholder for the movie from the slide.

ADD A MOVIE

You can add a movie stored on your computer to a slide in your presentation. The most common types of movies include AVI and MPEG files.

Adding a movie is useful if you want to add a movie clip from a television commercial, news broadcast, sporting event or film.

ADD A MOVIE FROM A FILE

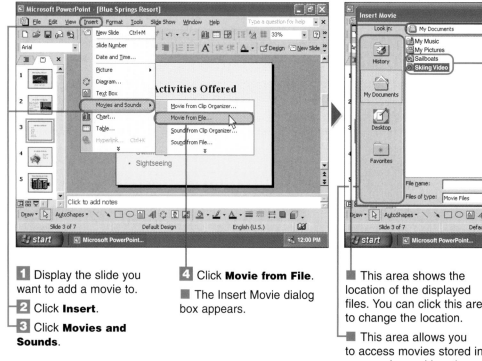

1 Display the slide you want to add a movie to.

2 Click **Insert**.

3 Click **Movies and Sounds**.

4 Click **Movie from File**.

■ The Insert Movie dialog box appears.

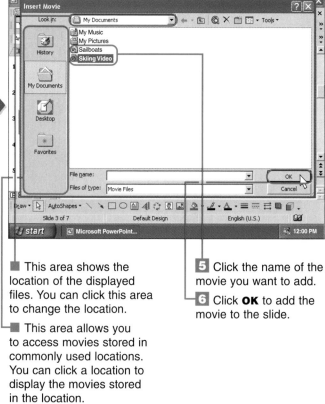

■ This area shows the location of the displayed files. You can click this area to change the location.

■ This area allows you to access movies stored in commonly used locations. You can click a location to display the movies stored in the location.

5 Click the name of the movie you want to add.

6 Click **OK** to add the movie to the slide.

I double-clicked the movie on my slide to preview the movie in the Normal view, but the movie did not play. What is wrong?

The movie you added to your slide may be an animated GIF file. You cannot preview this type of movie in the Normal view. An animated GIF file will play automatically when you view the slide during a slide show. To view a slide show, see page 266.

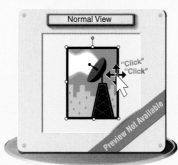

Why does the movie on my slide appear grainy?

Most movies are designed to play best at their original size. If you increased the size of the movie, the movie may become jerky, appear grainy or display other visual distortions.

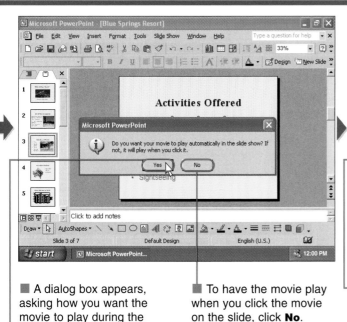

■ A dialog box appears, asking how you want the movie to play during the slide show.

7 To have the movie play automatically when the slide is displayed, click **Yes**.

■ To have the movie play when you click the movie on the slide, click **No**.

■ The first frame of the movie appears. The handles (o) around the movie let you resize the movie. To move or resize the movie, see page 170.

8 To hide the handles, click outside the movie.

■ To play the movie in the Normal view, double-click the movie.

Note: To view a slide show, see page 266.

■ To delete the movie from the slide, see page 195.

197

PLAY A MUSIC CD DURING A SLIDE SHOW

You can play tracks from a music CD during a slide show to add background music to your slides.

The music CD tracks you add to a slide will automatically stop playing when you display the next slide in a slide show.

You need a computer with sound capabilities to play a music CD during a slide show.

PLAY A MUSIC CD FOR ONE SLIDE

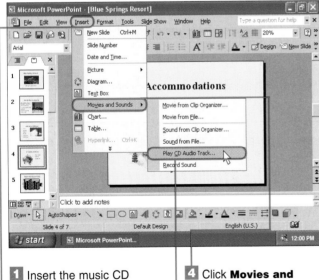

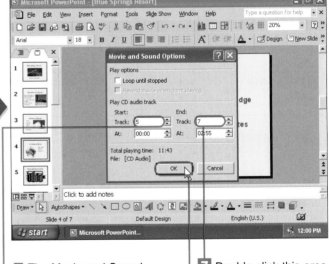

■1 Insert the music CD into your CD-ROM drive.

■2 Display the slide you want to play the music CD.

■3 Click **Insert**.

■4 Click **Movies and Sounds**.

■5 Click **Play CD Audio Track**.

Note: If Play CD Audio Track does not appear on the menu, position the mouse ⌖ over the bottom of the menu to display the menu option.

■ The Movie and Sound Options dialog box appears.

■6 Double-click this area and type the number of the first track you want to play on the music CD.

■7 Double-click this area and type the number of the last track you want to play.

■8 Click **OK** to confirm your changes.

Why did this dialog box appear when I inserted a music CD into my CD-ROM drive?

If you are running the Windows XP operating system on your computer, the Audio CD dialog box may automatically appear when you insert a music CD. Click **Cancel** to close the dialog box. To prevent the dialog box from appearing when you insert a music CD, press and hold down the Shift key as you insert the CD into the CD-ROM drive.

How do I play a music CD during a slide show?

You must insert the music CD into the CD-ROM drive before you start the slide show. If you selected **Yes** in step 9 below, the music CD will start to play automatically when you display the slide containing the CD icon (🎵). If you selected **No**, click the CD icon on the slide to start playing the music CD. To view a slide show, see page 266.

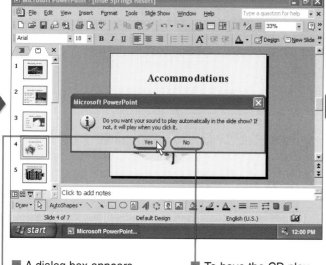

■ A dialog box appears, asking how you want the music CD to play during the slide show.

9 To have the CD play automatically when the slide is displayed, click **Yes**.

■ To have the CD play when you click the CD icon (🎵) on the slide, click **No**.

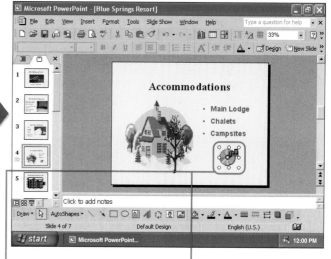

■ A CD icon (🎵) appears.

Note: To move or resize the CD icon, see page 170.

■ To play the music CD in the Normal view, double-click the CD icon.

■ If you no longer want to play a music CD for a slide, click the CD icon and then press the Delete key.

CONTINUED

PLAY A MUSIC CD DURING A SLIDE SHOW

You can choose to have a music CD play for several slides during a slide show.

Playing a music CD for multiple slides can help set a particular mood for your presentation or for a self-running slide show at a kiosk. Kiosks are often found at trade shows and shopping malls.

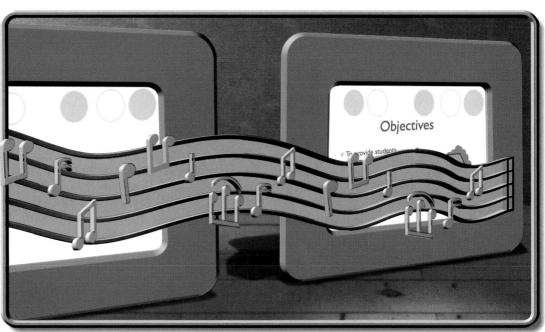

PLAY A MUSIC CD FOR MULTIPLE SLIDES

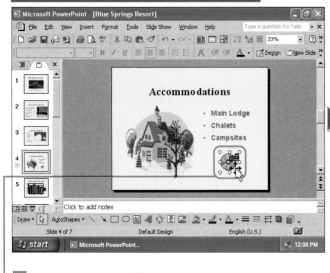

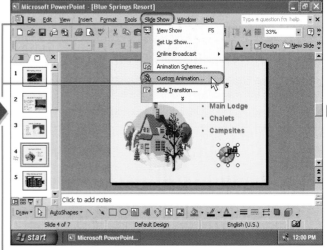

1 Click the CD icon (🎵) for the music CD you want to play for multiple slides. Handles (o) appear around the icon.

Note: To set up a music CD to play during a slide show, perform steps 1 to 9 starting on page 198.

2 Click **Slide Show**.

3 Click **Custom Animation**.

■ The Custom Animation task pane appears.

How do I change the volume of the music CD?

Your speakers may have a volume dial you can use to increase or decrease the volume of the music CD. You can also adjust the system volume for your operating system to change the volume of the CD. To change the system volume, consult the documentation that came with your operating system.

My slide also contains animations and other sounds and videos. How can I ensure that the music CD will start playing before the other items on the slide?

You can use the Custom Animation task pane to change the order of the items on the slide to ensure the music CD will start playing before any animations or other sounds or videos on the slide. For more information on changing the order of the items in the Custom Animation task pane, see page 208.

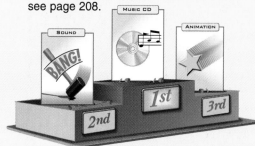

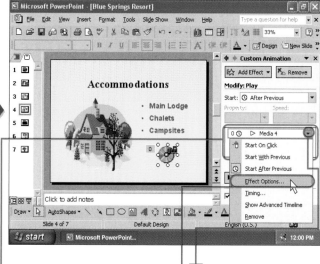

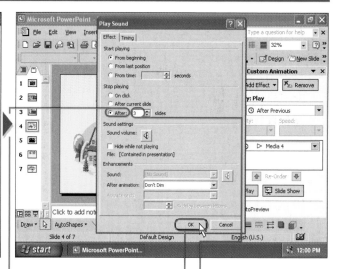

■ This area displays the sounds, movies and animations you have added to the slide.

Note: For information on adding animations to slides, see pages 214 to 219.

■ Click the sound for the music CD in this area. An arrow (▾) appears.

5 Click the arrow (▾) to display a list of options for the sound.

6 Click **Effect Options**.

■ The Play Sound dialog box appears.

7 Click **After** to specify that you want the music CD to play for multiple slides (○ changes to ◉).

8 Type the number of slides you want the music to play for.

9 Click **OK** to confirm your changes.

Note: To play the music CD during a slide show, see the top of page 199.

ADD A RECORDED SOUND

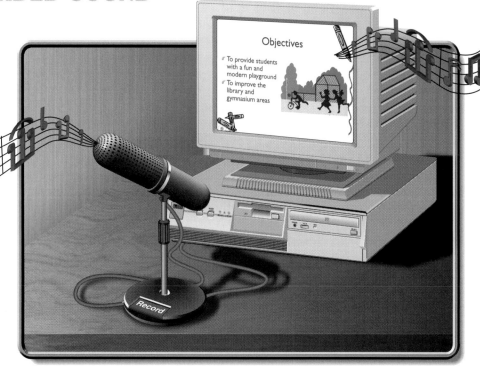

You can record your own sound and then add it to a slide. Adding a recorded sound is useful if you need to include a statement from a colleague who is unable to attend your presentation.

You need a computer with sound capabilities to add a recorded sound to your presentation.

ADD A RECORDED SOUND

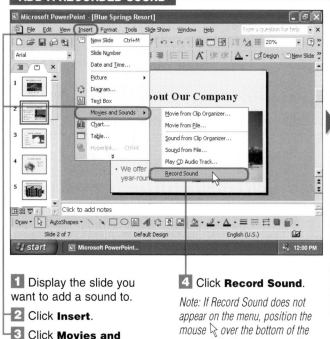

1 Display the slide you want to add a sound to.

2 Click **Insert**.

3 Click **Movies and Sounds**.

4 Click **Record Sound**.

Note: If Record Sound does not appear on the menu, position the mouse over the bottom of the menu to display the menu option.

■ The Record Sound dialog box appears.

5 To specify a name for the sound, drag the mouse I over this area and then type the name.

6 Click ● to start recording.

7 Speak into your microphone or start your sound device.

What devices can I record sounds from?

You can record sounds from any sound device you can connect to your computer, such as a microphone, CD player, stereo or VCR.

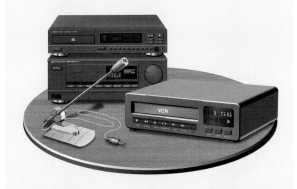

How do I play a recorded sound during a slide show?

To play the recorded sound during a slide show, click the speaker icon (🔊) for the sound on the slide. To view a slide show, see page 266.

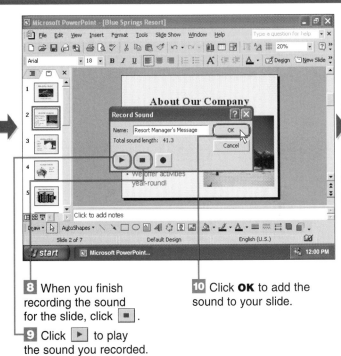

8 When you finish recording the sound for the slide, click ■ .

9 Click ▶ to play the sound you recorded.

10 Click **OK** to add the sound to your slide.

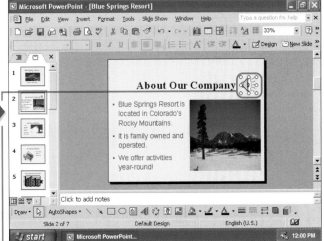

■ A speaker icon (🔊) appears. To move or resize the speaker icon, see page 170.

■ To play the sound in the Normal view, double-click the speaker icon (🔊).

■ To delete the sound from the slide, see the top of page 189.

ADD NARRATION TO A SLIDE SHOW

You can record voice narration and add it to a slide show. This is ideal for a presentation that will run on the Web or a self-running slide show at a kiosk.

Kiosks are often found at trade shows and shopping malls.

ADD NARRATION TO A SLIDE SHOW

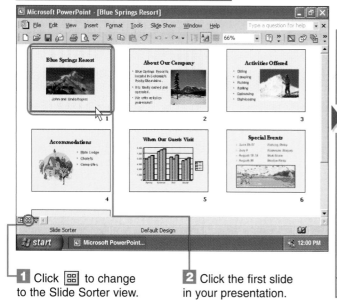

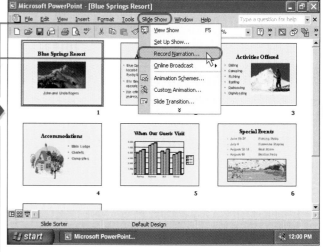

1 Click ⊞ to change to the Slide Sorter view.

2 Click the first slide in your presentation.

3 Click **Slide Show**.

4 Click **Record Narration**.

Note: If Record Narration does not appear on the menu, position the mouse ⊗ over the bottom of the menu to display the menu option.

■ The Record Narration dialog box appears.

What should I do to prepare for recording narration?

You should prepare and rehearse a script that includes the information you want to record for each slide in your slide show. This can help you avoid awkward pauses that may distract the audience.

 How can I ensure that my microphone is working properly?

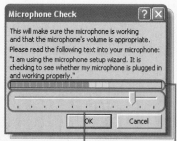

1 Before you begin recording, click the **Set Microphone Level** button in the Record Narration dialog box.

■ The Microphone Check dialog box appears.

■ If the microphone is working, this area displays movement when you speak into the microphone.

■ As you speak, PowerPoint may automatically move the slider ( ) in this area to adjust the recording volume to an appropriate level.

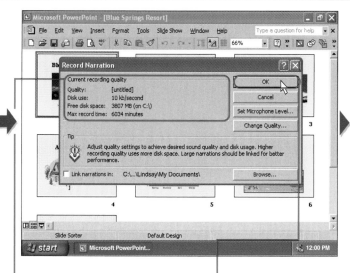

■ This area displays the recording quality, amount of hard disk space required for each second of narration, amount of free space on your hard disk and amount of recording time available.

5 Click **OK** to start recording.

■ The first slide in the slide show appears.

6 Speak into your microphone to record narration for the slide.

7 To display the next slide, click the current slide or press the **Spacebar**.

CONTINUED

ADD NARRATION TO A SLIDE SHOW

You can have PowerPoint record the amount of time you spent narrating each slide. PowerPoint will use these timings to advance the slides automatically during your slide show.

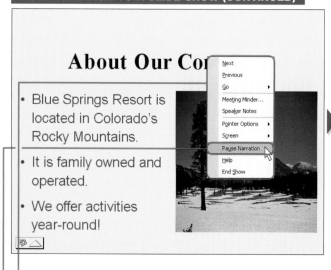

8 To pause recording the narration at any time, right-click the current slide. A menu appears.

9 Click **Pause Narration**.

10 To resume recording, repeat steps **8** and **9**, except select **Resume Narration** in step **9**.

■ When you finish the slide show, a dialog box appears, stating that the narrations have been saved with each slide.

11 To record the time you spent narrating each slide and use the timings when you later view the slide show, click **Save**.

Can I turn off the narration for a slide show?

Yes. You can temporarily turn off the narration for a slide show without deleting the narration you recorded for the slides. To temporarily turn off the narration, see page 259.

Can I preview the narration I added to a slide in the Normal view?

Yes. To preview the narration in the Normal view, double-click the speaker icon (🔊) at the bottom right corner of the slide. For information on the views, see page 42.

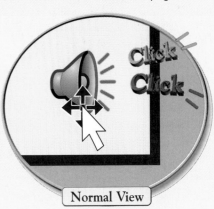

Normal View

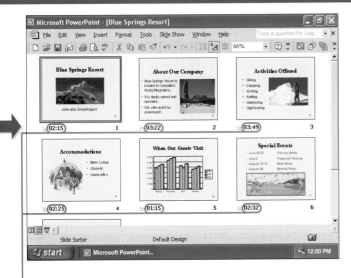

■ The time you spent narrating each slide appears below the slides.

■ When you view the slide show, you will hear the narration you recorded. To view the slide show, see page 266.

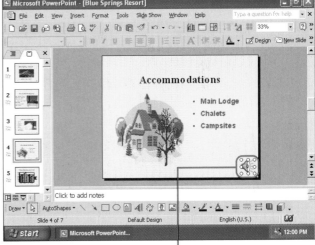

DELETE NARRATION FROM A SLIDE

1 Display the slide you no longer want to play a narration in the Normal view. For information on the views, see page 42.

2 To delete the narration, click the speaker icon (🔊) at the bottom right corner of the slide. Then press the Delete key.

207

You can change
when and how a
sound or movie
will start playing
during a slide
show.

CHANGE HOW A SOUND OR MOVIE PLAYS

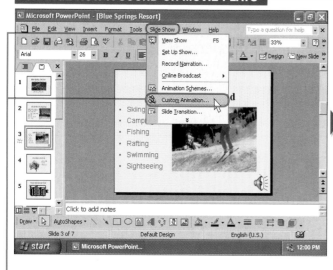

1 Click **Slide Show**.

2 Click **Custom Animation**.

■ The Custom Animation
task pane appears.

3 Click the movie or the
icon (or) for the
sound you want to change.
Handles (o) appear around
the object.

■ This area displays
the sounds, movies and
animations you have added
to the slide. The sound
or movie you selected in
step **3** is highlighted.

*Note: For information on adding
animations to slides, see pages 214
to 219.*

Can I change how an animated GIF movie plays in my presentation?

No. An animated GIF movie begins playing as soon as the slide is displayed in a slide show. You cannot change when or how the movie starts. For information on adding an animated GIF movie to your presentation, see page 192.

 Why does a gray Trigger bar appear above a sound or movie in the Custom Animation task pane?

When you add a sound or movie to a slide, PowerPoint may set up the sound or movie as a triggered effect. A triggered effect is an item, such as a movie, that will play when you click the specified item on a slide during a slide show. You can change how a triggered effect plays as you would change any sound or movie.

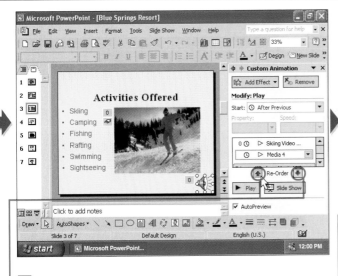

4 To change the order of the selected sound or movie in the list, click one of the following buttons.

⬆ Move up
⬇ Move down

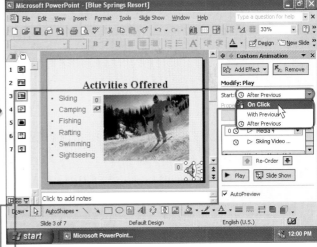

5 To change the way the selected sound or movie will start in a slide show, click this area.

6 Click the way you want the sound or movie to start.

On Click – Sound or movie starts when you click the slide

With Previous – Sound or movie starts at the same time as the previous action

After Previous – Sound or movie starts after the previous action ends

CHAPTER 11

Add Special Effects

Do you want to add special effects to your presentation? This chapter teaches you how to use interesting transitions to introduce slides, animate objects and more.

ADD SLIDE TRANSITIONS

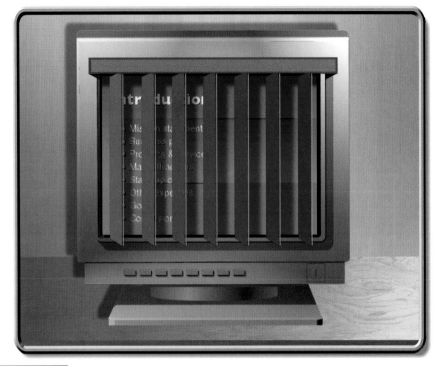

You can add transitions to slides in your presentation. A transition is a visual effect that appears when you move from one slide to the next.

Using transitions can help you introduce each slide during an on-screen slide show and signal your audience that new information is appearing.

ADD SLIDE TRANSITIONS

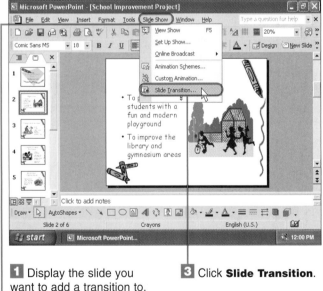

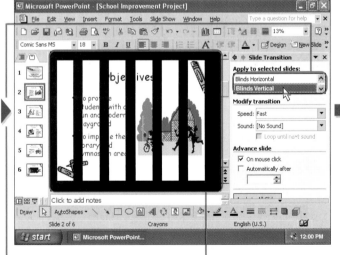

1 Display the slide you want to add a transition to.

2 Click **Slide Show**.

3 Click **Slide Transition**.

■ The Slide Transition task pane appears.

■ This area displays the available transitions. You can use the scroll bar to browse through the transitions.

4 Click the transition you want to use.

■ PowerPoint adds the transition to the current slide and displays a preview of the transition.

Note: To view the transition again, repeat step 4.

What should I consider when adding transitions to slides?

Although PowerPoint allows you to add a different transition to each slide in your presentation, using too many different transitions may distract the audience. The audience may focus on how each slide is introduced, rather than the information you are presenting.

How do I remove a transition from a slide?

Display the slide you want to remove a transition from and then perform steps **2** to **4** below, selecting **No Transition** in step **4**.

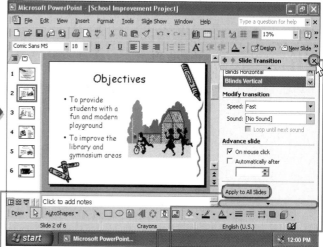

5 To change the speed of the transition, click this area to display a list of speed options.

6 Click the speed you want to use.

■ PowerPoint displays a preview of the transition with the speed you selected.

Note: To view the transition with the speed again, repeat steps 5 and 6.

7 To add the transition to all the slides in your presentation, click **Apply to All Slides**.

Note: To apply the transition only to the slide you displayed in step 1, skip to step 8.

■ If you cannot see the **Apply to All Slides** button, click ▼ to browse through the information in the task pane.

8 When you finish selecting a transition, you can click ⨯ to hide the Slide Transition task pane.

ADD AN ANIMATION SCHEME

You can add an animation scheme to a slide in your presentation. Animation schemes add movement to titles, bulleted text and paragraphs on a slide and can help keep your audience's attention throughout a presentation.

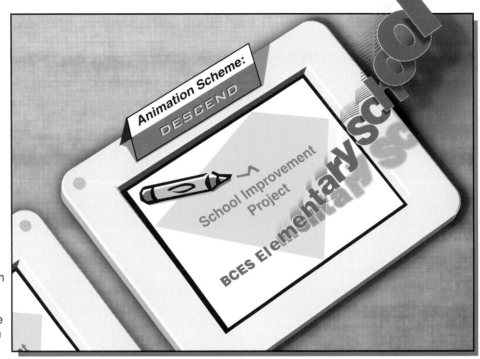

Although PowerPoint allows you to add a different animation scheme to each slide in your presentation, using too many different schemes may take the audience's attention away from the information you present.

ADD AN ANIMATION SCHEME

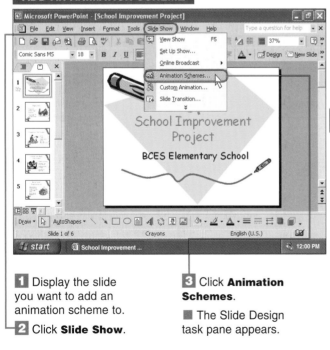

1 Display the slide you want to add an animation scheme to.

2 Click **Slide Show**.

3 Click **Animation Schemes**.

■ The Slide Design task pane appears.

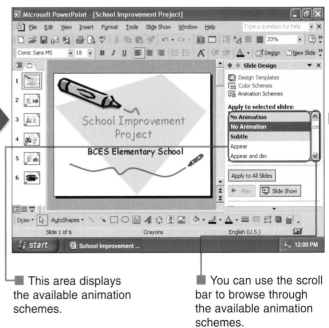

■ This area displays the available animation schemes.

■ You can use the scroll bar to browse through the available animation schemes.

How do I preview an animation scheme in a slide show?

You can click the **Slide Show** button in the Slide Design task pane to preview the animation scheme in a slide show. You may need to click the current slide to display each animated item on the slide during the slide show. For more information on viewing a slide show, see page 266.

How do I remove an animation scheme from a slide?

To remove an animation scheme from a slide, repeat steps **1** to **4** below, except select **No Animation** in step **4**.

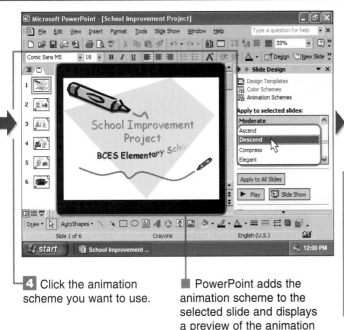

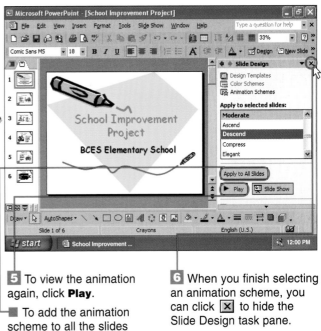

4 Click the animation scheme you want to use.

■ PowerPoint adds the animation scheme to the selected slide and displays a preview of the animation in this area.

Note: To select a different animation scheme, repeat step 4.

5 To view the animation again, click **Play**.

■ To add the animation scheme to all the slides in your presentation, click **Apply to All Slides**.

6 When you finish selecting an animation scheme, you can click ☒ to hide the Slide Design task pane.

215

ADD CUSTOM ANIMATIONS

You can add custom animations to the objects on your slides. Creating custom animations allows you to specify a different animation for each object on a slide.

You can animate objects such as titles, lists of points, AutoShapes, WordArt and clip art images.

ADD CUSTOM ANIMATIONS

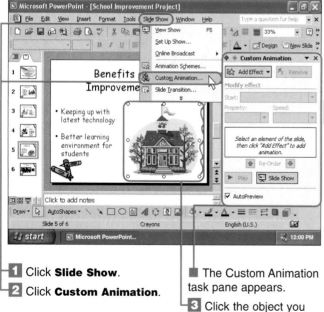

1 Click **Slide Show**.

2 Click **Custom Animation**.

■ The Custom Animation task pane appears.

3 Click the object you want to animate on the slide. Handles (o) appear around the object.

4 Click **Add Effect** to display the types of animations you can add.

5 Click the type of animation you want to add.

Note: For information on the types of animations, see the top of page 217.

6 Click the animation you want to add.

Note: The available animations depend on the type of object you selected in step 3.

216

What types of animations can I add to objects on my slides?

Entrance

Animations that change how an object is displayed on a slide.

Emphasis

Animations that draw attention to an object on a slide.

Exit

Animations that change how an object disappears from a slide.

Motion Paths

Animations that move an object on a slide.

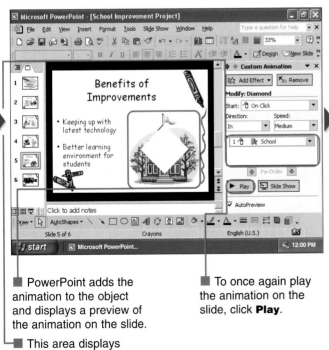

■ PowerPoint adds the animation to the object and displays a preview of the animation on the slide.

■ This area displays information about the animation.

■ To once again play the animation on the slide, click **Play**.

■ To add an animation to other objects on the slide, repeat steps **3** to **6** for each object.

■ A number appears beside each animated object on the slide to indicate the order the animations will play on the slide.

Note: The numbers will not appear on the slide during a slide show or when you print the presentation.

CONTINUED

ADD CUSTOM ANIMATIONS

You can change the order of the animations in the slide show. You can also change the way an animation will start.

PowerPoint offers three ways you can have an animation start in your slide show.

On Click
Animation starts when you click the slide.

With Previous
Animation starts at the same time as the previous animation.

After Previous
Animation starts after the previous animation ends.

ADD CUSTOM ANIMATIONS (CONTINUED)

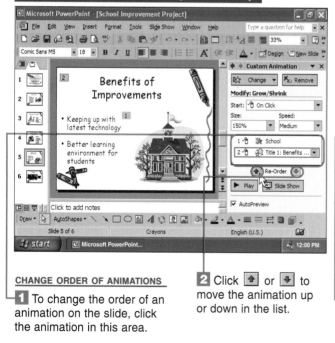

CHANGE ORDER OF ANIMATIONS

1 To change the order of an animation on the slide, click the animation in this area.

2 Click ⬆ or ⬇ to move the animation up or down in the list.

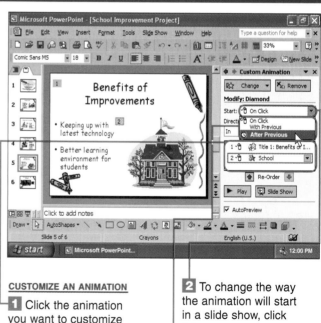

CUSTOMIZE AN ANIMATION

1 Click the animation you want to customize in this area.

2 To change the way the animation will start in a slide show, click this area.

3 Click the way you want the animation to start.

What information is displayed for each animation listed in the Custom Animation task pane?

PowerPoint provides information about the animations you added to the slide.

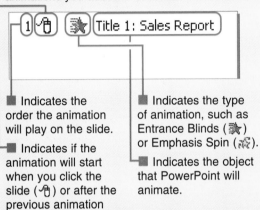

■ Indicates the order the animation will play on the slide.

■ Indicates if the animation will start when you click the slide (🖱) or after the previous animation ends (⏲).

■ Indicates the type of animation, such as Entrance Blinds (🎦) or Emphasis Spin (🌀).

■ Indicates the object that PowerPoint will animate.

Can I add more than one animation to an object?

Yes. You can perform steps **1** to **6** on page 216 to add more than one animation to an object on a slide. For example, you may want one animation to display the object on the slide and another animation to remove the object from the slide.

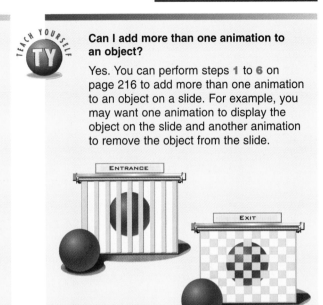

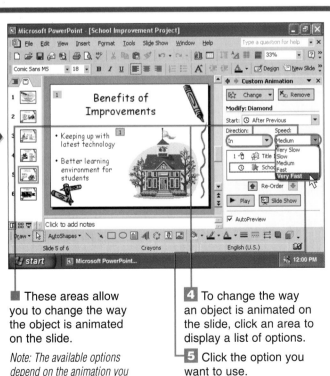

■ These areas allow you to change the way the object is animated on the slide.

Note: The available options depend on the animation you selected in step 6 on page 216.

4 To change the way an object is animated on the slide, click an area to display a list of options.

5 Click the option you want to use.

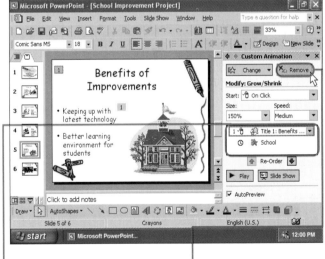

DELETE AN ANIMATION

1 Click the animation you want to delete in this area.

2 Click **Remove** to delete the animation.

Note: Deleting an animation from an object will not remove the object from your slide.

ADD SOUND EFFECTS TO CUSTOM ANIMATIONS

You can add sound effects to custom animations on your slides. Adding sound effects to animations can help set the mood of your presentation and keep the audience's attention.

You can add sound effects such as applause, an explosion or wind.

ADD SOUND EFFECTS TO CUSTOM ANIMATIONS

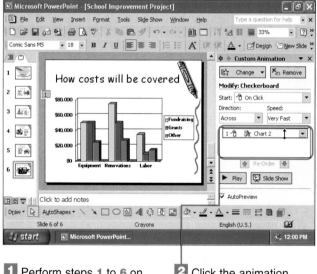

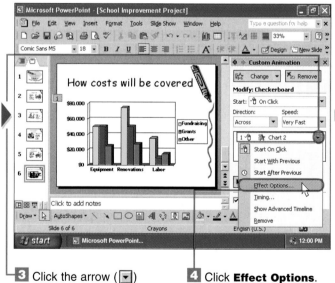

1 Perform steps **1** to **6** on page 216 to add a custom animation to an object on your slide.

2 Click the animation you want to add a sound effect to in this area. An arrow (▾) appears.

3 Click the arrow (▾) to display a list of options.

4 Click **Effect Options**.

Why did a dialog box appear when I tried to select a sound effect for an animation?

A dialog box appears if the sound effects are not installed on your computer. Insert the CD-ROM disc you used to install PowerPoint into your computer's CD-ROM drive. Then click **Yes** to install the sound effects.

Note: A window may appear on your screen. Click ✕ *in the top right corner of the window to close the window.*

How do I remove a sound effect from a custom animation?

To remove a sound effect from a custom animation, repeat steps **2** to **8** below, except select **[No Sound]** in step **6**.

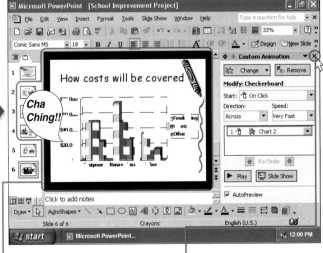

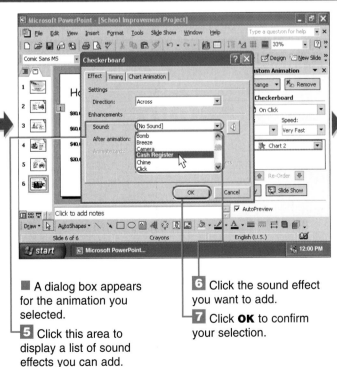

■ A dialog box appears for the animation you selected.

5 Click this area to display a list of sound effects you can add.

6 Click the sound effect you want to add.

7 Click **OK** to confirm your selection.

■ PowerPoint plays the sound effect and displays a preview of the animation on the slide.

8 When you finish adding sound effects, you can click ✕ to hide the Custom Animation task pane.

CHANGE HOW A CHART IS ANIMATED

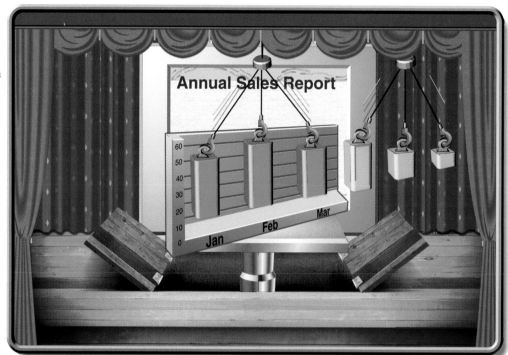

After you add a custom animation to a chart, you can change how the chart is animated. For example, you can introduce each series in a chart individually during a slide show.

By default, PowerPoint animates a chart as a single object on a slide.

Introducing the parts of a chart individually allows you to present the chart in a dramatic way during a slide show.

CHANGE HOW A CHART IS ANIMATED

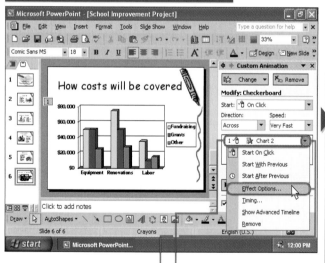

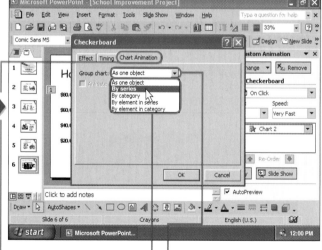

■1 Perform steps 1 to 6 on page 216 to add a custom animation to a chart on your slide.

■2 To change how the chart is animated, click the animation for the chart in this area. An arrow (▼) appears.

■3 Click the arrow (▼) to display a list of options.

■4 Click **Effect Options**.

■ A dialog box appears for the animation you selected.

■5 Click the **Chart Animation** tab.

■6 Click this area to display a list of ways you can introduce the parts of the chart during the slide show.

■7 Click the way you want to introduce the parts of the chart.

Note: If the options are not available, you cannot change how the chart is animated.

**How can I introduce the parts
of a chart during a slide show?**

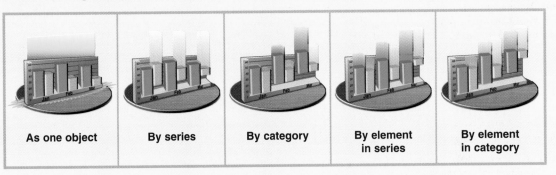

| As one object | By series | By category | By element in series | By element in category |

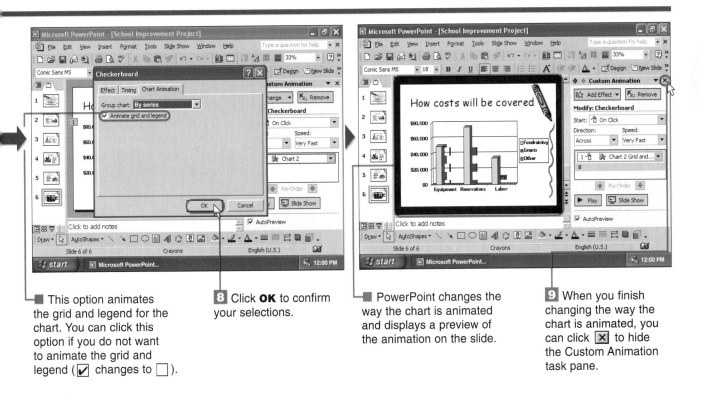

■ This option animates
the grid and legend for the
chart. You can click this
option if you do not want
to animate the grid and
legend (☑ changes to ☐).

8 Click **OK** to confirm
your selections.

■ PowerPoint changes the
way the chart is animated
and displays a preview of
the animation on the slide.

9 When you finish
changing the way the
chart is animated, you
can click ☒ to hide
the Custom Animation
task pane.

An action button allows you to jump to another slide in your presentation. This can help make your presentation easier to browse through.

Adding action buttons to slides is useful if people will view your presentation at a kiosk. Kiosks are often found at trade shows and shopping malls.

ADD AN ACTION BUTTON

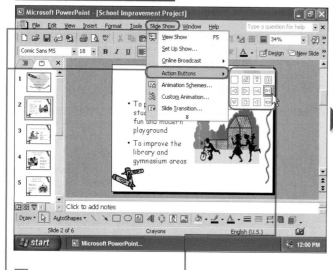

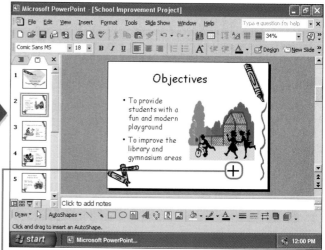

1 Display the slide you want to add an action button to.

2 Click **Slide Show**.

3 Click **Action Buttons**.

Note: If Action Buttons does not appear on the menu, position the mouse ⟍ over the bottom of the menu to display the menu option.

4 Click the action button you want to add to the slide.

5 Click the location on the slide where you want the action button to appear.

■ The Action Settings dialog box appears.

What are some of the action buttons I can add to slides in my presentation?

The image on an action button helps identify where the button will take you in the presentation.

◀	Previous Slide
▶	Next Slide
◀	First Slide
▶	Last Slide
↩	Last Slide Viewed

Should I test the action buttons I add to my slides?

Yes. Before presenting a slide show that contains action buttons, you should preview the slide show to test all the action buttons. This allows you to ensure that the action buttons will take you to the intended destinations.

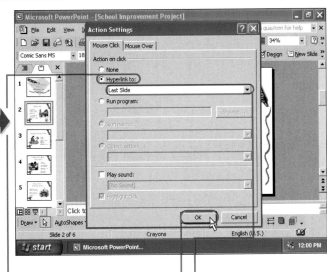

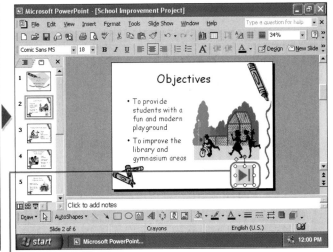

■ **6** Click this option to be able to jump to another slide in the presentation when you click the action button (○ changes to ⊙).

■ This area indicates the slide you will jump to when you click the action button. You can click this area to select another slide.

7 Click **OK** to confirm your changes.

■ The slide displays the action button.

■ When you view the slide show, you can click the action button to jump to the slide you specified. To view a slide show, see page 266.

Note: To move, resize or delete an action button, see pages 170 to 173.

CHAPTER 12

Fine-Tune a Presentation

Are you ready to put the finishing touches on your presentation? Read this chapter to learn how to create notes, preview and print your presentation, track changes made by reviewers and more.

REORDER SLIDES

You can change the order of the slides in your presentation. This is useful when you want to reorganize the ideas in your presentation.

REORDER SLIDES

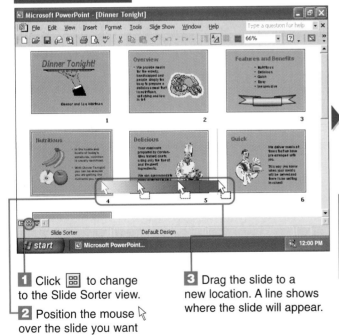

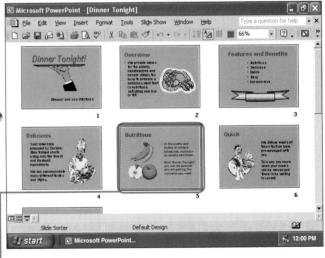

1 Click 🔡 to change to the Slide Sorter view.

2 Position the mouse ⌖ over the slide you want to move.

3 Drag the slide to a new location. A line shows where the slide will appear.

■ The slide appears in the new location.

■ PowerPoint automatically renumbers the slides in your presentation.

DELETE A SLIDE

You can remove a
slide you no longer
need from your
presentation. This
is useful if a slide
contains incorrect
or outdated
information.

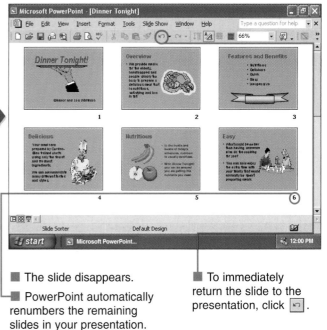

DELETE A SLIDE

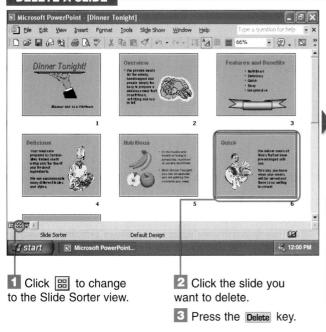

1 Click 🔳 to change
to the Slide Sorter view.

2 Click the slide you
want to delete.

3 Press the Delete key.

■ The slide disappears.

■ PowerPoint automatically
renumbers the remaining
slides in your presentation.

■ To immediately
return the slide to the
presentation, click 🔙.

HIDE A SLIDE

You can hide a slide in your presentation. Hiding a slide allows you to include supporting information in your slide show, but not display the information unless the audience requires clarification.

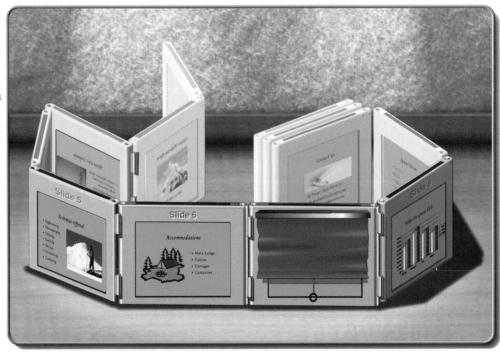

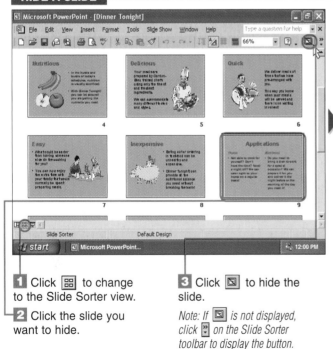

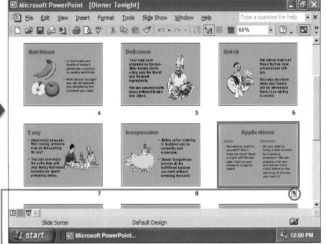

1 Click to change to the Slide Sorter view.

2 Click the slide you want to hide.

3 Click 🔲 to hide the slide.

Note: If 🔲 is not displayed, click »› on the Slide Sorter toolbar to display the button.

■ A symbol (🔲) appears through the slide number.

■ If you no longer want to hide the slide, repeat steps **1** to **3**.

■ To display a hidden slide during a slide show, press the **H** key when viewing the slide before the hidden slide. To view a slide show, see page 266.

230

VIEW SLIDES IN BLACK AND WHITE

PowerPoint allows you to view how your slides will look in grayscale or pure black and white. This is useful if you will be presenting your slide show on equipment that does not support color.

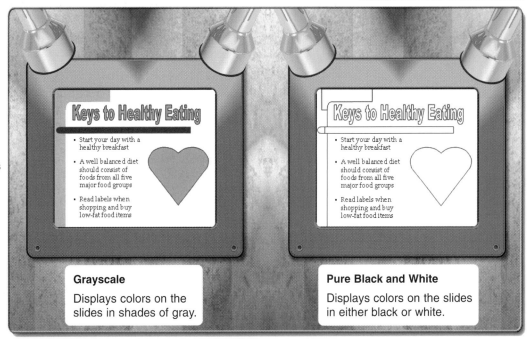

Grayscale

Displays colors on the slides in shades of gray.

Pure Black and White

Displays colors on the slides in either black or white.

VIEW SLIDES IN BLACK AND WHITE

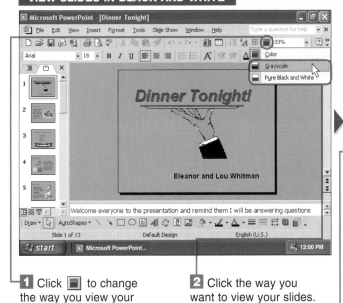

1 Click ▦ to change the way you view your slides.

Note: If ▦ is not displayed, click ⁂ on the Standard toolbar to display the button.

2 Click the way you want to view your slides.

■ The Grayscale View toolbar appears.

■ The current slide appears in grayscale or pure black and white.

■ You can use this scroll bar to view the other slides in your presentation.

3 Click **Close** to once again view the slides in color.

CREATE A SUMMARY SLIDE

You can create a summary slide that lists the titles of all the slides in your presentation. A summary slide is useful for introducing the contents of your presentation to the audience.

CREATE A SUMMARY SLIDE

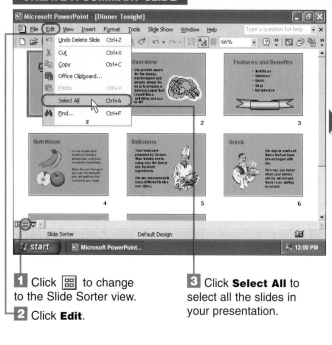

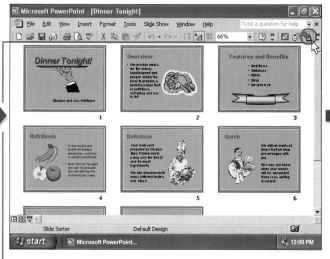

1 Click ▦ to change to the Slide Sorter view.

2 Click **Edit**.

3 Click **Select All** to select all the slides in your presentation.

■ A thick border appears around each slide in your presentation.

4 Click ▦ to create a summary slide.

Note: If ▦ is not displayed, click ▸ on the Slide Sorter toolbar to display the button.

Why did two summary slides appear at the beginning of my presentation?

PowerPoint can only fit a certain amount of information on each slide. If your presentation contains many slides, PowerPoint may need to create more than one summary slide to list all the titles in the presentation.

Can I move the summary slide to a different location in my presentation?

Yes. You can move the summary slide to a location in your presentation that better suits your needs. For example, you may want the summary slide to appear at the end of your presentation to encourage questions from the audience on the topics you discussed. To move a slide, see page 228.

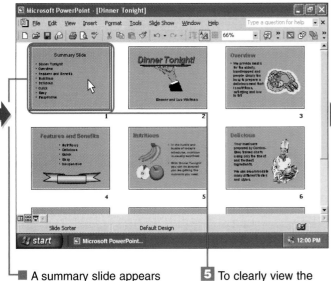

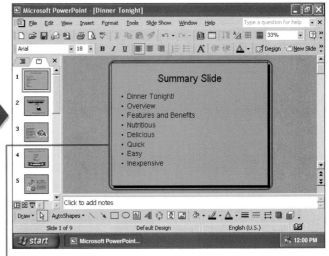

■ A summary slide appears at the beginning of your presentation, listing the title of each slide.

5 To clearly view the contents of the summary slide, double-click the slide.

■ The summary slide appears in the Normal view. You can edit the summary slide as you would edit any slide in your presentation.

You can add slides
to your current
presentation from
a presentation you
previously created.

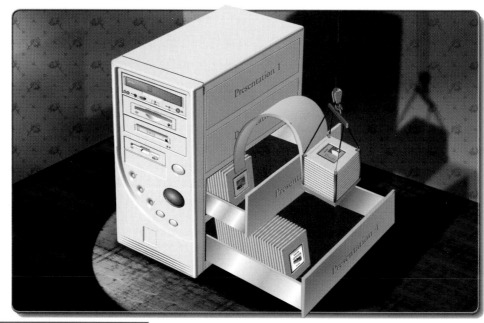

ADD SLIDES FROM ANOTHER PRESENTATION

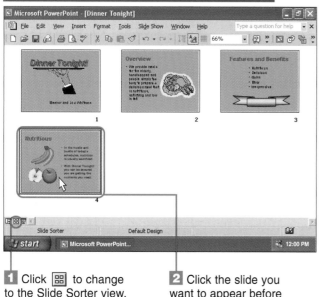

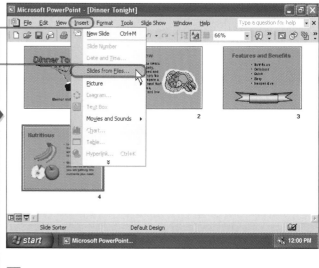

1 Click 🔢 to change
to the Slide Sorter view.

2 Click the slide you
want to appear before
the new slides.

3 Click **Insert**.

4 Click **Slides from Files**.

*Note: If Slides from Files does
not appear on the menu, position
the mouse ⟋ over the bottom of
the menu to display the menu
option.*

When I add slides from another presentation, does PowerPoint remove the slides from the other presentation?

No. PowerPoint makes a copy of each slide you select in the original presentation and places the copies in your current presentation. The slides in the original presentation do not change.

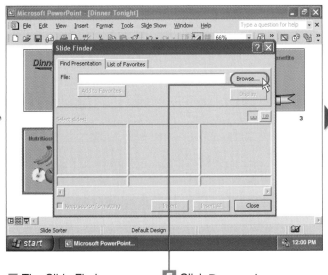

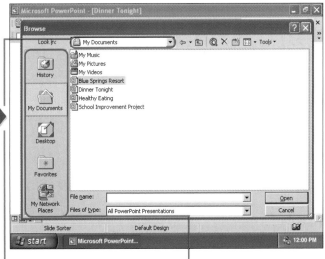

■ The Slide Finder dialog box appears.

5 Click **Browse** to locate the presentation that contains the slides you want to use.

■ The Browse dialog box appears.

■ This area shows the location of the displayed presentations. You can click this area to change the location.

■ This area allows you to access presentations in commonly used locations. You can click a location to display the presentations stored in the location.

Note: For information on the commonly used locations, see the top of page 27.

CONTINUED

ADD SLIDES FROM ANOTHER PRESENTATION

When you add slides from another presentation, PowerPoint automatically changes the design of the slides to match the design of the current presentation.

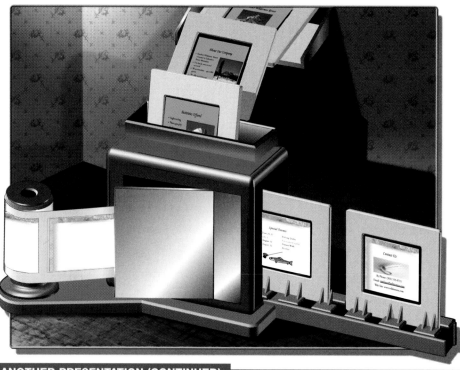

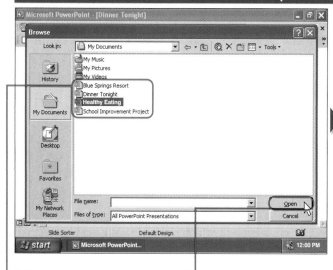

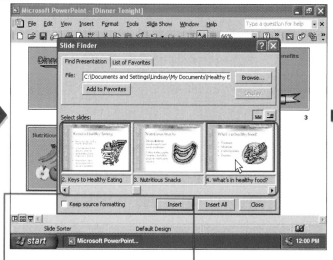

6 Click the name of the presentation that contains the slides you want to add to the current presentation.

7 Click **Open**.

■ The slides in the presentation appear in this area. The slide title appears below each slide. You can use the scroll bar to browse through the slides.

8 Click each slide you want to add to the current presentation. A blue border appears around each slide you select.

Note: To deselect a slide you accidentally selected, click the slide again.

Can I move the slides I added to my presentation?

After adding slides to your presentation, you can change the order of the slides. To reorder slides in a presentation, see page 228.

Can I stop PowerPoint from changing the design of the slides I add from another presentation?

Yes. Perform steps **1** to **8** starting on page 234 to add the slides from another presentation. In the Slide Finder dialog box, click the **Keep source formatting** option (☐ changes to ☑) to have the slides you add display their original design in the current presentation. Then perform steps **9** and **10** below.

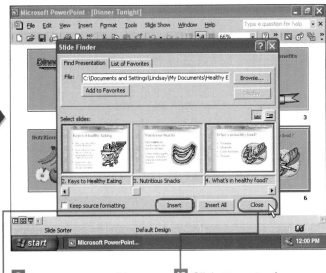

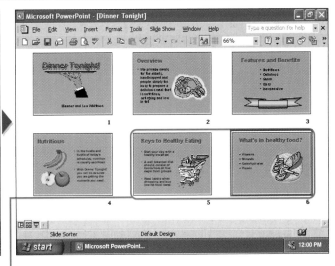

9 Click **Insert** to add the slides you selected to the current presentation.

10 Click **Close** to close the Slide Finder dialog box.

■ The slides appear in the current presentation.

■ PowerPoint automatically changes the design of the slides to match the design of the current presentation.

CREATE NOTES

You can create notes that contain the ideas you want to discuss for each slide in your presentation. You can use your notes as a guide when delivering your presentation.

Notes can include statistics and information that you may need to answer questions from the audience.

CREATE NOTES

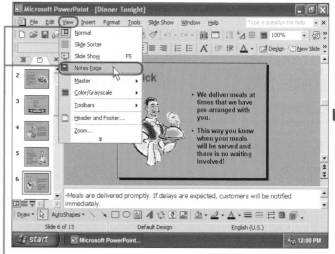

USING THE NORMAL VIEW

1 Display the slide you want to create notes for.

2 Click this area and then type the notes for the slide.

■ If you type more than one line of text, you can use the scroll bar to browse through the text.

USING NOTES PAGES

1 Click **View**.

2 Click **Notes Page** to display your notes pages.

Note: If Notes Page does not appear on the menu, position the mouse ⟨₂ over the bottom of the menu to display the menu option.

When using the Normal view to create notes, how do I increase the size of the notes area?

To increase the size of the notes area in the Normal view, position the mouse I over the top border of the area (I changes to $\updownarrow$) and then drag the border to a new location.

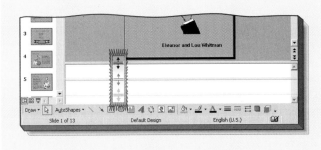

Can I print my notes pages?

You can print your notes pages so you will have a paper copy of the notes to refer to while delivering your presentation. Printing notes pages is also useful if you want to use the pages as handouts to help your audience follow your presentation. For information on printing notes pages, see page 244.

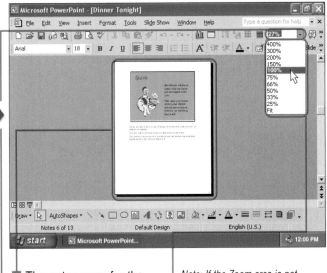

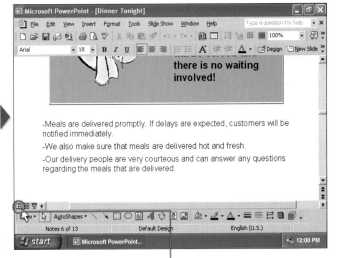

■ The notes page for the current slide appears.

Note: You can use the scroll bar to view the notes pages for other slides in the presentation.

3 To magnify the notes page so you can clearly view the notes, click ▼ in this area.

Note: If the Zoom area is not displayed, click ▶ on the Standard toolbar to display the area.

4 Click the magnification you want to use.

■ The notes page appears in the new magnification.

■ You can edit and format the text on the notes page as you would any text in your presentation.

*Note: To once again display the entire notes page, repeat steps 3 and 4, selecting **Fit** in step 4.*

5 When you finish reviewing your notes pages, click 🔲 to return to the Normal view.

SET UP A PRESENTATION FOR PRINTING

Before printing your presentation, you can specify how you want to output the presentation, such as on paper, 35mm slides or overheads.

You can also specify the orientation you want to use when printing your presentation. You should review your presentation after changing the orientation of slides to ensure that the information on the slides still appears the way you want.

SET UP A PRESENTATION FOR PRINTING

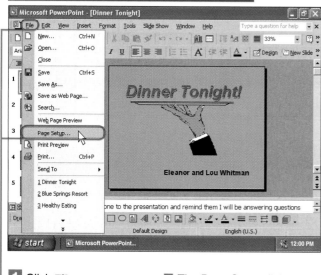

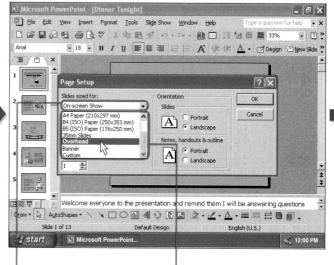

1 Click **File**.

2 Click **Page Setup**.

■ The Page Setup dialog box appears.

3 Click this area to display the ways you can output the slides.

4 Click the way you want to output the slides.

What is the difference between landscape and portrait orientation?

Landscape orientation prints information across the long side of a page. This is the standard orientation for slides.

Portrait orientation prints information across the short side of a page. This is the standard orientation for notes, handouts and the outline of the presentation.

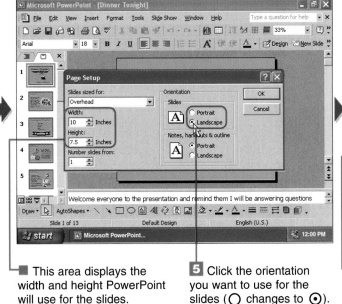

■ This area displays the width and height PowerPoint will use for the slides.

5 Click the orientation you want to use for the slides (○ changes to ⊙).

6 Click the orientation you want to use for notes, handouts and the outline of the presentation (○ changes to ⊙).

7 Click **OK** to confirm your changes.

PREVIEW A PRESENTATION BEFORE PRINTING

You can use the
Print Preview
feature to see how
your presentation
will look when
printed. This allows
you to confirm that
the presentation
will print the way
you want.

You can choose
the part of your
presentation
that you want to
preview, such as
slides, handouts,
notes pages or
an outline.

PREVIEW A PRESENTATION BEFORE PRINTING

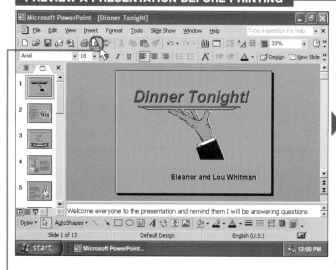

1 Click 🔍 to preview
your presentation before
printing.

*Note: If 🔍 is not displayed,
click ⏩ on the Standard toolbar
to display the button.*

■ The Print Preview
window appears.

■ This area displays a
preview of the slide that
will appear on the first
printed page.

2 To view the slides that
will appear on the other
printed pages, click one
of the following buttons.

📤 Display previous page

📥 Display next page

■ You can also use the
scroll bar to view the
slides that will appear
on other printed pages.

How do I magnify an area of a page I am previewing?

Position the mouse ⍩ over the area of the page you want to magnify (⍩ changes to ⊕) and then click the area to display a magnified view of the area. To once again display the entire page, you can click anywhere on the page.

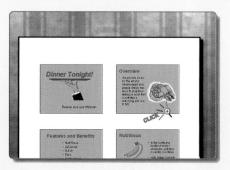

How do I quickly print my presentation while working in the Print Preview window?

You can click the Print button (🖨Print...) to quickly print the presentation you are previewing.

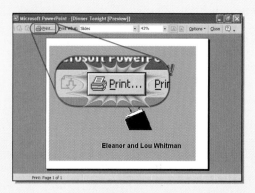

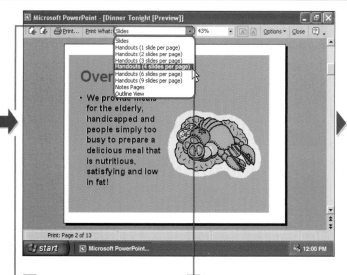

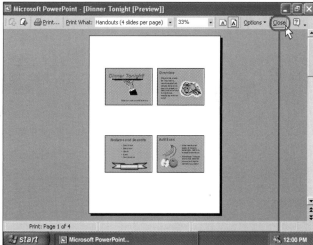

3 To preview a different part of your presentation before printing, click this area.

4 Click the part of the presentation you want to preview. For information on the parts of your presentation that you can print, see the top of page 245.

■ A preview of the part of the presentation you selected appears.

5 When you finish previewing your presentation, click **Close** to close the Print Preview window.

PRINT A PRESENTATION

You can produce a paper copy of a presentation for your own use or to hand out to your audience.

Before printing your presentation, make sure your printer is turned on and contains paper.

PRINT A PRESENTATION

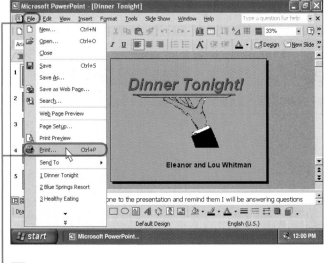

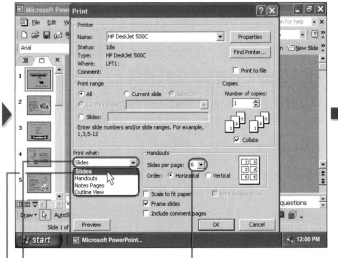

1 Click **File**.

2 Click **Print**.

■ The Print dialog box appears.

3 Click this area to select the part of the presentation you want to print.

4 Click the part of the presentation you want to print.

Note: For information on the available options, see the top of page 245.

■ If you selected **Handouts** in step **4**, you can click this area to change the number of slides that will print on each page.

What parts of my presentation can I print?

Slides

Prints one slide on each page. This is useful when you are printing transparencies for an overhead projector.

Handouts

Prints one or more slides on each page. You can give handouts to your audience to help them follow your presentation.

Notes Pages

Prints one slide and any notes you added to the slide on each page. You can use notes pages as a guide when delivering your presentation. To add notes to your slides, see page 238.

Outline View

Prints the text displayed in the Outline view of your presentation. For information on the Outline view, see page 42.

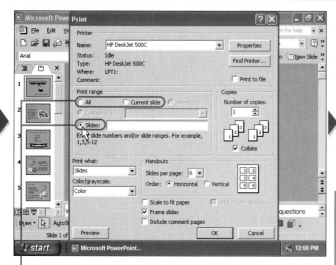

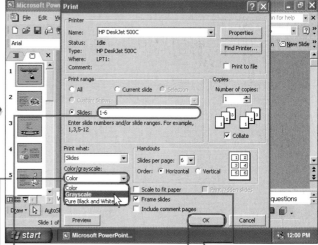

5 Click an option to specify which slides you want to print (○ changes to ⊙).

All – Print every slide in your presentation

Current slide – Print the slide displayed on your screen

Slides – Print the slides you specify

6 If you selected **Slides** in step **5**, type the numbers of the slides you want to print in this area (example: 1,2,4 or 1-4).

7 Click this area to specify if you want to print your slides in color, grayscale or pure black and white.

8 Click the way you want to print the slides.

9 Click **OK** to print your presentation.

WORK WITH A PRESENTATION IN MICROSOFT WORD

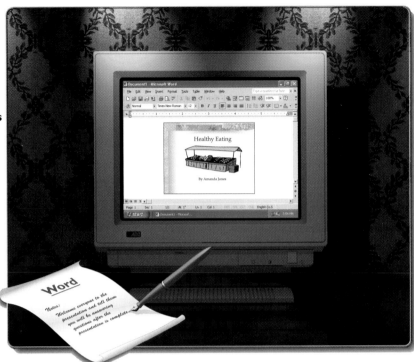

You can work with your presentation as a Microsoft Word document. This gives you more flexibility when creating and printing handouts or notes for your presentation.

To work with a presentation in Microsoft Word, you need Microsoft Word installed on your computer.

WORK WITH A PRESENTATION IN MICROSOFT WORD

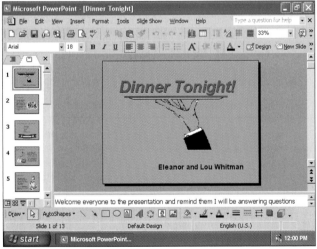

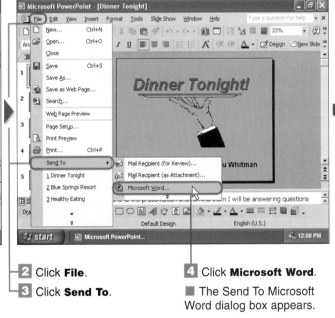

1 Open the presentation you want to work with in Microsoft Word. To open a presentation, see page 28.

2 Click **File**.

3 Click **Send To**.

4 Click **Microsoft Word**.

■ The Send To Microsoft Word dialog box appears.

What page layouts can I choose from to display my presentation in Microsoft Word?

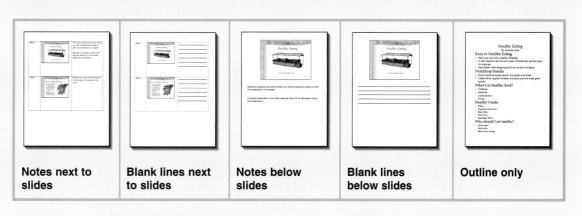

| Notes next to slides | Blank lines next to slides | Notes below slides | Blank lines below slides | Outline only |

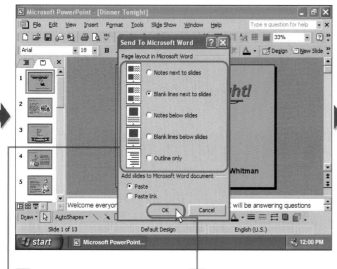

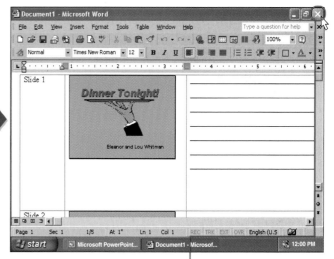

5 Click the page layout you want the presentation to display in Microsoft Word (○ changes to ⊙).

Note: For information on the available page layouts, see the top of this page.

6 Click **OK** to confirm your selection.

■ Microsoft Word opens and your presentation appears in a Word document.

■ You can edit, save and print the document as you would any Word document.

Note: You can use the scroll bars to view other areas of the document.

7 Click ☒ to exit Microsoft Word.

ADD A COMMENT

You can add a comment to a slide in your presentation. A comment can be a note, explanation or reminder about information you need to verify later.

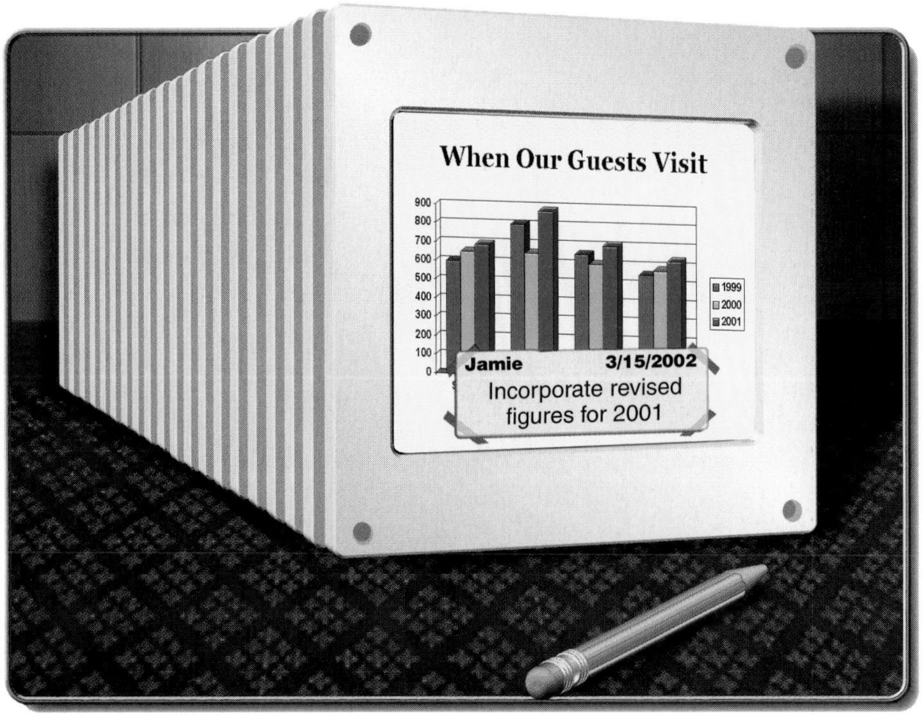

Comments you add to your slides will not be displayed during the slide show or when you print the slides.

ADD A COMMENT

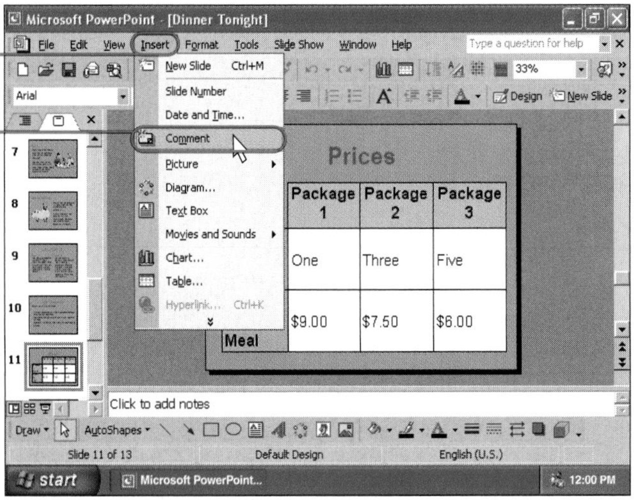

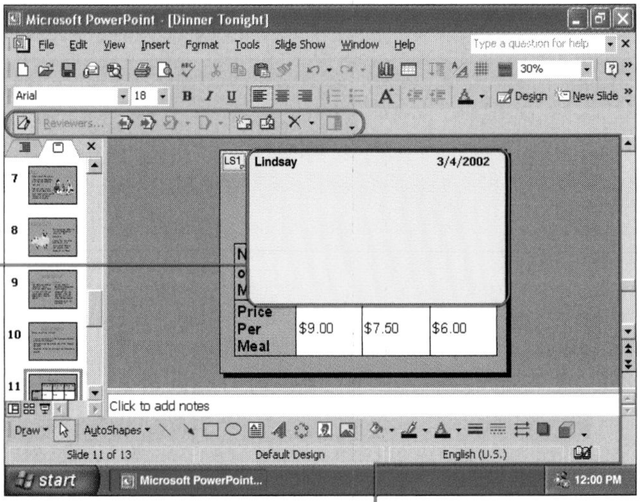

1 Display the slide you want to add a comment to.

2 Click **Insert**.

3 Click **Comment**.

Note: If Comment does not appear on the menu, position the mouse over the bottom of the menu to display the menu option.

■ A yellow comment box appears, displaying your name and the current date.

■ The Reviewing toolbar also appears.

Can I edit a comment?

You can edit a comment to update the information in the comment. Double-click the comment marker for the comment you want to edit. You can then edit the text in the comment box as you would edit any text in a presentation.

How can I delete a comment I no longer need?

■1 Right-click the comment marker for the comment you want to delete.

■2 Click **Delete Comment**.

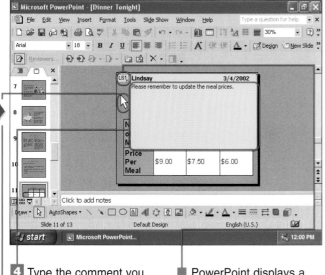

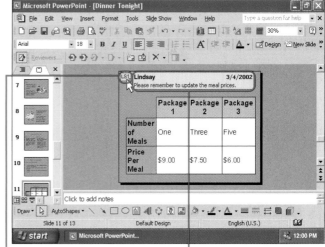

■4 Type the comment you want to add.

■5 When you finish typing the comment, click outside the comment box to hide the box.

■ PowerPoint displays a comment marker containing your initials and the number of the comment on the slide to indicate the slide contains a comment.

VIEW A COMMENT

■1 Display the slide you want to view the comment for.

■2 Position the mouse ⌖ over the comment marker for the comment you want to view.

■ After a few seconds, the comment box appears.

■3 When you finish viewing the comment, move the mouse ⌖ away from the comment marker to once again hide the comment box.

You can save a presentation that you want other people to review. PowerPoint will keep track of the editing and formatting changes the reviewers make to the presentation.

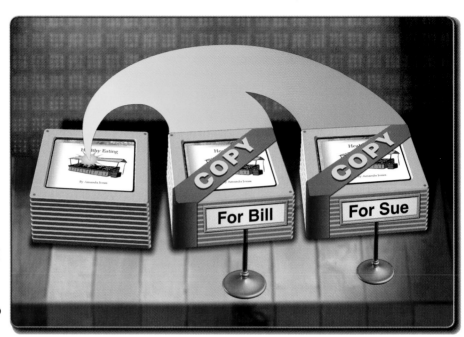

To prevent multiple reviewers from changing the same copy of your presentation, you should save a separate copy for each reviewer. You can later combine all the reviewed presentations with your original presentation to review all the changes at once.

TRACK CHANGES FROM MULTIPLE REVIEWERS

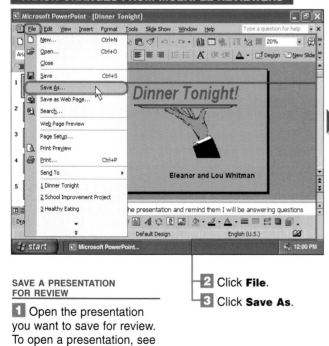

SAVE A PRESENTATION FOR REVIEW

1 Open the presentation you want to save for review. To open a presentation, see page 28.

2 Click **File**.

3 Click **Save As**.

■ The Save As dialog box appears.

4 Type a name for the presentation.

Note: The presentation name should be personalized for each reviewer and cannot contain the * : ? > < | or " characters.

How do the reviewers make changes to my presentation?

Reviewers can open and edit their copy of the presentation as they would open and edit any PowerPoint presentation. When each reviewer finishes making changes, they should save their copy of the presentation and notify you that the changes are ready for your review.

The reviewers cannot access some of the features in my presentation. What is wrong?

Reviewers may not be able to access the sound file needed to play a sound in your presentation. After you save your presentation for review, you should save any sound files you added to your presentation in the same location so your reviewers will be able to play the sounds.

If the reviewers are using an older version of PowerPoint, they will also not be able to access any features of PowerPoint that their version does not support.

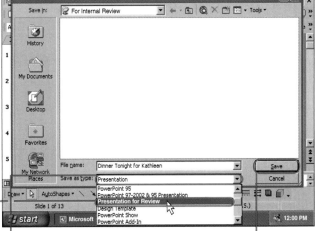

■ This area shows the location where PowerPoint will store your presentation. You can click this area to change the location.

■ This area allows you to access commonly used locations. You can click a location to save your presentation in the location.

Note: For information on the commonly used locations, see the top of page 27.

5 Click this area to specify that you want to save the presentation for review.

6 Click **Presentation for Review**.

7 Click **Save** to save your presentation.

8 Repeat steps **2** to **7** to save a copy of the presentation for each person who will review your presentation.

CONTINUED

After the reviewers have made changes to the copies of your presentation, you can combine the reviewed presentations with your original presentation. Combining the presentations allows you to review the changes from all the reviewers at once.

PowerPoint displays markers on the slides to indicate where changes were made. The changes for each reviewer are displayed in a different color.

TRACK CHANGES FROM MULTIPLE REVIEWERS (CONTINUED)

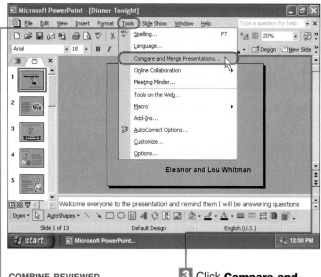

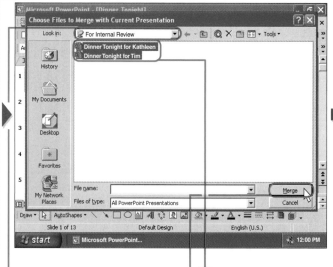

COMBINE REVIEWED PRESENTATIONS

1 Open the original presentation. To open a presentation, see page 28.

2 Click **Tools**.

3 Click **Compare and Merge Presentations**.

Note: If Compare and Merge Presentations does not appear on the menu, position the mouse ⌦ over the bottom of the menu to display the menu option.

■ The Choose Files to Merge with Current Presentation dialog box appears.

■ This area shows the location of the displayed presentations. You can click this area to change the location.

4 Press and hold down the **Ctrl** key as you click each reviewed presentation you want to combine with the original presentation.

5 Click **Merge**.

252

How do I hide the Reviewing toolbar?

You can hide or display the Reviewing toolbar as you would hide or display any toolbar. To hide or display a toolbar, see page 51.

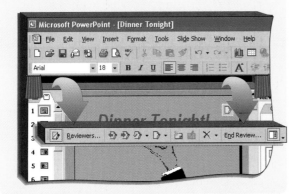

How can I temporarily hide the markers on my slides?

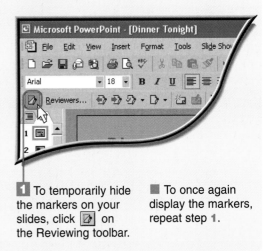

1 To temporarily hide the markers on your slides, click 📝 on the Reviewing toolbar.

■ To once again display the markers, repeat step **1**.

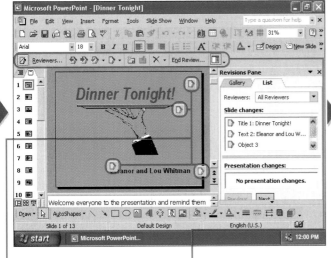

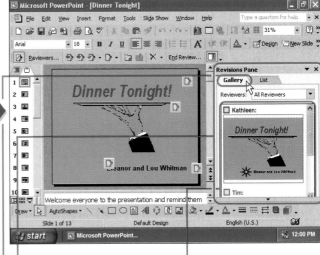

■ PowerPoint combines the reviewed presentations with your original presentation.

■ A marker appears in each location where a reviewer made a change to the presentation. Each reviewer's changes are displayed in a different color.

■ The Reviewing toolbar appears, displaying buttons you can use to review the changes made to the presentation.

■ The Revisions Pane also appears.

6 To preview how the current slide will appear with a reviewer's changes, click **Gallery**.

■ Previews of the slide appear in this area. Each preview contains all the changes made by one reviewer.

CONTINUED

253

TRACK CHANGES FROM MULTIPLE REVIEWERS

After you have combined the reviewed presentations with your original presentation, you can review all the changes in the presentation and choose whether you want to apply or ignore each change.

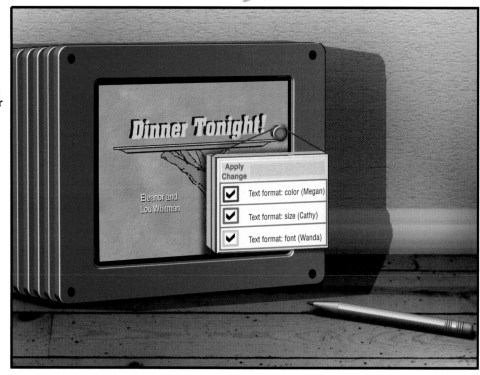

TRACK CHANGES FROM MULTIPLE REVIEWERS (CONTINUED)

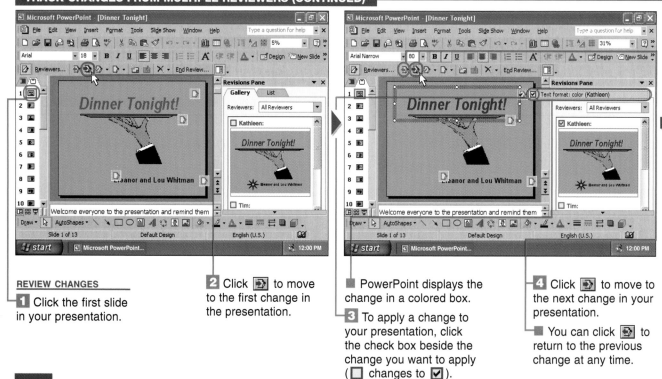

REVIEW CHANGES

1 Click the first slide in your presentation.

2 Click ⮞ to move to the first change in the presentation.

■ PowerPoint displays the change in a colored box.

3 To apply a change to your presentation, click the check box beside the change you want to apply (☐ changes to ☑).

4 Click ⮞ to move to the next change in your presentation.

■ You can click ⮞ to return to the previous change at any time.

How can I apply all the changes to a slide at once?

1 Click the **Gallery** tab in the Revisions Pane.

2 Click the preview of the slide that contains all the reviewer's changes you want to apply to the current slide.

What happens when one reviewer makes a change that conflicts with a change made by another reviewer?

PowerPoint displays the 🔁 marker on the slide where the changes made by the reviewers conflict. When reviewing the changes for your presentation, you can choose which change you want to apply to the slide.

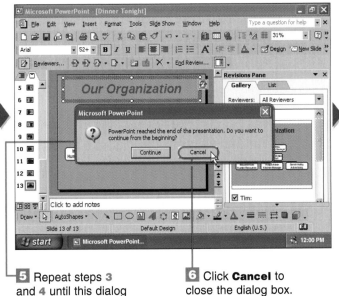

5 Repeat steps **3** and **4** until this dialog box appears.

6 Click **Cancel** to close the dialog box.

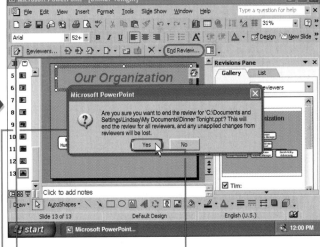

7 When you have finished applying or ignoring all the changes, click **End Review**.

■ A dialog box appears, confirming that you want to end the review.

8 Click **Yes** to end the review and remove all the markers from the slides in the presentation.

255

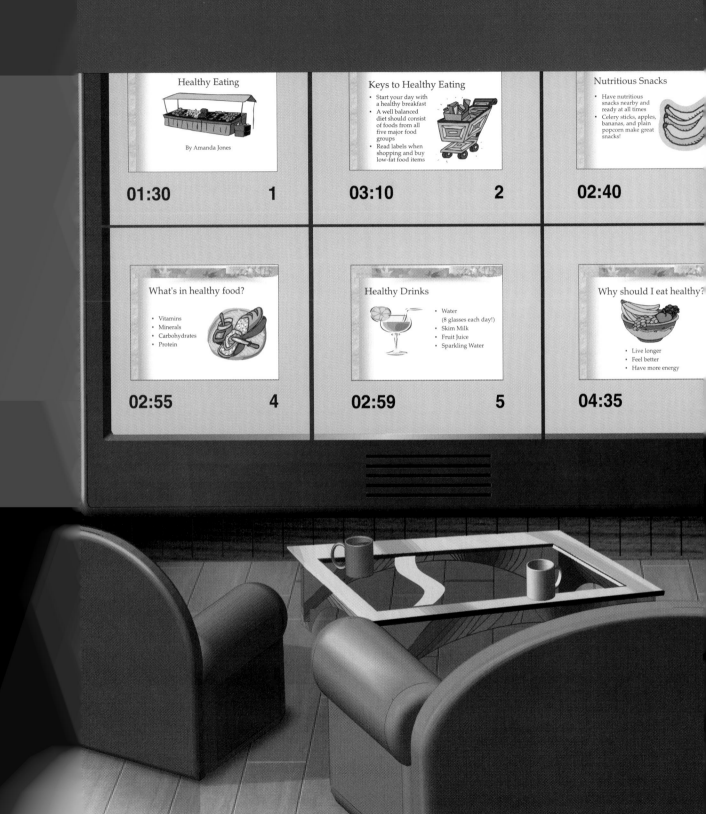

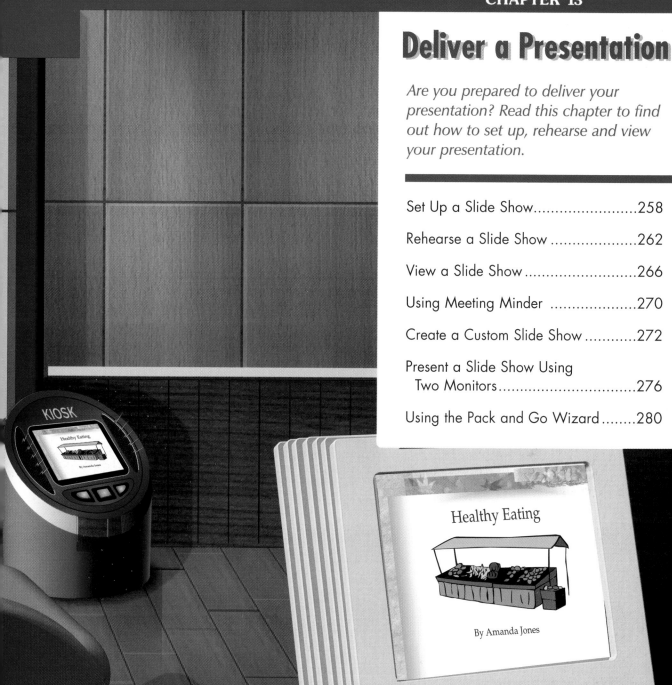

CHAPTER 13

Deliver a Presentation

Are you prepared to deliver your presentation? Read this chapter to find out how to set up, rehearse and view your presentation.

SET UP A SLIDE SHOW

You can specify how you want to present a slide show on a computer. For example, you can deliver the slide show yourself or allow other people to browse through the slide show on their own.

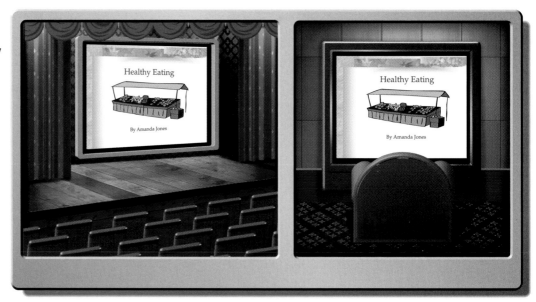

SET UP A SLIDE SHOW

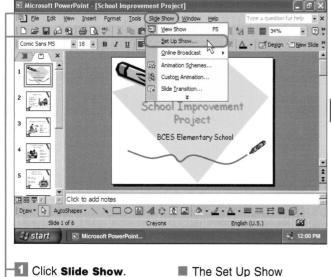

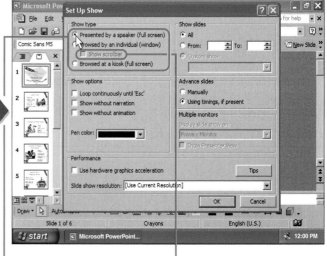

1 Click **Slide Show**.

2 Click **Set Up Show**.

■ The Set Up Show dialog box appears.

3 To specify how the slide show will be presented, click one of these options (○ changes to ◉).

■ If you selected **Browsed by an individual** in step **3**, you can click this option to display a scroll bar people can use to browse through the slides (☐ changes to ☑).

How can I present my slide show?

Presented by a speaker

Select this option if you plan to deliver a full-screen slide show to an audience.

Browsed by an individual

Select this option if a person will view the slide show on their own. The slide show will appear in a window that displays menus and buttons the person can use to browse through the slides.

Browsed at a kiosk

Select this option if you plan to present a full-screen, self-running slide show at a kiosk. Kiosks are often found at trade shows and shopping malls.

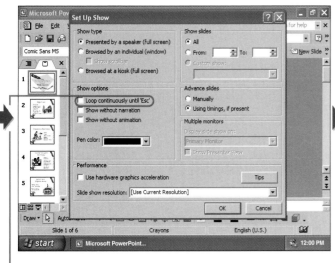

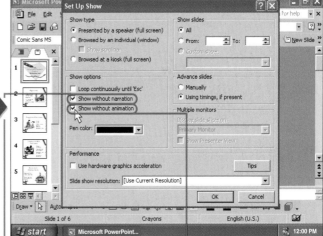

4 To have the slide show run continuously until you press the `Esc` key, click this option (☐ changes to ☑).

*Note: PowerPoint automatically turns on this option if you selected **Browsed at a kiosk** in step 3.*

5 If you added narration to the slides, you can click this option to run the slide show without the narration (☐ changes to ☑).

Note: To add narration to slides, see page 204.

6 If you added animations to the slides, you can click this option to run the slide show without the animations (☐ changes to ☑).

Note: To add animations to slides, see pages 214 to 219.

CONTINUED

SET UP A SLIDE SHOW

You can select which slides you want to display during the slide show.

SET UP A SLIDE SHOW (CONTINUED)

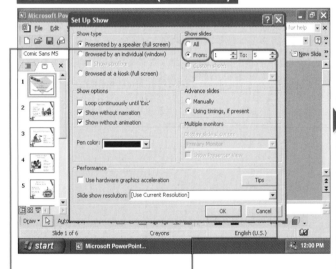

7 To specify which slides you want to include in the slide show, click one of these options (○ changes to ⊙).

8 If you selected **From** in step **7**, type the number of the first slide you want to display. Then press the `Tab` key and type the number of the last slide you want to display.

9 To specify how you want to advance the slides, click one of these options (○ changes to ⊙).

Note: For information on how you can advance slides, see the top of page 261.

How can I advance the slides during a slide show?

Manually

The method you use to advance slides manually depends on the way you selected to present the slide show in step **3** on page 258. If the show is presented by a speaker, clicking the left mouse button moves to the next slide. If the show is browsed by an individual, pressing the [Page Down] key moves to the next slide. If the show is browsed at a kiosk, you can add action buttons to the slides that people can use to move through the slides. To add action buttons to slides, see page 224.

Using timings, if present

The slides will advance automatically using timings you have set. To rehearse a slide show and set timings, see page 262.

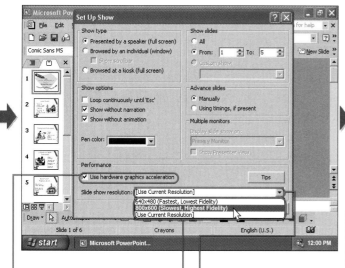

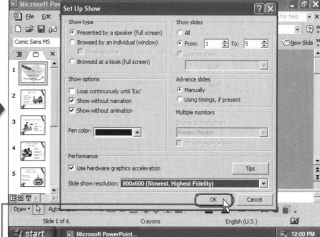

10 If your computer supports hardware graphics acceleration, you can click this option to have the computer try to improve the performance of the slide show (☐ changes to ✔).

11 To change the screen resolution PowerPoint will use to display the slide show, click this area.

12 Click the new resolution you want PowerPoint to use.

13 Click **OK** to confirm your changes.

■ PowerPoint will use the settings you specified when you view the slide show. To view a slide show, see page 266.

REHEARSE A SLIDE SHOW

You can rehearse your slide show and have PowerPoint record the amount of time you spend on each slide.

Rehearsing your slide show and recording the timings can help you determine if you need to add or remove information from your presentation.

REHEARSE A SLIDE SHOW

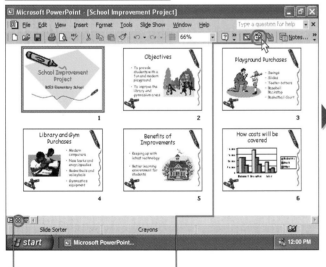

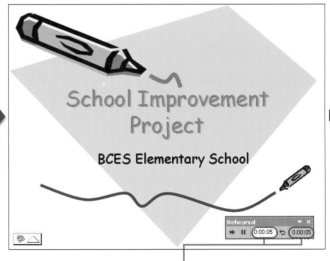

1 Click ⊞ to change to the Slide Sorter view.

2 Click 🕮 to rehearse your slide show.

Note: If 🕮 is not displayed, click 🔋 on the Slide Sorter toolbar to display the button.

■ The first slide in the slide show appears.

■ The Rehearsal toolbar displays the time spent on the current slide and the total time spent on the slide show.

How does PowerPoint use the timings I record?

PowerPoint will use the recorded timings to advance your slides automatically during a slide show. This is useful if you want to set up a self-running slide show for a kiosk. Kiosks are often found at trade shows and shopping malls. If you do not want PowerPoint to advance your slides automatically, see page 260.

Can I quickly set the timing for the current slide?

Yes. When rehearsing your slide show, you can set a specific length of time that you want the current slide to appear on your screen.

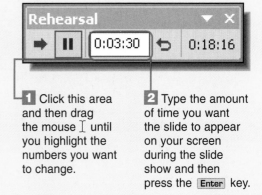

1 Click this area and then drag the mouse I until you highlight the numbers you want to change.

2 Type the amount of time you want the slide to appear on your screen during the slide show and then press the Enter key.

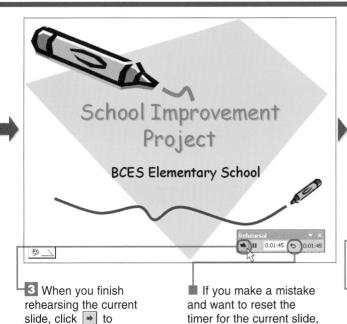

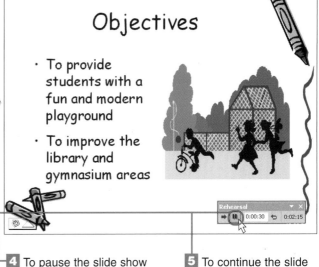

3 When you finish rehearsing the current slide, click ➡ to display the next slide.

■ If you make a mistake and want to reset the timer for the current slide, click ↺.

4 To pause the slide show at any time, click ❚❚.

5 To continue the slide show, click ❚❚ again.

CONTINUED

REHEARSE A SLIDE SHOW

When you finish rehearsing your slide show, you can review the time you spent on each slide to determine if you have set an appropriate pace for your presentation.

REHEARSE A SLIDE SHOW (CONTINUED)

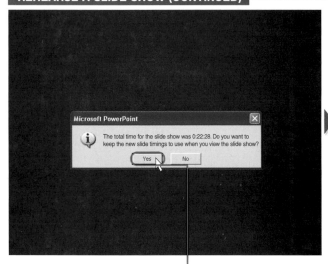

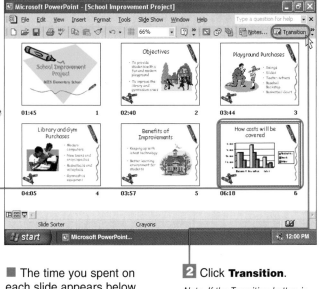

■ When you finish rehearsing the slide show, a dialog box appears, displaying the total time for the slide show.

6 To record the time you spent on each slide and use the timings when you later view the slide show, click **Yes**.

■ The time you spent on each slide appears below the slides.

CHANGE SLIDE TIMINGS

1 Click the slide you want to change the timing for.

2 Click **Transition**.

Note: If the Transition button is not displayed, click ⟩⟩ on the Slide Sorter toolbar to display the button.

Why would I want to change the slide timings?

Changing the slide timings is useful when you want a slide to appear during a slide show for a longer or shorter time than you originally rehearsed. You may also want to change the slide timings to ensure your presentation runs for a specific length of time.

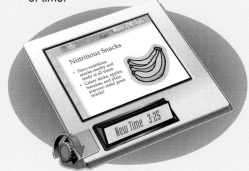

How can I change the slide timings for all the slides in my presentation at once?

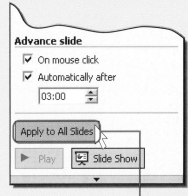

1 Perform steps **1** to **3** below to specify the amount of time you want each of the slides to appear.

2 Click **Apply to All Slides** to add the slide timings to all the slides.

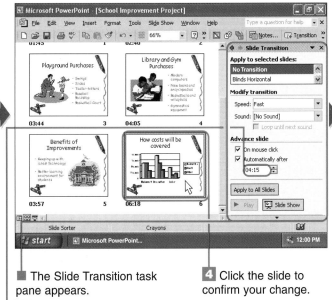

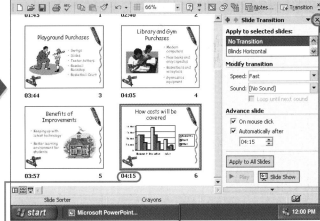

■ The Slide Transition task pane appears.

3 Drag the mouse I over this area until you highlight the numbers you want to change. Then type the amount of time you want the slide to appear on your screen during the slide show.

4 Click the slide to confirm your change.

■ The slide displays the new timing.

5 When you finish changing the slide timings, you can click ✕ to hide the Slide Transition task pane.

VIEW A SLIDE SHOW

You can view a slide show of your presentation on a computer screen. A slide show displays one slide at a time using the entire screen.

Before presenting a slide show to an audience, you can view the slide show to rehearse your presentation.

VIEW A SLIDE SHOW

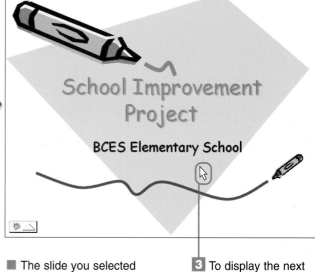

1 Click the first slide you want to view in the slide show.

2 Click 🖳 to start the slide show.

■ The slide you selected fills your screen.

Note: You can press the **Esc** *key to end the slide show at any time.*

3 To display the next slide, click anywhere on the current slide.

How can I use my keyboard to move through a slide show?

Task:	Press this key:
Display the next slide	Spacebar
Display the previous slide	+Backspace
Display any slide	Type the number of the slide and then press Enter
End the slide show	Esc
Pause the slide show and turn the screen black	B (Press B again to return to the slide show)
Pause the slide show and turn the screen white	W (Press W again to return to the slide show)

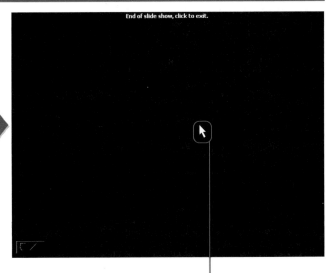

End of slide show, click to exit.

■ The next slide appears.

■ To return to the previous slide, press the +Backspace key.

4 Repeat step **3** until this screen appears, indicating you have reached the end of the slide show.

5 Click the screen to exit the slide show.

CONTINUED

VIEW A SLIDE SHOW

During a slide show, you can instantly display any slide in your presentation. You can also draw on the slides to emphasize information you are presenting.

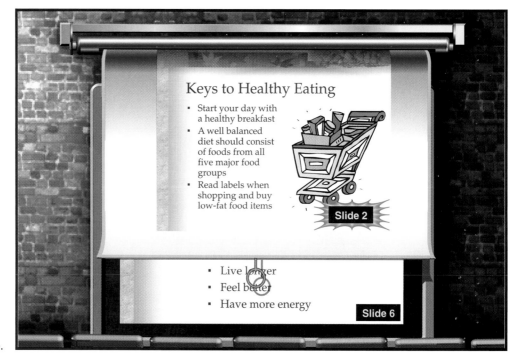

Lines you draw during a slide show are temporary and will disappear when you move to another slide.

VIEW A SLIDE SHOW (CONTINUED)

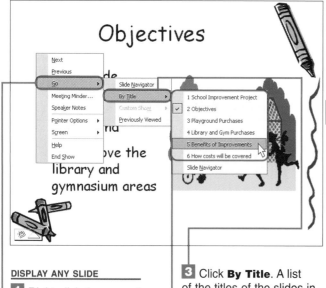

DISPLAY ANY SLIDE

1 Right-click the current slide. A menu appears.

2 Click **Go**.

3 Click **By Title**. A list of the titles of the slides in your presentation appears.

4 Click the title of the slide you want to display.

Note: A check mark (✔) appears beside the title of the current slide.

■ The slide you selected appears.

268

Can I erase the drawings on the current slide?

Yes. If your slide becomes cluttered with drawings, you can quickly erase all the drawings to clearly display the information on the slide. To erase all the drawings on the slide at any time, press the [E] key.

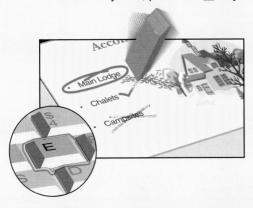

How do I change the color of the pen I use to draw on a slide?

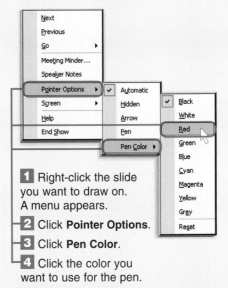

1 Right-click the slide you want to draw on. A menu appears.

2 Click **Pointer Options**.

3 Click **Pen Color**.

4 Click the color you want to use for the pen.

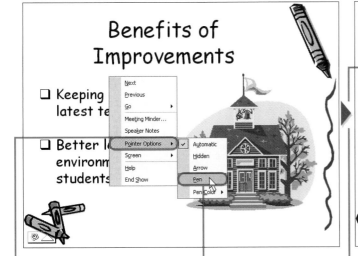

Benefits of Improvements

❑ Keeping [ ] latest te[ ]

❑ Better l[ ] environm[ ] students[ ]

Benefits of Improvements

☑ eeping up with latest technology

❑ Better learning environment for students

DRAW ON A SLIDE

1 Right-click the slide you want to draw on. A menu appears.

2 Click **Pointer Options**.

3 Click **Pen** to activate the pen.

Note: You can also press and hold down the [Ctrl] *key and then press the* [P] *key to activate the pen.*

4 Position the mouse where you want to start drawing on the slide.

5 Drag the mouse to draw on the slide.

*Note: When drawing on a slide, you must press the **Spacebar** to display the next slide. To once again use the mouse pointer to move through slides, repeat steps 1 to 3, except select **Automatic** in step 3.*

You can record meeting minutes during a slide show to take notes on important ideas discussed during your presentation. You can also assign tasks, called action items, to your colleagues during your slide show.

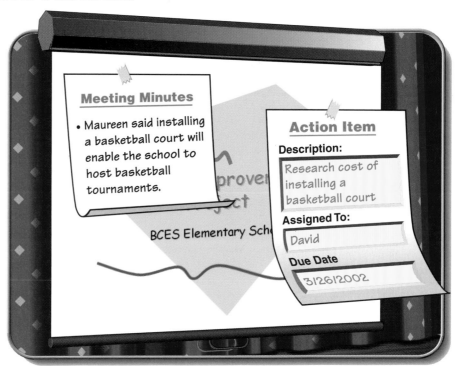

USING MEETING MINDER

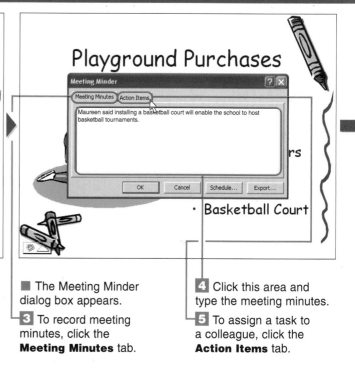

1 During the slide show, right-click a slide on your screen. A menu appears.

Note: To view a slide show, see page 266.

2 Click **Meeting Minder**.

■ The Meeting Minder dialog box appears.

3 To record meeting minutes, click the **Meeting Minutes** tab.

4 Click this area and type the meeting minutes.

5 To assign a task to a colleague, click the **Action Items** tab.

How can I review the tasks I assigned during my slide show?

PowerPoint creates a new slide at the end of the slide show listing the tasks you assigned during the slide show. This allows the audience to review the tasks and take note of the items that are their responsibility.

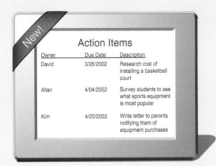

How do I later review the meeting minutes created during my presentation?

You can review the meeting minutes you created during a slide show in the Normal view of your presentation.

1 Display your presentation in the Normal view. For information on the views, see page 42.

2 Click **Tools**.

3 Click **Meeting Minder** to redisplay the meeting minutes you recorded in the Meeting Minder dialog box.

Note: If Meeting Minder does not appear on the menu, position the mouse ⌖ over the bottom of the menu to display the menu option.

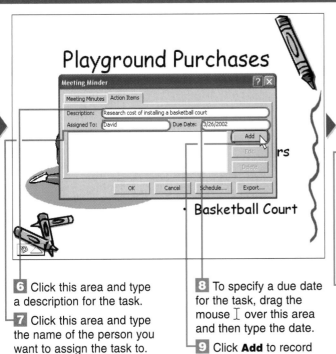

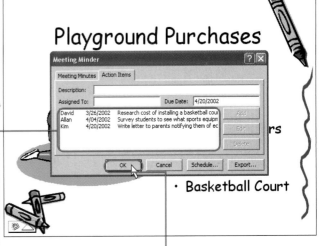

6 Click this area and type a description for the task.

7 Click this area and type the name of the person you want to assign the task to.

8 To specify a due date for the task, drag the mouse ⌶ over this area and then type the date.

9 Click **Add** to record the task.

■ The task appears in this area.

10 Repeat steps **6** to **9** for each task you want to assign.

11 When you finish recording meeting minutes and assigning tasks, click **OK** to close the Meeting Minder dialog box.

Note: To redisplay the dialog box at any time during the slide show, repeat steps 1 and 2.

CREATE A CUSTOM SLIDE SHOW

You can create a custom slide show that includes only some of the slides in a presentation. This is useful if you want to customize your presentation to suit specific audiences.

CREATE A CUSTOM SLIDE SHOW

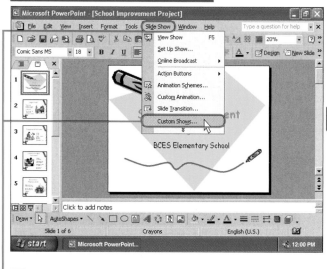

1 Click **Slide Show**.

2 Click **Custom Shows**.

Note: If Custom Shows does not appear on the menu, position the mouse ⍀ over the bottom of the menu to display the menu option.

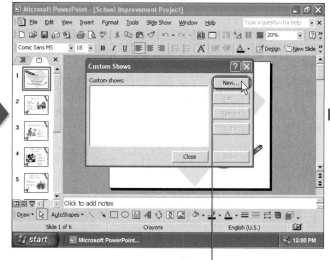

■ The Custom Shows dialog box appears.

3 Click **New** to create a custom slide show.

Can I create several custom slide shows from one presentation?

Yes. You can create several custom slide shows from a presentation containing all your ideas and information. For example, you may want to use a presentation about a new product to create a detailed custom slide show for the sales department and a shorter custom slide show for the executive committee.

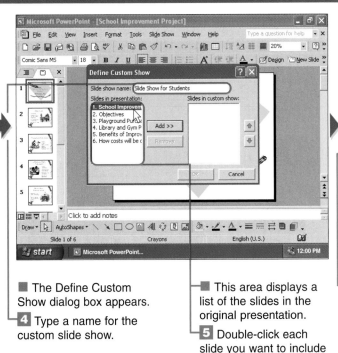

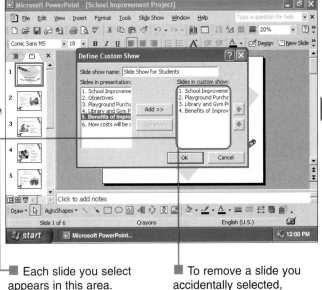

■ The Define Custom Show dialog box appears.

4 Type a name for the custom slide show.

■ This area displays a list of the slides in the original presentation.

5 Double-click each slide you want to include in the custom slide show.

■ Each slide you select appears in this area.

■ To remove a slide you accidentally selected, double-click the slide in this area.

CONTINUED

CREATE A CUSTOM SLIDE SHOW

You can rearrange the order of the slides in a custom slide show to suit your needs.

Changing the order of the slides in a custom slide show does not affect the order of the slides in the original presentation.

CREATE A CUSTOM SLIDE SHOW (CONTINUED)

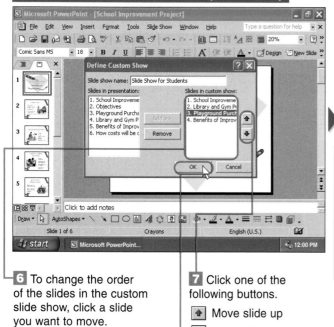

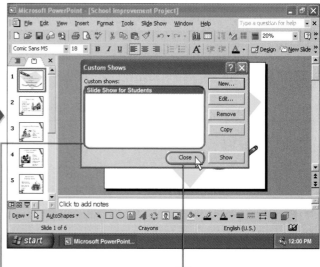

6 To change the order of the slides in the custom slide show, click a slide you want to move.

7 Click one of the following buttons.

⬆ Move slide up

⬇ Move slide down

8 When you finish creating the custom slide show, click **OK** to confirm your changes.

■ The name of the custom slide show you created appears in this area.

9 Click **Close** to close the Custom Shows dialog box.

How do I make changes to the slides in a custom slide show?

When you make changes to the slides in the original presentation, the slides in the custom slide show automatically display the changes.

Can I later add or remove slides in the custom slide show?

Yes. You can edit a custom slide show to change the slides that you want to include in the show.

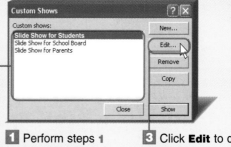

1 Perform steps **1** and **2** below to display the Custom Shows dialog box.

2 Click the custom slide show you want to edit.

3 Click **Edit** to display the Define Custom Show dialog box.

4 Perform steps **5** to **9** starting on page 273 to edit the custom slide show.

VIEW A CUSTOM SLIDE SHOW

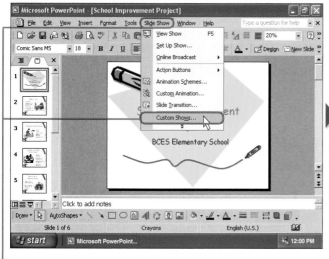

1 Click **Slide Show**.

2 Click **Custom Shows**.

Note: If Custom Shows does not appear on the menu, position the mouse ⟍ over the bottom of the menu to display the menu option.

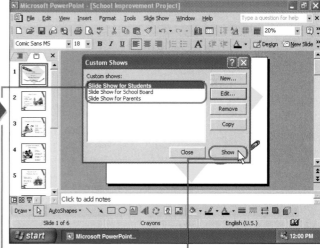

■ The Custom Shows dialog box appears.

3 Click the custom slide show you want to view.

4 Click **Show** to view the custom slide show.

Note: For information on moving through a slide show, see the top of page 267.

PRESENT A SLIDE SHOW USING TWO MONITORS

You can present a slide show to an audience using one monitor while you view the presentation and your notes on another monitor.

PRESENT A SLIDE SHOW USING TWO MONITORS

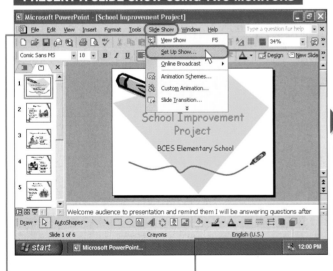

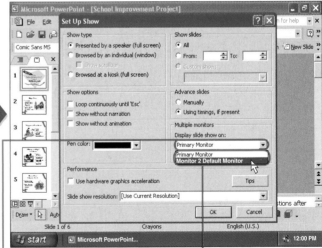

1 Open the presentation you want to view using two monitors. To open a presentation, see page 28.

2 Click **Slide Show**.

3 Click **Set Up Show**.

■ The Set Up Show dialog box appears.

4 Click this area to display a list of monitors set up on your computer.

Note: If this area is not available, your computer is not set up to use two monitors. For more information, see the top of page 277.

5 Click the monitor the audience will view.

How can I set up my computer to use two monitors?

To set up your computer to use two monitors, your computer and operating system must have dual-monitor capabilities. For more information on setting up your computer to use two monitors, refer to your operating system documentation.

Do I have to use the presenter tools?

When you present a slide show using two monitors, PowerPoint provides presenter tools, such as buttons that let you move through the slides, a miniature version of each slide and the notes for the current slide. If you do not want to use the presenter tools when presenting your slide show on two monitors, perform steps **1** to **8**, except skip step **6**. Your monitor will display the presentation in the Normal view. You can view the slide show on the audience's monitor as you would view any slide show. For information on viewing a slide show, see page 266.

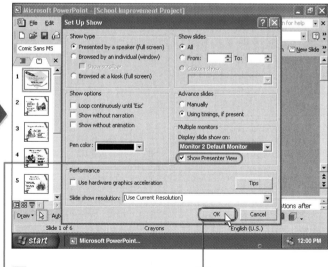

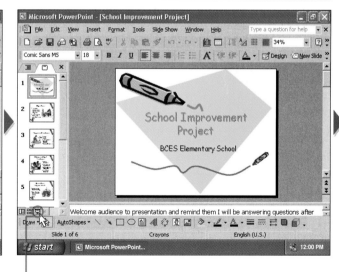

6 Click this option to display presenter tools on your monitor that you can use to deliver the slide show (☐ changes to ✔).

7 Click **OK** to confirm your change.

8 Click 🖳 to begin the slide show.

CONTINUED

PRESENT A SLIDE SHOW USING TWO MONITORS

When presenting a slide show using two monitors, you can use the presenter tools displayed on your monitor to move through the slides and review your notes.

PRESENT A SLIDE SHOW USING TWO MONITORS (CONTINUED)

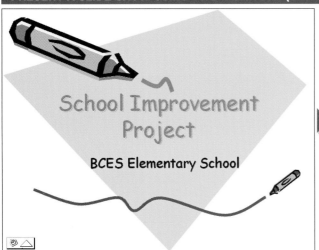

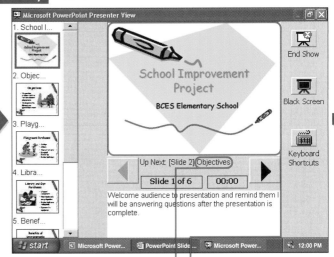

AUDIENCE'S MONITOR

■ The audience's monitor displays the slide show.

YOUR MONITOR

■ The Microsoft PowerPoint Presenter View window appears on your screen, displaying tools you can use to present the slide show.

■ This area displays the slide that is currently displayed on the audience's monitor.

■ This area displays the name of the next slide or animation in the slide show.

How do I pause the slide show?

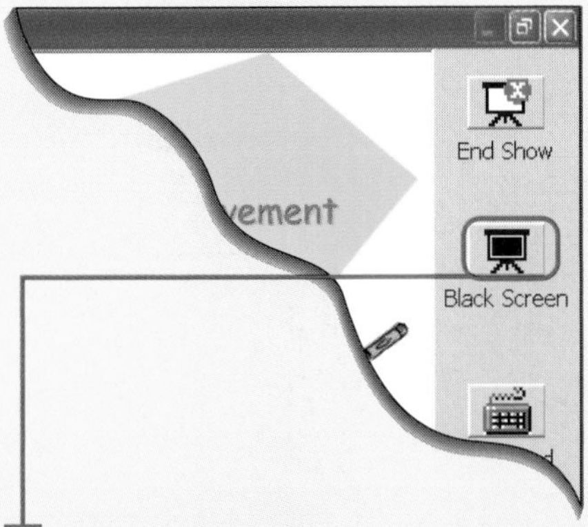

1 Click the Black Screen button (▣) to pause the slide show and turn the screen black (▣ changes to ▣).

■ To once again resume the slide show, click the Resume Show button (▣).

I set up a sound and movie to play when they are clicked on a slide. How do I play the sound and movie on the monitor displaying the slide show?

To play a sound or movie, move the mouse ☝ over the speaker icon (🔊) or movie on the monitor displaying the slide show and then click the speaker icon or movie on the slide. To add a sound to a slide, see page 186. To add a movie to a slide, see page 196.

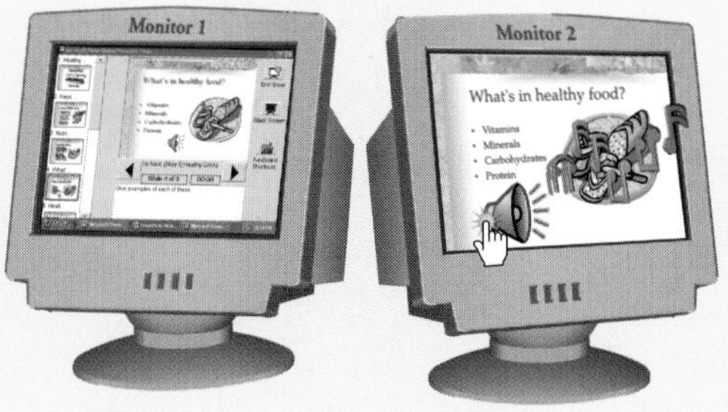

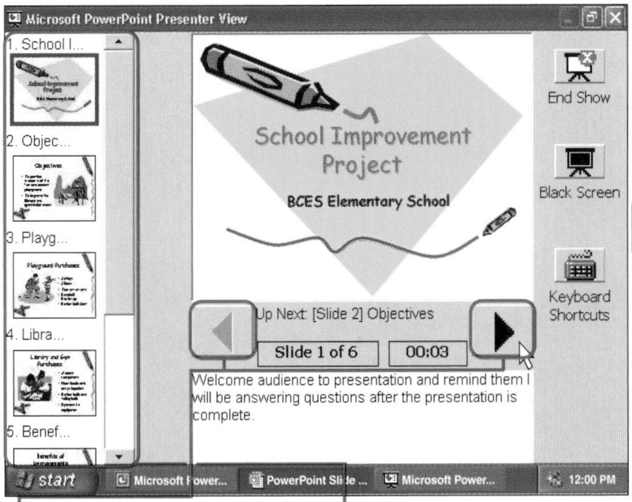

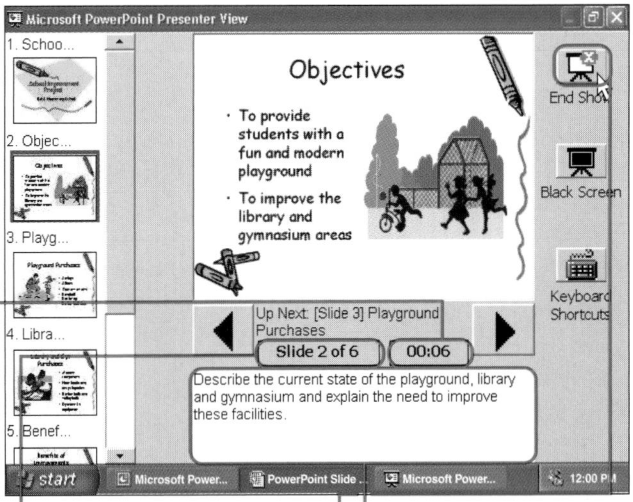

9 To move through the slides or animations, click one of the following buttons.

◀ Display previous slide or animation

▶ Display next slide or animation

■ This area displays a miniature version of all the slides in your presentation. You can click a slide in this area to immediately display the slide on the audience's monitor.

■ This area displays the number of the slide that is currently displayed and the total number of slides in the presentation.

■ This area displays the amount of time that has passed since the start of the slide show.

■ This area displays the notes for the current slide. To add notes to your slides, see page 238.

10 To end the slide show at any time, click ▣.

USING THE PACK AND GO WIZARD

You can use the Pack and Go Wizard to package your presentation onto a floppy disk and transport it to another computer.

The Pack and Go Wizard packages your presentation and all the files associated with the presentation, such as sound files. The wizard then compresses, or squeezes, the entire presentation to make the presentation easier to transport.

PACKAGE A PRESENTATION

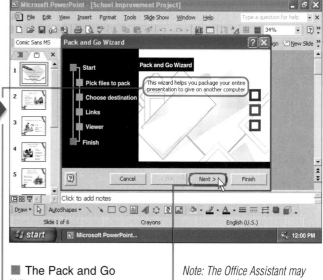

1 Open the presentation you want to package and transport to another computer. To open a presentation, see page 28.

2 Click **File**.

3 Click **Pack and Go**.

Note: If Pack and Go does not appear on the menu, position the mouse ⟍ over the bottom of the menu to display the menu option.

■ The Pack and Go Wizard appears.

■ This area describes the wizard.

*Note: The Office Assistant may also appear. Click **No** to remove the Office Assistant from your screen.*

4 Click **Next** to continue.

Can I package my presentation onto a recordable CD disc?

You can package the presentation to a location on your computer so you can later copy the packaged presentation to a recordable disc. In the Pack and Go Wizard, click **Choose destination** (○ changes to ⊙) and then type **C:** in the area provided to store the presentation on your hard drive. You can then use the software that came with your recordable CD drive or Windows XP to copy the presentation to a recordable CD. For more information, see the documentation that came with your CD drive or Windows XP.

 Can I make changes to my presentation after I run the Pack and Go Wizard?

Yes. If you make changes to your presentation after you package it, you must run the Pack and Go Wizard again to make sure that the latest changes are included in the packaged presentation.

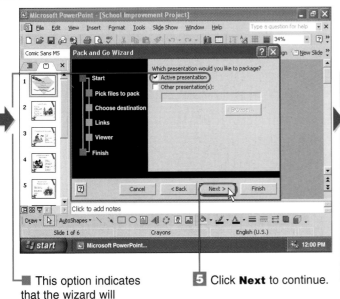

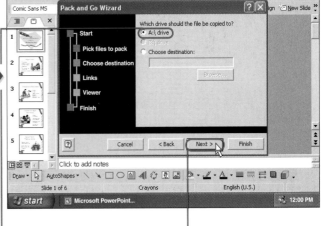

■ This option indicates that the wizard will package the presentation displayed on your screen.

5 Click **Next** to continue.

■ This option indicates that the wizard will copy the presentation to your floppy drive.

6 Click **Next** to continue.

CONTINUED

The Pack and Go
Wizard allows
you to include
linked files and
TrueType fonts
in your packaged
presentation.

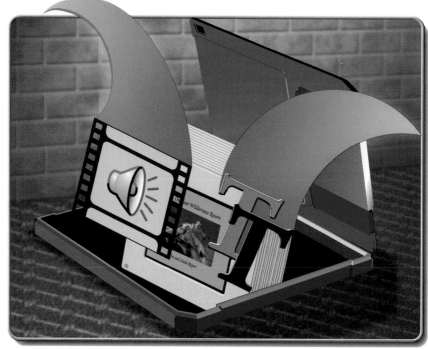

Including linked files
allows you to open
files included in
your presentation,
such as sounds
and movies, on the
other computer.

Including TrueType
fonts ensures that
the text in your
presentation will be
displayed correctly,
even if the other
computer does not
have the same fonts
installed.

PACKAGE A PRESENTATION (CONTINUED)

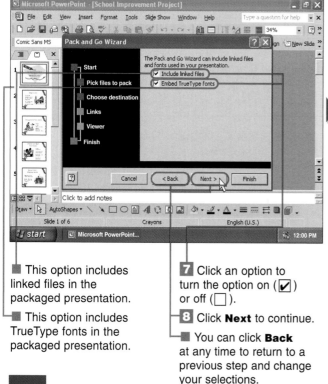

■ This option includes
linked files in the
packaged presentation.

■ This option includes
TrueType fonts in the
packaged presentation.

7 Click an option to
turn the option on (✔)
or off (☐).

8 Click **Next** to continue.

■ You can click **Back**
at any time to return to a
previous step and change
your selections.

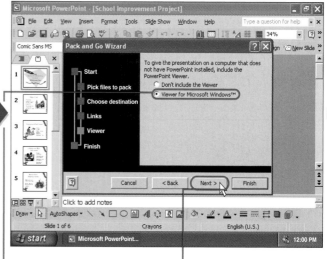

■ The PowerPoint Viewer
allows you to deliver your
presentation on a computer
that does not have PowerPoint
installed.

9 To include the PowerPoint
Viewer in the packaged
presentation, click this
option (◯ changes to ⦿).

*Note: If this option is not
available, see the top of page 283.*

10 Click **Next** to continue.

Why isn't the Viewer for Microsoft Windows option available in the wizard?

VIEWER IS NOT INSTALLED

You must install the Viewer on your computer. Click the **Download the Viewer** button to connect to the Microsoft Office Web site and then download the **PowerPoint Viewer 97 (2000 Release)** to your computer. Double-click the file you downloaded and then follow the instructions on your screen to install the Viewer.

PRESENTATION IS PROTECTED

If you have protected your presentation with a password, the Pack and Go Wizard will not allow you to include the Viewer with the presentation. For information on protecting a presentation, see page 34.

Why does this dialog box appear after I finish selecting options in the Pack and Go Wizard?

This dialog box appears if the Pack and Go Wizard is not installed on your computer. Insert the CD-ROM disc you used to install PowerPoint into your computer's CD-ROM drive. Then click **Yes** to install the wizard.

Note: A window may appear on your screen. Click ☒ *in the top right corner of the window to close the window.*

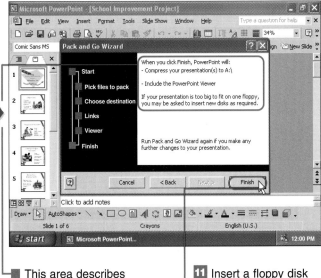

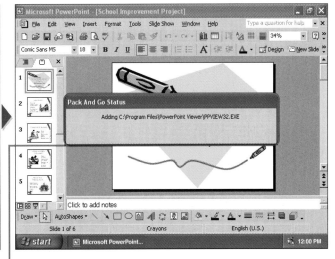

■ This area describes the tasks PowerPoint will perform to package the presentation.

11 Insert a floppy disk into your floppy drive.

12 Click **Finish**.

■ The Pack And Go Status dialog box appears, indicating the tasks PowerPoint is performing to package the presentation. This dialog box will disappear when PowerPoint is finished packing the presentation.

Note: If your presentation is too large to fit on one floppy disk, a dialog box will appear, asking you to insert another disk.

CONTINUED ▶

USING THE PACK AND GO WIZARD

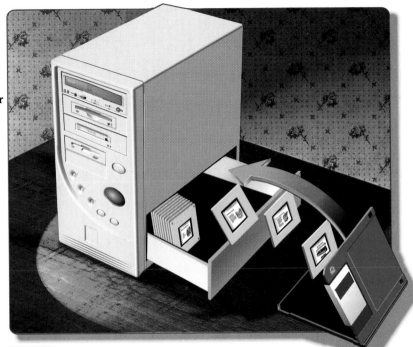

When you arrive at your destination, you can unpack your presentation on the computer you will use to deliver the presentation.

If you included the PowerPoint Viewer in your packaged presentation, PowerPoint will install the Viewer on the other computer when you unpack the presentation.

UNPACK A PRESENTATION

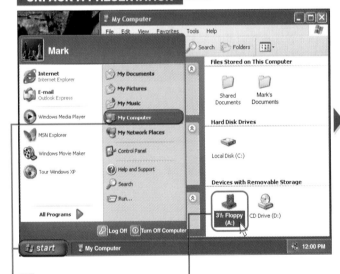

1 Insert the floppy disk into the floppy drive on the computer you will use to deliver the presentation.

2 Click **start**.

3 Click **My Computer**.

■ The My Computer window appears.

4 Double-click the drive containing the floppy disk.

Note: If you are using an older version of Windows, refer to the Windows documentation for information on displaying the contents of your floppy drive.

■ The contents of the floppy disk appear.

5 Double-click **PNGSETUP**.

Should I preview the presentation I unpacked?

Yes. Before presenting the slide show to the audience, you should preview the presentation you unpacked to make sure the slide show works the way you intended.

How do I view the slide show again later?

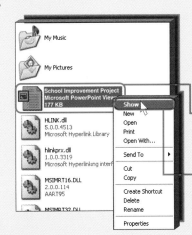

1 Display the contents of the location where you saved the presentation you unpacked.

2 Right-click the presentation you want to view. A menu appears.

3 Click **Show**.

Note: For information on viewing a slide show, see page 266.

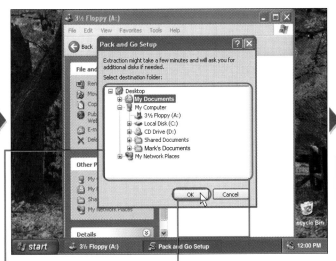

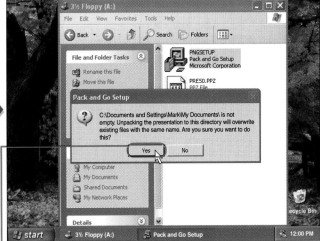

■ The Pack and Go Setup dialog box appears.

■ This area displays the locations where you can save the presentation. A location displaying a plus sign (⊞) contains hidden locations.

6 To display the hidden locations within a location, click the plus sign (⊞) beside the location.

7 Click the location where you want to save the presentation.

8 Click **OK** to continue.

■ A warning dialog box appears, stating that saving the presentation will replace any existing files with the same name in the location.

9 Click **Yes** to continue.

Note: If you used more than one disk to package the presentation, a dialog box will appear, asking you to insert the next disk.

■ A dialog box will appear when the presentation has been successfully installed. Click **Yes** to preview the slide show.

CHAPTER 14

PowerPoint and the Internet

Are you interested in sharing your presentation with other people on the Internet? In this chapter, you will learn how to e-mail a presentation, save a presentation as a Web page and more.

E-MAIL A PRESENTATION

You can e-mail a presentation to a friend, family member or colleague.

Before you can e-mail a presentation, an e-mail program, such as Microsoft Outlook, must be set up on your computer.

E-MAIL A PRESENTATION

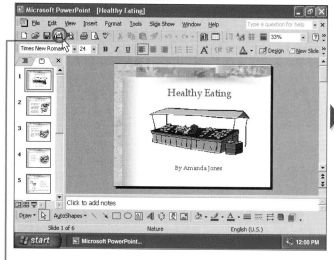

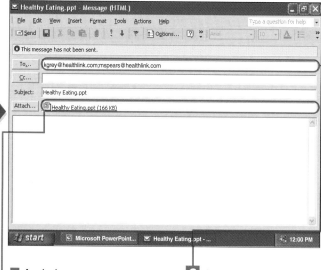

1 Click 🖳 to e-mail the current presentation.

Note: If 🖳 is not displayed, click » on the Standard toolbar to display the button.

■ The Choose Profile dialog box may appear. Click **OK** to close the dialog box.

■ A window appears for the e-mail message.

■ This area displays the name and size of the presentation.

2 Click this area and type the e-mail address of each person you want to receive the message. Separate each address with a semicolon (;).

288

How can I address an e-mail message?

To

Sends the message to each person you specify.

Carbon Copy (Cc)

Sends a copy of the message to a person who is not directly involved but would be interested in the message.

Why can't the person I sent my presentation to view the information?

When you e-mail a presentation, the presentation is sent as an attached file. The recipient must have PowerPoint 2000 or a later version of PowerPoint installed to open the file.

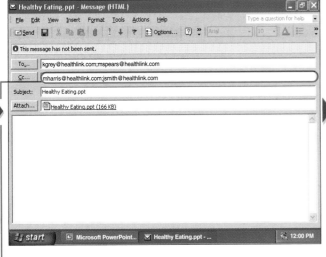

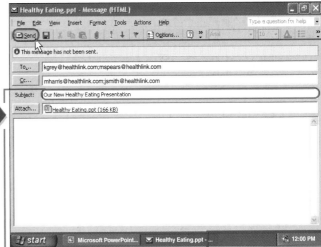

3 To send a copy of the message, click this area and type the e-mail address of each person you want to receive a copy. Separate each address with a semicolon (;).

4 Click this area and type a subject for the message.

Note: If a subject already exists, you can drag the mouse I over the existing subject and then type a new subject.

5 Click **Send** to send the message.

CREATE A HYPERLINK

You can create a hyperlink, also called a link, to connect a word, phrase or object in your presentation to another file or Web page on your computer, network or the Internet.

Creating a hyperlink allows you to quickly display the file or Web page connected to the hyperlink during a slide show.

CREATE A HYPERLINK

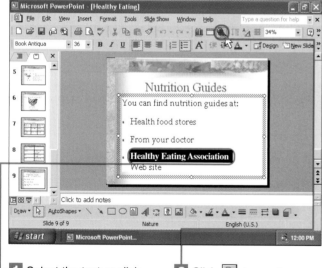

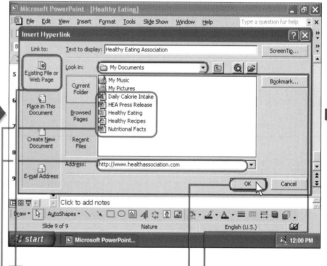

1 Select the text or click the object you want to link to another file or Web page. To select text, see page 56.

2 Click 🔗 to create a hyperlink.

Note: If 🔗 is not displayed, click ⮞ on the Standard toolbar to display the button.

■ The Insert Hyperlink dialog box appears.

3 Click **Existing File or Web Page**.

4 To create a hyperlink to a Web page, click this area and type the address of the Web page.

■ To create a hyperlink to a file on your computer or network, click the file in this area.

■ This area shows the location of the displayed files. You can click this area to change the location.

5 Click **OK** to create the hyperlink.

Can PowerPoint automatically create a hyperlink for me?

When you type the address of a Web page and then press the **Spacebar** or the `Enter` key, PowerPoint will automatically change the address to a hyperlink.

www.bluesprings.com

How can I remove a hyperlink?

To remove a hyperlink completely, select the text or click the object and then press the `Delete` key. To select text, see page 56.

To remove a hyperlink but keep the text or graphic on the slide, right-click the hyperlink and then select **Remove Hyperlink** from the menu that appears.

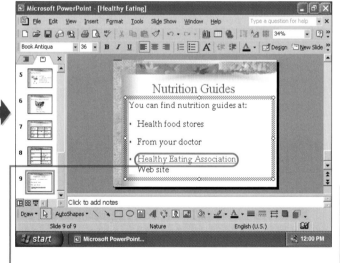

■ PowerPoint creates the hyperlink. A text hyperlink appears underlined and in color.

■ To deselect text, click outside the selected area.

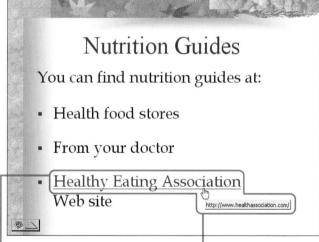

SELECT A HYPERLINK

1 View the slide show that contains the hyperlink. To view a slide show, see page 266.

■ When you position the mouse 🖑 over the hyperlink, a yellow box appears, displaying the Web page address or the location and name of the file that the hyperlink will display.

2 Click the hyperlink to display the Web page or file connected to the hyperlink.

PREVIEW A PRESENTATION AS A WEB PAGE

You can preview how your presentation will look as a Web page. This allows you to see how the presentation will appear on the Internet or your company's intranet.

An intranet is a small version of the Internet within a company.

PREVIEW A PRESENTATION AS A WEB PAGE

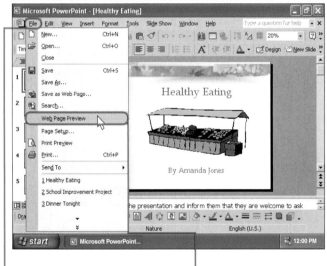

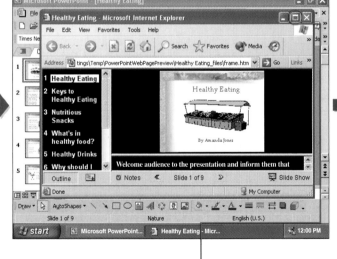

1 Open the presentation you want to view as a Web page. To open a presentation, see page 28.

2 Click **File**.

3 Click **Web Page Preview** to preview your presentation as a Web page.

■ Your Web browser window opens, displaying your presentation as a Web page.

■ To maximize the Web browser window to fill your screen, click ▣.

Will a Web browser window display my presentation exactly as it appears in PowerPoint?

No. Some of the features available in PowerPoint will not work in a Web browser window. For example, most Web browsers do not support shadow text styles or animation effects.

When people view my presentation on the Internet, will they be able to view a full-screen version of my presentation?

Yes. When viewing your presentation as a Web page, people can click the **Slide Show** button in the bottom right corner of their Web browser window to view the full-screen version of the presentation. People viewing the presentation can click the current slide to move forward through the slides or press the Esc key to end the presentation at any time.

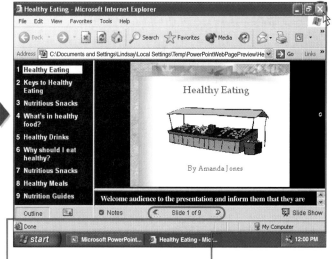

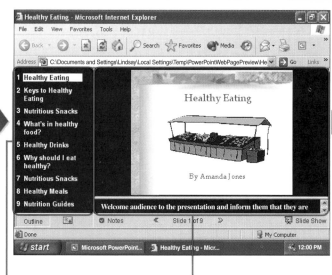

■ This area displays the title of each slide in your presentation. You can click a title to display a different slide.

■ This area displays the current slide and any notes for the current slide.

■ You can click ≪ or ≫ in this area to move backward or forward through the slides in your presentation.

4 When you finish previewing your presentation as a Web page, click ✕ to close the Web browser window.

SAVE A PRESENTATION AS A WEB PAGE

You can save a
presentation as a
Web page. This
allows you to place
the presentation
on the Internet or
your company's
intranet.

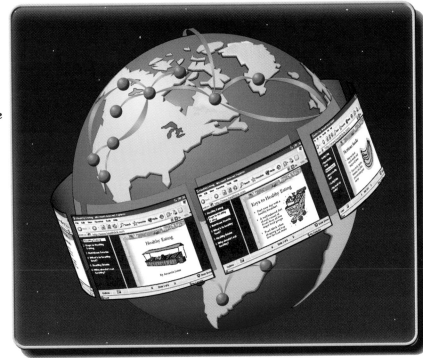

An intranet is a
small version of
the Internet within
a company.

SAVE A PRESENTATION AS A WEB PAGE

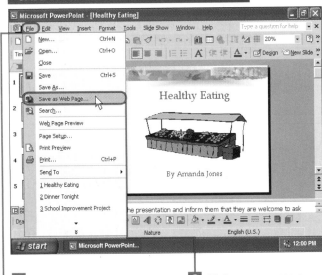

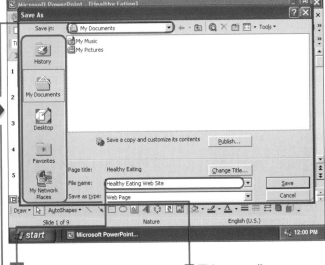

1 Open the presentation
you want to save as a
Web page. To open a
presentation, see page 28.

2 Click **File**.

3 Click **Save as Web
Page**.

■ The Save As dialog
box appears.

4 Type a file name for
the Web page.

■ This area shows the
location where PowerPoint
will store the Web page.
You can click this area to
change the location.

■ This area allows you
to access commonly used
locations. You can click a
location to save the Web
page in the location.

Note: For information on the
commonly used locations,
see the top of page 27.

What is the difference between the file name and the title of a Web page?

The file name is the name you use to store the Web page on your computer. The title is the text that will appear at the top of the Web browser window when a person views your Web page.

How do I make my Web page available for other people to view?

After you save a presentation as a Web page, you can transfer the page to a computer that stores Web pages, called a Web server. Once the Web page is stored on a Web server, the page will be available for other people to view. For information on transferring a Web page to a Web server, contact your network administrator or Internet service provider.

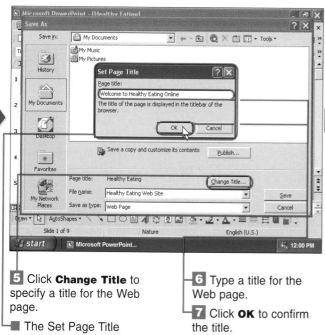

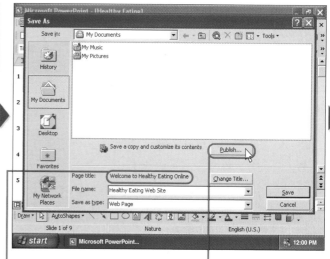

5 Click **Change Title** to specify a title for the Web page.

■ The Set Page Title dialog box appears.

Note: A default title may appear in the dialog box.

6 Type a title for the Web page.

7 Click **OK** to confirm the title.

■ This area displays the title you specified for the Web page.

8 Click **Publish** to customize the Web page to suit your needs.

CONTINUED

SAVE A PRESENTATION AS A WEB PAGE

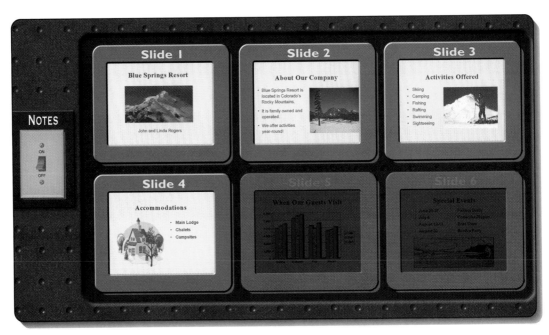

You can customize your Web page to display only specific slides. You can also choose not to display your notes on the Web page.

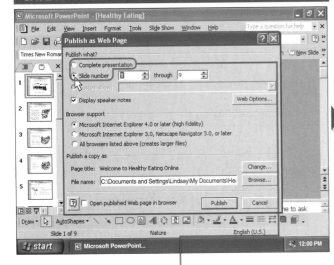

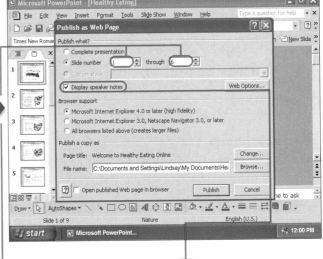

■ The Publish as Web Page dialog box appears.

*Note: The Office Assistant may appear. Click **No** to hide the Office Assistant.*

9 Click an option to specify whether you want to save the entire presentation or only specific slides as a Web page (○ changes to ◉).

10 If you selected **Slide number** in step **9**, double-click this area and type the number of the first slide you want to save. Press the Tab key and type the number of the last slide you want to save.

11 PowerPoint will display your notes on each Web page. If you do not want to display your notes, click this option (☑ changes to ☐).

Which Web browser(s) should I choose to display my Web page?

You should choose the Web browser(s) that most people will use to view your Web page. The most popular browsers on the Web are currently Microsoft Internet Explorer and Netscape Navigator.

Older versions of Web browsers will not be able to display objects such as sound and movies in your presentation. To ensure that most people will be able to view your Web page, select the **All browsers listed above** option in step **12** below.

Will my Web page look the same to everyone who views the page?

Different Web browsers may display your Web page differently. For example, Microsoft Internet Explorer and Netscape Navigator may display your Web page differently.

Internet Explorer

Netscape Navigator

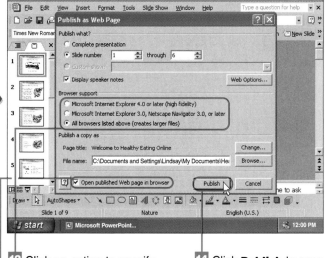

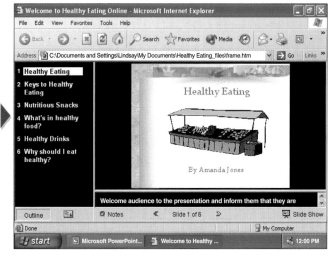

12 Click an option to specify which Web browser(s) you want to be able to display your Web page (○ changes to ⊙).

13 To preview the Web page in your Web browser, click this option (☐ changes to ☑).

14 Click **Publish** to save your presentation as a Web page.

■ Your Web browser opens and displays the Web page. For information on viewing a Web page in a Web browser, see page 292.

INDEX

INDEX

INDEX

INDEX

Teach Yourself VISUALLY **YOGA**

ISBN: 0-7645-2580-8
Price: $24.99 US; $36.99 CDN; £14.99 UK
Page count: 320

Teach Yourself VISUALLY **GUITAR**

ISBN: 0-7645-2581-6
Price: $24.99 US; $36.99 CDN; £14.99 UK
Page count: 320

Other Visual Series That Help You Read Less - Learn More™

Teach Yourself VISUALLY™

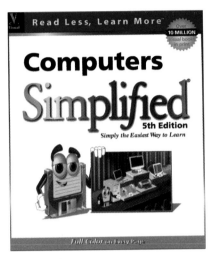

Simplified®

Master VISUALLY™

Visual Blueprint™

In an Instant

Available wherever books are sold

To view a complete listing of our publications, please visit **www.maran.com**

Wiley Publishing, Inc.